VALUES IN EDUCATION

Following the perceived breakdown of moral and social fabric and the diminishing role of traditional arbiters of morality and standards, more and more is being expected of schools and teachers in the guidance and control of children. It is a daunting task for educators at all levels of the education system to decide what values are appropriate, whose values are appropriate and how such values are to be addressed in the curriculum.

Based upon an empirical study involving training and practising teachers from seven countries, this book investigates the various attitudes and practices towards the teaching of values and their place in the curriculum. The findings from each of the countries are compared and contrasted in the light of the diverse cultural conditions which are apparent.

This book brings together various approaches currently taken in values education and also suggests a theoretical foundation for decision making. It culminates in practical examples, drawn from the evidence of the research project, which teachers can adapt for use with their own pupils.

The authors offer a challenging and imaginative perspective on values in education at a time when educators face a new era which demands dynamic, transformative and reflective approaches.

Joan Stephenson is Head of the Education Department at De Montfort University, Bedford. **Lorraine Ling** and **Eva Burman** are Lecturers in Education in the Graduate School of Education at La Trobe University, Bundoora, Australia, and **Maxine Cooper** is Senior Lecturer in Education at the University of Melbourne.

VALUES IN EDUCATION

*Edited by Joan Stephenson, Lorraine Ling
Eva Burman and Maxine Cooper*

London and New York

First published 1998
by Routledge
11 New Fetter Lane, London EC4P 4EE

Simultaneously published in the USA and Canada
by Routledge
29 West 35th Street, New York, NY 10001

Typeset in Garamond by RefineCatch Limited, Bungay, Suffolk

Printed and bound in Great Britain by
Hartnolls Ltd, Bodmin, Cornwall

British Library Cataloguing in Publication Data
A catalogue record for this book is available from the British Library

Library of Congress Cataloging in Publication Data
A catalogue record for this book has been requested

ISBN 0–415–15737–4 (hbk)
ISBN 0–415–15738–2 (pbk)

For tomorrow's children and all who teach them

CONTENTS

CONTENTS

Part IV Reflections

FIGURES

TABLES

CONTRIBUTORS

Eva Burman is Lecturer in Education, co-ordinator of secondary and acting director of primary education programmes at La Trobe University, Victoria, Australia. An active member of the Indonesia/IBRD scheme, she has experience of working in different cultures and has researched and written on classroom discipline. Research interests include school management and discipline, the literacy needs of female non-native speakers and values education.

Maxine Cooper is Senior Lecturer in Education at the University of Melbourne. She is an experienced classroom teacher and past president of the Australian Teacher Education Association. Co-author of *STAGES: Steps Toward Addressing Gender in Educational Settings*, she is presently working on a research-council-funded longitudinal study on gender in teacher education.

Esther Gottlieb is Director of Research and Economic Development, West Virginia University, USA, and a research fellow at the State Teachers College – Seminar Hakibbutzim, Tel Aviv, Israel. Her research has focused on comparative and international education, in the fields of academic professoriate and the analysis of pragmatic discourse. Her most recent publications include *Mapping the Utopia of Professionalism: The Carnegie International Survey of the Academic Profession in Social Cartography* (Garland, 1996).

Hans Ulrich Grunder, when this study was undertaken, was Vice-Director for the training of secondary school teachers at the University of Berne.

Maureen Killeavy is Lecturer in the Education Department at University College Dublin. She works in the areas of professional development, IT, group dynamics, communication studies and learning difficulties. She has taught in primary, secondary and tertiary education.

Lorraine Ling has taught in the primary, secondary and tertiary education sectors. She is currently employed at La Trobe University in Victoria, Australia, as a teacher educator. Her research interests focus upon policy construction, change and restructuring of education systems, values in education and the socio-political context of education.

Peter Ling is Associate Professor in the Educational Programme Improvement Group at Royal Melbourne Institute of Technology. He has been Senior Lecturer in Teacher Education and Head of the Department of Community Studies, responsible for inter-cultural studies, criminology and youth work. He is co-editor of the *Higher Education Research and Development Journal* and has undertaken national and international projects on education policy. His research interests include the role of teacher educators in values education.

Alenka Polak works in the Faculty of Education at the University of Ljubljana, Slovenia, as subject assistant in educational psychology. Her interests lie within the field of self-reflective thinking and awareness in the professional development of teachers.

David Purpel is Professor in the Department of Educational Leadership and Cultural Studies at the University of North Carolina, Greensboro, USA. He is author of *The Moral and Spiritual Crises in Education*.

Cveta Razdevsek-Pucko works in the Faculty of Education at the University of Ljubljana, Slovenia, as Assistant Professor for Educational Psychology. Besides her interest in values in education her special fields of interest are teacher education and assessment in the primary school. She is part of the team preparing a new assessment system for schools following new legislation.

Joan Stephenson is Head of the Department of Education at De Montfort University, UK. Her research and writing interests include children's moral, social and economic education, and mentoring.

Ruth Yakir teaches at the State Teachers College – Seminar Hakibbutzim in Tel Aviv, Israel, where she is also director of the Segal Institute of Research and Development, and heads the Department of Educational Administration. Her research interests include teacher education and higher education, teacher role orientations and school administration.

Ruth Zuzovsky is Head of Pedagogical Studies, Science Department, State Teachers College – Seminar Hakibbutzim, Tel Aviv, Israel, where she has worked since 1962, and concurrently from 1970 at the Israel Science Teaching Centre, School of Education, Tel Aviv University. Her professional areas of interest in regard to teacher education are: professional development of teachers and student teachers, pre- and in-service training programmes, supervision and mentoring, and values education.

PREFACE

The existence of this book is an example of the increasing emphasis and importance being given to education and training throughout the developed and developing world. It also illustrates co-operative inquiry and problem-solving in practice. Through membership of the Association for Teacher Education in Europe the contributors were able to exchange issues of concern and interest not only with near neighbours but also with those from the other side of the world. The countries involved represent democracies at many stages in their evolution. All have long and varied programmes of mass education and an established tradition of training future and practising teachers. Most have recently undergone changes in their social, cultural, economic and political make-up. In some cases, as in Slovenia, these have been of major proportions; in others the changes occurred longer ago or are in detail rather than fundamental change. Schools, schooling and educational aims are being challenged. The underlying purpose of their remit and function is being subjected to conflicting interpretations. The curriculum in schools is also under debate, reflecting the pressing needs in modern times for a workforce which is able to adapt itself to the escalating rate of change in technology, and to the transfer of labour from man to machines. These issues are reflected in the mores and demands of the societies in which we live, work and study. In a time of transition and disjunction, such as is being experienced at a global level as we enter the twenty-first century, traditional approaches and attitudes are constantly challenged and confronted. This radical change in an era of transformation is also likely to affect the area of values. The traditional values on which social, political and economic elements of society are premised, are being renewed and reconstructed in non-traditional ways. New relationships are occurring through the breaking and blurring of boundaries between nations, groups and ideologies. These new relationships result in the stretching of time and space and in instantaneous communication world-wide. The events in one part of the world will instantly impact upon other parts of the world. In this kind of context, then, it is the multinational corporations which are able to set the agenda across the continents, and therefore economic rationalism operates everywhere.

This poses new challenges and dilemmas at all levels of society. Some are more prevalent in particular societies, others are common to all. Today's children, the future generation of decision makers, are at the centre of this process.

In this rationalist economic climate, values which previously underpinned social contexts are no longer applicable. The seeming certainties of what are being viewed by some as more ordered times are failing to provide the answers. The social fabric is seen by some commentators to be in danger of collapse. A concern is that old prejudices and 'historical' or nationalistic solutions will gain dominance if a vacuum is allowed to develop. It is necessary therefore to devise new approaches to a new era. In the area of values in education, this task is urgent. We are already educating learners for a future whose prevailing features are not clear. It is thus a daunting task for educators at all levels of the education system to influence the decision about what values are appropriate, whose values are appropriate, how such values will be addressed in the education curriculum, and what the answers to these questions mean for particular groups and individuals in society.

It is timely, therefore, that a book which addresses the topic of values in education at an international level should be available. Based upon an empirical study in seven countries, and involving students and teachers in real-life situations, the investigation has gathered the perceptions of teachers about the teaching of values and its place in the curriculum of formal schooling. Each country has its own diverse cultural conditions, and this gives added value to the comparisons and contrasts of the findings.

By using the conclusions drawn from the international research study, this book provides a synthesis of the current approaches of educators in the values area, and also suggests a theoretical foundation for decision making. A chapter is devoted to practical classroom activities based upon the theoretical framework proposed in this book. These activities can be used to address a range of concepts in values education.

This book provides an innovative, challenging and imaginative perspective on the area of values in education and comes at a time when educators face a new era which demands approaches that are dynamic, transforming and reflective.

> The school *is* in the business of values education, unavoidably. Right now, . . . schools must become more than knowledge factories, and assessment more than apple-sorting, for students are more than disincarnate minds, and so are teachers. (B.V. Hill, *Values Education in Australian Schools*, 1991, Melbourne, ACER, p. 168).

Our thanks to the many colleagues in education, too numerous to mention by name, who have made this book possible.

Lorraine M. Ling and Joan Stephenson

Part I
BEGINNINGS

1

INTRODUCTION AND THEORETICAL PERSPECTIVES

Lorraine Ling and Joan Stephenson

> Everyone knows what they want from education – until they are asked
> to spell it out. Then it becomes apparent that many people simply have
> a 'warm fuzzy' feeling about education.
>
> (Hill, 1991: 1)

There is an immense diversity of opinion regarding the place of values in the
curriculum and also regarding the strategies and approaches to be employed
when teaching values. In times of economic crisis or social upheaval there
are inevitably conflicting demands for specific interests and viewpoints to be
favoured when the curriculum of schooling is being constructed and
reconstructed. One of the areas in which the greatest tension and conflict
occurs may be seen to be that of values education. In order to clarify the
term 'values', the definition supplied by Hill (1991: 4) will be used as the basis
for this discussion.

> When people speak of values they are usually referring to those beliefs
> held by individuals to which they attach special priority or worth, and
> by which they tend to order their lives. A value is, therefore, more than
> a belief; but it is also more than a feeling.

Theorists have attempted to itemize values, and typologies of values have
resulted. Two such typologies are provided by Taylor (1961) and by De Witt
H. Parker (1931). Parker distinguishes two kinds of values – 'Real Life' and
'Imagination', Jarrett (1991: 13), in his discussion of Parker's typology, lists
the two types as:

[Real Life] health and comfort; ambition; love and friendship; ethical
or moral; knowledge; technological (efficiency)

[Imagination] play; art; religion.

In outlining the categories of values as listed by Taylor (1961), Jarrett
notes 'the moral; the aesthetic; the intellectual; the religious; the economic;
the political; the legal; etiquette or custom' (1991: 13). He also notes that
these typologies do not include sensual values. For the purposes of this

3

project the values which are predominantly referred to are moral or ethical values.

In the current era, educators face a dilemma as they are pressured by particular interest groups to favour particular value positions and thus to re-establish some form of social stability and cohesion in times of upheaval or transition. Yet while this demand for stability is strong there is a concurrent agenda which stems from the fact that in times of change and upheaval the established, traditional values may no longer be appropriate or relevant.

The period of the 1990s leading to the twenty-first century in so-called 'developed' countries is being labelled variously as an interregnum (Eco, 1986), a divide (Drucker, 1993) a transformation (Drucker, 1993; Giddens, 1991) and a period of high modernity (Giddens, 1991). Some social theorists contend that the period of post-modernity has arrived (Baudrillard, 1981; Lyotard, 1984) and thus that we have already entered a new era. The stance adopted in this book, however, is to assert that we are in a transition period between eras and that continuous change and renewal, restructure and reconstruction, reform and transformation are dominant features. The current era has brought a breaking and blurring of all kinds of boundaries – national, social, political, technological and in communication. An era of globalization has begun in which the traditional boundaries that separated ideologies and communities are being broken so that the values that may have been context-specific and unique in a particular social milieu are being challenged in the light of a global perspective. Knowledges and multiple discourses and literacies are a feature of the current period, and thus the voices of many groups, hitherto silent or at least faint, are being heard. The growth of new social movements such as environmental groups, feminist groups, gay liberation, civil rights groups and the like has led to a social context in which there are multiple agendas, discourses and interests con-tinuously interacting with each other and with the existing social pattern. Approaches to social processes, such as education, which may have been appropriate in past eras, are no longer appropriate and thus new ways are being explored to deal with the challenges of the twenty-first century.

When considering the concept of values in education, then, educators are faced with multiple agendas and a plethora of interests, motivations, tensions and conflicts about values and the teaching of values. It has always been essential for educators to have a firm, considered and well articulated theo-retical framework within which to function effectively. It is now, however, even more important for educators to draw upon a well synthesized, soundly conceived theoretical perspective to inform their decisions regarding cur-riculum and their interaction with it. Theory is apparently a frightening and awe-inspiring word, if the fear and anxiety which it engenders in some educators is any indication. Educators need to be concerned with practical issues and that is not in question here. It is asserted that in order to deal most effectively and critically with practical issues, educators are required to base their practice upon firmly constructed theoretical positions. This demands that educators reflect, read, think critically and analytically, select and synthesize a variety of stances and that they selectively and reflectively construct for themselves a firm theoretical position from which to proceed. Unless this is done, the work of educators at all levels of the system is in danger of being *ad hoc*, of lacking in cohesion and consistency, of being eclectic and haphazard and thus potentially ineffective. While it may be the case that curriculum decisions generally are under-theorized, the area of values in education reflects an even greater theoretical void. Values teaching is often avoided in classrooms or is *ad hoc* and unstructured.

> Values education is the poor cousin of other core areas in the curriculum ... The openness of value debates, in which clinching proof of a position is often hard to pin down, easily leads to the view that such studies are 'soft' and 'vague'. ... Values education remains a vague and woolly notion. This state of affairs is reflected in the nickname given by students [at a school] to social studies – they call it 'social slops'.
>
> (Hill, 1991: 3)

There is, then, an urgent demand to provide, for educators, theoretical perspectives which inform the teaching of values and the place of values education in schools, so that they may themselves selectively and critically construct a theoretical foundation for their practice in the area of values. In this chapter a brief sketch of a variety of theoretical positions is presented, and a specific framework for the interpretation of the data collected in each country throughout the course of the research project is articulated.

THEORETICAL PERSPECTIVES

The ancient Greeks, and Socrates in particular, seem to be an accepted starting point for considering theoretical perspectives on values. Central to Socrates' philosophy were the two elements of morality and logic. These two elements were seen to be congruent in that when moral issues were considered, logic was called upon as the basis for action and decisions. Socrates based his theory upon the notion that we all want and seek 'the good' but a lack of logic leads to our doing things which we ought not to do. Therefore in order to avoid acting immorally, people are required to clarify their thinking logically. Thus, from a Socratic perspective, values teaching may involve such strategies as values clarification, critical thinking exercises and conversation in which values positions are articulated and critically appraised.

Aristotle, however, was concerned with moral virtues which included friendliness, honesty, justice and courage. For Aristotle, people were able to decide upon a moral course of action by considering the extremes of two actions or attitudes, for example honesty–dishonesty, patience–impatience, courage–cowardice, hard work–slothfulness. After considering the extremes

5

people were then able to arrive at an understanding of a middle or appropriate course of action. Action follows a rational assessment of a situation, and choices are made after a consideration of the extremes of responses available. Taking Aristotle as a basis for teaching values, strategies may include comparing and contrasting behaviours and actions, role plays of situations where opposite actions are taken in a given situation, debates and activities where choices are provided and options are available.

A pervasive stream of thought running parallel with the philosophy of the ancient Greeks and also especially evident at the beginning of the nineteenth century was 'hedonism'. The most extreme version of hedonism may be traced back to the fourth century BC to the Cyrenaics, who

> claimed that the art of living consists in maximizing the enjoyment of each moment through pleasures of the senses and of the intellect. In contrast, the Epicureans laid emphasis on the attainment of enduring pleasures and the avoidance of pain, stressing the role of prudence and discipline in securing the supreme good.
>
> (*A Dictionary of Philosophy*, 1979: 138)

Bentham's version of hedonism towards the end of the eighteenth century became known as 'utilitarianism'. Bentham claimed that there were two masters governing the universe – pleasure and pain. In order to act to produce the greatest possible happiness one is required to consider the possible good for the greatest number of people. This may involve a reduction of one's own personal pleasure for the sake of the greatest good for the greatest number. Following the thinking of Bentham, John Stuart Mill (1806–73) introduced the notion of a qualitative distinction between higher and lower pleasures. Mill considered that there was a need to distinguish between pleasures which were qualitatively different and then to choose action. These utilitarian concepts form the basis of ideological stances taken by governments in the framing of laws to protect people from the actions of others and also from their own actions. If this kind of theoretical framework were to be used as the basis for the teaching of values in classrooms the strategies employed might involve the study of democratic principles, activities involving voting and determining the consequences of action for groups and individuals.

In the nineteenth century, Friedrich Nietzsche's writings became significant and have exerted an influence on the theory underpinning moral and values education. For Nietzsche the basic drive behind all human action is power or, in his terms, 'the will to power'.

> Appeals to reason and truthfulness are merely one means among others (such as physical force) by which one 'will' can, in appropriate circumstances, assert its power over another. All reason . . . is rationalization; all 'truth' a perspective issuing from the centre of some ascendant 'will'. . . . What actually matters about a belief is not so much

whether or not it is 'true', but whether or not it is 'life-affirming', that is, capable of giving to those who entertain it, feelings of strength, power and freedom.

(A Dictionary of Philosophy, 1979: 248)

Here then the assertion is that it is necessary to be strong. If educators were to employ the Nietzschean philosophy in the teaching of values, activities might include discussions about power and authority, about dilemmas involving power struggles and tensions between opposing viewpoints or motivations, and about the ability to make a strong and 'tough' decision based upon one's belief that strong and creative people are those who control and dominate in society.

If we were to adopt a Kantian perspective based upon the thinking of Immanuel Kant (1724–1804) we would base our actions upon our sense of duty and responsibility and upon the fact that such action could become a universal principle for action. Kant refers to 'categorical imperatives' for action which provides a source for moral principles and action. For Kant it is never morally correct to act according to feeling or emotions. On the basis of Kantian thought, the teaching of values would involve consideration of universal principles and a development of a sense of duty and responsibility. Here strategies which might be employed in classrooms could include discussion of global issues which affect the population of the world, civil and human rights, environmental issues, moral dilemma situations based on universal principles as distinct from personal gain or good, and development of a sense of the consequences of one's actions through role-play and discussion.

For John Dewey (1859–1952) the context was the central concern rather than direct instruction in values.

> Direct instruction in morals has been effective only in social groups where it was part of the authoritative control of the many by the few. Not the teaching of it but the reinforcement of it by the whole regimen of which it is an aspect made it effective. To attempt to get similar results from lessons about morals in a democratic society is to rely upon sentimental magic.
>
> (Dewey, 1916 quoted in Jarrett, 1991: 57)

Dewey is not opposed to moral education so long as it is seen in the whole context of the environment and so long as morals are viewed as social relationships. For Dewey, then, there should be no separate area of the curriculum for dealing with values and moral education. Rather these areas of the development of the individual should be an integral and inevitable part of all of the experiences and activities through which a learner passes. Thus if an educator takes a stance based upon Dewey's thought, the values dimension would be seen as part of all teaching and learning activities.

Any place where 'intercourse, communication, and co-operation' go on, any situation that extends the 'perception of connections' is educational, morally educational . . anything that promotes 'growth' is an instance of moral education.

(Jarrett, 1991: 57)

It is also pertinent to note that, for Dewey, there could be no predetermined curriculum in a learning context as it is necessary for the learner to learn through experiences, and thus the curriculum is emergent and non-prescriptive.

In the late 1930s the 'emotivist' perspective came into prominence as discussed by Ayer in *Language, Truth and Logic* (1936) and by C.L. Stevenson in *Ethics and Language* (1944). The emotivist stance contends that 'all moral utterances are essentially an attempt to persuade others to share one's own attitude'. Stevenson concludes that 'the purpose of moral discussion is to reach agreement through persuasion' (*A Dictionary of Philosophy*, 1979: 104). Thus in the emotivist perspective, all value judgements are made on the basis of a moral imperative and an emotional commitment to a specific point of view. This view involves a belief that moral reasoning is not subject to logic, reason or rationality nor is it grounded in fact or knowledge. If this perspective is to provide the basis for the teaching of values in schools, activities may include debates, persuasive presentations and writing, and development of techniques to expound a position or opinion lucidly.

The thought of Emile Durkheim (1858–1917) has been especially influential in shifting the emphasis from the individual in society to the group as a social entity.

Durkheim argued that society was not 'a mere sum of individuals', and that 'the system formed by their association represents a specific reality which has its own characteristics. . .' 'If we begin with the individual', Durkheim maintained, 'we shall be able to understand nothing of what takes place in the group.'

(Beilharz, 1991: 72)

If appeal is made to the concepts of Durkheim as a basis for the teaching of values in schools, then it is upon group interactions and group decision-making strategies that the syllabus would focus. Activities might include team building where all members have a specific role to play in the successful product of a group action; group projects and assignments where the negotiation of meanings and goals is paramount; and heterogeneous classroom groupings across the curriculum where the views of all are negotiated and incorporated.

Recent moral theorizing has incorporated many of the stances outlined here but has also proceeded according to a conception that, though moral convictions may be shaken by the dynamics of the current era, it is not possible for an educator to be value-free – or even value-neutral. Thus strategies have been devised for the teaching or the development of values in schools such as that of Values Clarification as presented by Raths (1971). This approach has some congruence with the phenomenological perspective where the negotiation of meanings is of central importance.

> The middle ground is constantly being redefined by a continuously negotiated consensus, and is in no sense based on a final blueprint or a political resolution. That is why it has been said that the price of liberty is 'eternal vigilance'. The secular school stands on this middle ground. The value judgements which underlie it, as one strategy amongst several in the lives of the citizenry, include beliefs in the right of all citizens to be given adequate educational opportunity, to be made critically aware of the kind of society and world they live in, and to be initiated into democratic processes of rational negotiation, persuasion and mutual care. This is, in effect, a minimum value charter for the state school.
>
> (Hill, 1991: 16)

The middle ground, in a complex of viewpoints, is not necessarily co-herent. If educators adhere to this perspective the strategies and activities for the values area of the curriculum may include values clarification exercises, or discussions where meanings and viewpoints are articulated and negotiated as the basis for group action. The Values Clarification Approach (Raths, Harmin and Simons, 1966) involves students in examining their own behaviour according to a specific process and then articulating their emotions and feelings openly and in a public forum. Such a process includes the following steps: 'Choosing from alternatives; choosing thoughtfully; choosing freely; prizing one's choice; affirming one's choice; acting repeatedly over time' (Raths, Harmin and Simons, 1966: 38–9). Here then the emphasis is upon prioritizing choices and options in the context of real-life dilemmas or simulations of real-life situations, creative activities such as songs and the arts, and also through systems of voting. In discussing the Values Clarification approach Purpel and Ryan (1976: 122) state:

> Values clarification definitely values thinking, feeling, choosing, communicating and acting. Moreover, it values certain types of thinking, feeling, choosing, communicating and acting non-critically. Considering consequences is regarded as better than choosing glibly or thoughtlessly. Choosing freely is considered better than simply yielding to authority or peer pressure.

Part of the criticism which is implied in Purpel and Ryan's statement is that this approach is not only a process for the development of values, but that it also provides the content and thus is into the business of imposing values rather than evoking them. Values Clarification has also been accused of promoting conformist thinking; that in requiring students to assert their stance publicly, it is a form of pressure which endangers the rights of students to privacy. Despite these criticisms, however, values clarification is still regarded as a useful approach for the development of values in the classroom.

The theory of moral developmentalist thinkers such as Kohlberg in the 1960s and 1970s, following the work of Piaget in the 1960s, has exerted an influence upon the teaching of values in schools. Drawing on Piaget's stages of cognitive development, Kohlberg (1975) articulated a theory of the stages of moral reasoning. The environment is an important element in the framing and construction of the values an individual develops. Each individual will pass through a series of stages in moral development though the pace of progress will vary according to the individual. Moral reasoning is thought by Kohlberg to be based upon cognition and thus it is the task of the educator to create an environment which enhances an individual's movement through the stages of moral reasoning. Kohlberg's stages of moral reasoning are represented below.

Preconventional level

Stage 1 Avoidance of punishment and unquestioning obedience to superiors are valued.

Stage 2 Right action consists of that which instrumentally satisfies one's own needs and occasionally the needs of others (instrumentalist relativist orientation).

Conventional level

Stage 3 Good behaviour is that which pleases or helps others and is approved by them (interpersonal concordance orientation).

Stage 4 Authority, fixed rules and the maintenance of the social order are values.

Post-conventional level

Stage 5 Values agreed upon by the society, including individual rights, determine what is right.

Stage 6 Right is defined by one's conscience in accordance with self-chosen ethical principles (universal principle orientation).

Kohlberg's stages of moral reasoning (after Kohlberg, 1966, in Marsh and Stafford, 1988: 260)

Kohlberg claims that the highest stage of moral reasoning is to be desired and thus he establishes a hierarchy of moral reasoning. Strategies and activities derived from this approach to the teaching of values have included the moral dilemma approach. This strategy involves the creation of scenarios which involve a moral dilemma about appropriate choices for action. Discussion between students in a group occurs, perhaps following the role-play of the dilemma situation, and alternative approaches to the dilemma are raised and considered. This conflict situation is thought to stimulate students to form opinions and to be able to articulate their reasons for such opinions.

Criticisms of the moral developmental and moral dilemma approaches include concerns that individuals do not inevitably pass through all of the six stages which Kohlberg outlines. According to Marsh and Stafford, Gibbs (1977) claims that:

> The last two stages represent ideological and cultural points of view and can't be substantiated as universal to all cultures. If this is true then Kohlberg is simply perpetuating another form of values inculcation. Peters (1976) takes up a similar point when he criticizes Kohlberg for advocating that a morality based upon the concept of justice is the only type of morality that is defensible. Peters also argues that it may not be morally better for individuals to progress to stages 5 and 6. It may in fact be more important for citizens to be well bedded down in the other four stages.
>
> (Marsh and Stafford, 1988: 262)

Marsh and Stafford in their discussion of the criticisms of Kohlberg's approach also cite the writing of Perarsky (1980), who claims that moral dilemmas which are simulated in the classroom oversimplify the real-life dilemmas which people face and also that it requires considerable skill and sensitivity even to recognize that there is a moral problem that needs to be addressed (ibid.).

There are other critics such as Rest (1975) and Fraenkel (1977) who raise issues about Kohlberg's approach on pedagogical grounds in terms of their implications for the skills of matching and sequencing and the need to sequence dilemmas more rigorously than is traditionally the case.

Other strategies which have been evident in classrooms in the last two decades have focused upon the Values Analysis approach of Hunt and Metcalf (1968), Banks (1973) and Fraenkel (1977). In this approach a series of stages for decision making and moral reasoning are outlined as the basis for discussion and student activity in the area of values education. Analytical and

---

1 Students identify the issue or describe the problem.
2 Students identify alternative solutions to the problem or alternative positions on the issue.
3 Students hypothesize and/or collect data on the likely consequences of each alternative.
4 Students make a decision.
5 Students justify their decision.

(Marsh and Stafford, 1988: 263, after Hahn and Avery, 1985)

rational thought is a central concern in this approach. Marsh and Stafford provide the above list which outlines the steps to be worked through with students in the classroom.

In their discussion of the values analysis approach, Marsh and Stafford claim that Fraenkel's approach to values analysis, and especially his intake/organizational/demonstrative/expressive sequence, has been widely disseminated in curriculum documents. Critics such as Hahn and Avery (1985) suggest that the values analysis approach is difficult for teachers to adopt unless they receive adequate training sessions. It has also been noted that not all students are motivated to use or are capable of using this approach (Marsh and Stafford, 1988: 163).

There are, then, a number of different theoretical positions from which have developed specific approaches and strategies to be employed in classrooms for the teaching and development of values and for moral education programmes. The influence of religion and its supposed link with morals and values is also an element to be considered in a discussion of the theories which inform the teaching of values.

Influence

The relationship of morals and religion involves complex concepts and tensions which cannot be explored in depth here; however, a brief overview of some of the issues involved in this relationship will be provided. The secularist philosopher D.J. O'Connor addressed the issues of:

> deriving a moral 'ought' from a religious 'is'. In brief, if religion provides a description of the way the world is, one cannot from this logically deduce the way people ought to behave morally. O'Connor's second objection is that the claim that morality requires a religious base implies that people cannot be moral without being religious adherents, which ordinary observation would seem to refute.
>
> (O'Connor, 1957, cited in Hill, 1991: 23)

There is, then, a tension between the concepts of morality and religion and they are seen to be dependent upon one another in an unproblematic and inevitable way. It is presumed here, in admitting approaches to values education which are not based on religion, that one can act according to a moral or values base without resort to religion or religious beliefs as the basis for such moral action. People can thus act morally without any religious element underpinning their action. The position adopted here is that values may be prescribed by religion but religion is not required in order to establish values which bring about moral acts.

Having looked briefly at some of the possible theoretical positions which may provide a basis for the teaching and development of moral values, and having outlined the ramifications for the teaching of moral values in classrooms which may flow from an adherence to a particular theoretical position, we devote the following section of this chapter to a discussion of the way in which these theories may be consolidated and accommodated in a paradigmatic approach.

THEORIES INTO PRACTICE

A paradigm is taken here to refer to a group of theories or concepts which share a common element so as to make them in some way consonant with each other. When this approach is applied to the teaching of values in classrooms there is a variety of ways in which theories may be grouped. In the research project which is reported here, four paradigms have been employed to embrace the various approaches upon which strategies for values teaching may be based. The four paradigms are: religious monopolism; moral universalism; consensus pluralism, and moral vacuum. The first three of these paradigms are discussed in Hill (1991) while the moral vacuum paradigm, as it is construed in this study, has been constructed by the authors for the purposes of interpreting the data which have been collected. It is, then, according to these four paradigms that the data have been interpreted and the findings of each of the countries in the international study have been examined.

Religious monopolism

In this model, morality is considered to be directly dependent on one's religion which implies that it must be taught only within the framework of religious studies. The strong version of this argument is that there is only one true faith, and so only one efficacious morality.

(Hill, 1991: 22)

This model of thought may be considered an inappropriate and illegitimate basis for the totality of the teaching of values in a pluralistic society and thus be seen to be unsuited as a basis for devising and implementing values education programmes and approaches in secular settings. Within this paradigm the teaching and development of moral values is viewed as occurring legitimately only within the framework of religious beliefs. In some of the educational contexts in which this study has been conducted, for example in Australia where Christian schools have been established over the last two decades, or in Ireland where Catholicism, which is the dominant sect of Christianity, pervades education, this paradigm would have strong currency.

Moral universalism

Moral universalism ... maintains that religious disagreement is an undesirable and unnecessary complication in moral education and the

13

way ahead is to avoid it by identifying and teaching universal moral principles expected to command common agreement.

(Hill, 1991: 24)

Hill elaborates this concept by dividing the approach of moral universalism into two sub-concepts:

a) Substantivism – refers to the possibility of identifying moral principles common to all religions and which together form a basis for social values.
b) Formalism – relates to the way we talk about morality. Our discourse depends upon acceptance of the value of rationality and a willingness to place due weight upon the arguments of other people.

In this approach to the conceptualization of values and values education there is a search for common and universal meanings and understandings which provide a basis for teaching and learning and also for the development and implementation of values education programmes in educational contexts. The problematic elements in this approach are clearly the difficulty of arriving at agreed and universal moral values and the concern that what is universal or rational is itself a decision which is based upon particular values.

Consensus pluralism

The aim is to make students aware of the human quest for ultimate justifications and able to dialogue with persons of different persuasion without feeling threatened or hostile, while at the same time working with them to make the democratic community function morally. It is clear that, in this model, values education, so-called, is neither religious studies nor moral education alone, but embraces both ... It requires that students develop a critical awareness of the value domain and assume personal responsibility for the values they embrace.

(Hill, 1991: 28)

This model may be seen to be applicable in a democratic society where the processes of educational settings are required to model the processes of a democracy. In this model, the curriculum reflects values obtained through community negotiation and consensus regarding the values and principles which are necessary in order to maintain a secular, democratic and pluralist society. A question to be addressed when discussing this approach, however, is the applicability of this model to settings where the ideology of democracy and pluralism is not overtly espoused.

These three paradigms may allow for some organization of the findings of this study. It appears, however, that a fourth model may be proposed. This model resembles the so-called garbage-can model of administration as propounded by Cohen, March and Olsen (1972), which is based upon the

14

notion that strategies for administration can be best described as 'a loose collection of ideas [rather than] a coherent structure; preferences are discovered through action rather than on the basis of values' (Owens, 1981: 24). If we liken the basis on which decisions about the issue of values are made in education to this loose collection of ideas, which is not based in any clear structure or framework, a fourth model for interpreting the findings of this study may be defined. We have termed this eclectic and unstructured approach to the teaching of values the 'moral vacuum' paradigm.

If one reflects upon the notion of a vacuum, which is defined as 'space entirely devoid of matter', we can use this metaphor to address a situation where there may be a lack of substance evident in the way educators conceptualize values. If we extrapolate the notion of a vacuum to a modern-day example, we may use the analogy of a vacuum cleaner where a multiplicity of diverse elements are sucked in at one end and become a grey, amorphous mass of dust. If the vacuum cleaner is used in its blowing rather than its sucking mode, disparate and random elements are blown indiscriminately into the air. This may be seen to describe an approach to values education.

THE PLACE OF VALUES EDUCATION

In the public arena the concept of values is always contentious and underpins many of the media comments regarding education which are sometimes intelligent and at other times represent the pooling of ignorance. A day seldom passes without some news bulletin on television or radio or a leader or article in the popular or quality press mentioning, in the same breath, education and values. The story is usually one illustrating some real or imagined shortcoming in schools, pupils and their teachers, arising from or leading to less than desirable behaviour on a moral, social or personal front. Codes of ethics are publicly assumed to have been superseded or ignored. In media reports, standards of personal and community behaviour are demonstrated to have fallen and reasons and culprits are sought and identified. Media headlines in the various continents may be similar, even though the underlying causes identified may be different, as will be the suggested remedies. The responsibility of schools is acknowledged to be present in all societies and the school is traditionally seen as a tool in alleviating social problems.

With the growth of electronic communication systems, barriers of distance, nationality, culture and ideology are being challenged and recast. The values which would previously have been attributed to a specific milieu or locale are now being reformulated within a more global perspective according to the consequences of the stretching of time and space. With the rise of multinational companies and the internationalization of aspects of social, economic and political life, it is the system of values which informs such a process of internationalization that requires examination, critique and explanation. At the same time there is the tension created by often sizeable sections of a country's population striving to maintain their own 'higher' or stricter code of morals or behaviour in the face of influences from the dominant culture within both the country and the shrinking world. Instances of this can be seen in the multicultural populations of, for instance, the United Kingdom and, increasingly, Australia, where religious beliefs as well as ways of living are diverse. Israel is a further example, where religion may be shared by some but a consensus about acceptable values does not necessarily follow. As the formal schooling process constitutes the common vehicle for the development and reinforcement of basic social, moral, political and economic values, it is pertinent that such an examination of the internationalization of values begins at the schooling and teacher education level. As will be seen in later chapters of this book, the school system, within which values education operates, varies from country to country and is often diverse within the individual state.

The diversity of practice which exists between the countries represented in this study is not, however, as great as might have been expected given the different societies and the recent past history of the societies in which the schools are set. As revealed in the data, teachers' reactions to challenges show a degree of uniformity even when the impetus for action is quite different. Teachers' actions are, however, also constrained by aspects of their national situation, both within the school setting and in the wider community. Even here similarities outweigh differences. Similarities of principle should not be uncritically accepted, however, since it is the way these principles are affected by the historical, ideological, social and cultural mores of the context, as well as the particularities of the subject curriculum in which they are presented, which may provide a more accurate measure of their effect. The education systems involved in this study appear to be in a process of reform of their curricula, specifically in relation to areas which could be regarded as pertinent to values education. The hand of government as reflected in political philosophy and policy is also apparent, as is the increasingly diverse nature of the school population. The place of the teachers within their own society may have a bearing on this uniformity. Most respondents were of the prevailing ethnic and to some extent 'establishment' section of the population. The format of the Israeli study is of particular interest here, where teacher-respondents, as well as the schools, were designated by cultural area. A similarly diverse sample of the multi-ethnic and multi-faith teaching population, where they exist, in Australia and the United Kingdom might reveal more diversity.

Although formal religion, as part of education, appears in the curricula of most countries, this is not always reflected in the attitudes expressed by the teachers in their approach to values teaching in the classroom. The fact that religious beliefs form part and parcel of everyday thought and living is, however, acknowledged by the presenters in Ireland and Israel. The hidden influence of formative religious moral codes is also considered in Slovenia and the United Kingdom. The source of their own value judgements is not necessarily acknowledged or recognized by teachers. The concept of neutral or 'value-free' actions, though held to be universal by some respondents, is contradicted by the attitudes of other respondents. Each individual population of respondents does display its own diversity, though not to uniform degrees.

The practice of integration and discrete teaching of values was addressed in each country. Age and phase of development often seemed to affect the balance here. The permeation of values through all subjects was held to be desirable by most, despite the evidence of such diffusion becoming confusion in other areas of the curriculum. The sophistication of respondents' own values knowledge was questioned; if teacher educators seek to address the continuing needs of teachers through in-service support, the theoretical perspectives of teachers' values, beliefs and development may present an area for future research.

THE PRESENT STUDY

The researchers in this book are all attached to institutions of higher education which undertake the training of teachers as a specialized area. All modes of teacher training in the countries included have, as part of their course, practical periods spent in schools. These schools span the diversity of types, age phases, social and economic mixes found within the geographical areas in which the institutions are situated. Through their work with students in schools, the researchers had access to practising teachers who were willing to take part in the research study. This was particularly useful in allowing interview techniques as well as questionnaires to be used for data collection. The rapport already established between researcher and respondent helped in bringing about some free expression of beliefs and attitudes which might not have been so extensive had the entire project been conducted with unknown respondents.

The teachers and students taking part also see the situation *vis-à-vis* the position of schools and values education to be a matter of concern for their continuing or future careers. They felt positively involved and in most cases could see the relevance of the study to the demands that were being put on them in schools. It is in response to their involvement that the decision was taken to produce a publication which, while firmly based on research with practising and intending teachers, and primarily concerned with the data and issues raised by the research project, would go further than that and consider some ways in which the issues raised in classrooms could be developed and addressed in schools. The similarities and differences between countries add to the basis of understanding and shared knowledge of values, attitudes and practices demonstrated by these teachers in their schools and contribute to possible programmes to meet the demands of the communities in which teachers work. The question of whether the beliefs and practices of teachers in schools, the schools themselves and the values they seek to inculcate match those to be found in or demanded by the general public remains as a burning issue in each of the countries included.

This book does not aim to give a global picture of values education. What it constitutes is an attempt to explore within different geographic, cultural, religious, economic and political locales the values which are espoused in the curriculum of formal schooling in these particular contexts, and also to examine the teaching and learning strategies in the area of values education.

The book is divided into four parts: following this introduction and rationale, the second chapter covers the research methodology employed in this study. This addresses in detail the empirical element in the book. This is followed in Part II by accounts of the studies of values education under- taken in each of the countries involved. The contributors present and analyse their findings, within the social and cultural context, in their schools and societies. Part III looks at possible outcomes, in the classroom setting, in the form of activities which can be followed with students of all ages. These have been formulated to address the theoretical framework put forward as a result of the findings of the research project. Adaptations for age range and circumstance are suggested and possible extension activities are outlined. Much emphasis is placed upon their being aids and not prescriptions for teacher action and involvement. Part IV begins with an overview of values education in the United States. A decade or more has passed since the area of 'values' was an over-riding concern of educators in America, and by looking at the outcomes and challenges to theory and practice in the USA, the author is able to take a reflective stance on the issues surrounding the current debates in the societies in which the empirical study took place. The concluding chapter returns to the position of values education in our society today.

This chapter has been concerned with outlining a variety of theoretical foundations upon which values education in schools may be based. The values education component of a school programme will assume a different shape if the understanding of values in education differs, as indicated in the review of alternative values education positions. The concern which under- pins this chapter is that educators are required to examine and reflectively critique these theoretical stances and then to synthesize selectively a theo- retical position from which to function in the area of values and moral education. One of the tasks of teacher education, both at a pre-service and at an in-service level, may be to present these theoretical perspectives to teachers and to facilitate their critical reflection on them as a basis for classroom practice.

REFERENCES

Ayer, A.J. (1936) *Language, Truth and Logic* (London, Gollancz).

Banks, J.A. (ed.) (1973) *Teaching Ethnic Studies*, 43rd Year Book (Washington DC, National Council for Social Studies).

Baudrillard, J. (1981) *For a Critique of the Political Economy of the Sign* (St Louis, Telos Press).

Beilharz, P. (ed.) (1991) *Social Theory: A Guide to Central Thinkers* (Sydney, Allen & Unwin Pty Ltd).

Cohen, M.D., March, J.G. and Olsen, J.P. (1972) 'A Garbage Can Model of Organizational Choice', *Administrative Science Quarterly*, 17 (1): 1–25.

Dictionary of Philosophy (1979) (London, Pan Books).

Drucker, P.F. (1993) *Post Capitalist Society* (Oxford, Butterworth-Heinemann).

Eco, U. (1986) *Travels in Hyper-Reality* (London, Picador).

Fraenkel, J.R. (1977) *How to Teach about Values: An Analytic Approach* (Englewood Cliffs, New Jersey, Prentice-Hall).

Gibbs, J.C. (1977) 'Kohlberg's Stages of Moral Judgement: A Constructive Critique', *Harvard Educational Review*, 47 (1).

Giddens, A. (1991) *Modernity and Self Identity: Self and Society in the Late Modern Age* (Cambridge, Polity Press).

Hill, B.V. (1991) *Values Education in Australian Schools* (Melbourne, ACER).

Hunt, M.P. and Metcalf, L.E. (1968) *Teaching High School Social Studies* (New York, Harper & Row).

Jarrett, J.L. (1991) *The Teaching of Values: Caring and Appreciation* (London, Routledge).

Kohlberg, L. (1975) 'The Cognitive-Developmental Approach to Moral Education', *Phi Delta Kappan*, 56 (10).

Lyotard, J.-F. (1984) *The Post-modern Condition: A Report on Knowledge* (Manchester, Manchester University Press).

Marsh, C. and Stafford, K. (1988) *Curriculum: Practices and Issues*, 2nd edn (Roseville, Australia, McGraw-Hill).

O'Connor, D.J. (1957) *Introduction to the Philosophy of Education* (London, Routledge & Kegan Paul).

Owens, R.G. (1981) *Organizational Behaviour in Education*, 4th edn (Englewood Cliffs, New Jersey, Prentice-Hall).

Parker, De Witt H. (1931) *Human Values* (New York, Harper).

Perarsky, D. (1980) 'Moral Dilemmas and Moral Education', *Theory and Research in Social Education*, 8 (1).

Peters, R.S. (1976) 'Why Doesn't Lawrence Kohlberg Do His Homework?', *Phi Delta Kappan*, 56 (10).

Purpel, D. and Ryan, K. (1976) *Moral Education: It Comes with the Territory* (Berkeley, California, McCutcheon).

Raths, J. (1971) 'Teaching without Specific Educational Objectives', *Educational Leadership*, April: 714–20.

Raths, L., Harmin, M. and Simons, S.B. (1966) *Values and Teaching: Working with Values in the Classroom* (Columbus, Ohio, Charles E. Merrill).

Rest, J. (1975) 'The Validity of Tests of Moral Judgement', in J. R. Meyer (ed.) *Values Education Theory/Practice/Problems/Prospects* (Waterloo, Ontario, University Press).

Stevenson, C.L. (1944) *Ethics and Language* (London and New Haven, Yale University Press).

Taylor, P.W. (1961) *Normative Discourse* (Englewood Cliffs, New Jersey, Prentice-Hall).

2

INVESTIGATING VALUES
IN EDUCATION

Peter Ling

This chapter describes the methods adopted in investigating the approaches to values education taken by teachers in schools and in pre-service teacher education, their explicit positions and their underlying rationales. It deals also with investigating views about the most effective ways of preparing teachers to teach values and handle approaches to values in schools. The chapter concludes with some observations about the ways in which teachers can clarify for themselves their own position and that of people with whom they work as a basis for developing a coherent approach to the teaching of values in schools.

STRUCTURE OF THE INVESTIGATION

The empirical contributions to this book arise from a multiple-phase study conducted through independent investigations in a number of countries. The study proceeded through three phases.

Stage 1

An exploratory study was conducted in Australia surveying pre-service teacher education students in two universities in Melbourne on perceptions of the role of teachers in the area of attitudes and values; their perceptions of problems which they anticipated in relation to attitudes and values in classroom situations; their views on approaches which teachers could adopt; and their views on the preparation in this field provided by their teacher education courses. The exploratory study revealed several issues in values education which were reported at the 1993 Association for Teacher Education in Europe conference. The study appeared to be pertinent to other countries. It was decided to survey these issues among teacher education students and practising teachers in a number of countries. As a result the exploratory study was followed by a two-stage multinational study.

Stage 2

The first part of the multinational study surveyed the perceptions of teacher education students about teacher attitudes they regarded as necessary; the roles which they saw as appropriate for teachers in the area of values education; and their views on appropriate teacher approaches to values conflicts. The investigation was conducted in Australia by researchers at La Trobe University and the University of Melbourne, in Slovenia at the University of Ljubljana, in Switzerland at the University of Berne, in the United Kingdom at Bedford College of Higher Education (now De Montfort University), and in the USA at Central Missouri State University. Analysis of the results of this multinational survey allowed the generation of a four-category typology of approaches to values education.

Stage 3

The final phase of the empirical study (the second part of the multinational study) saw the employment of an open-ended questionnaire which explored teaching practices and approaches among final-year teacher education students and among practising teachers (mostly in-service teacher education students). The questionnaire provided a means to examine principles upon which teachers based their teaching of values; classroom strategies they employed; cultural issues which teachers perceived as influencing the values dimension of curriculum; teachers' perceptions of the origin, organization, and implementation of curriculum; and teachers' perceptions of the most important elements in values education in schools and in teacher education. It was translated where necessary. The questionnaire was supported by interview in some instances and by observations in others. Each of the participants reported his or her responses in terms of the typology which emerged from the first stage of the international study. The final phase of the project was conducted in Australia by La Trobe University and the University of Melbourne, in the Republic of Ireland by University College Dublin, in Israel by the University of Tel Aviv, in Slovenia by the University of Ljubljana, in Switzerland by the University of Berne and in the United Kingdom by De Montfort University.

INVESTIGATIVE TOOLS

The study involved an exploratory questionnaire used only in Australia, which focused on values education in teacher education programmes. This was modified in the first phase of the international study to address curriculum decision making. A final questionnaire was developed to focus on values education practice in the classroom with some consequences for teacher education. The questionnaires were complemented with one or more alternative exploratory techniques at each site. These included observations of classroom practice, semi-structured interviews, loosely structured interviews and document analysis. Information gleaned from these processes was used to help in assigning meaning to questionnaire responses as well as enriching commentary upon the context and substance of national responses.

The initial pilot questionnaire explored the following topics in an open-ended response format:

• the role of the teacher in the area of attitudes and values in the classroom;
• problems or issues which could be expected in classrooms with regard to the teaching of attitudes and values;
• approaches which should be adopted by teacher education courses for their role in the teaching of attitudes and values in the classroom;
• the strengths of existing teacher education courses in preparing future teachers to address values and attitudes in the classroom.

The first of the multinational studies employed a similar questionnaire but with two added topics relating to curriculum:

• the factors which should be taken into account when deciding upon the content to be included in or excluded from school curricula;
• the place of socially relevant topics, such as environmental education and peace studies, in school curriculum.

STRATEGIES

In the 1994 surveys in Australia, Slovenia and England respondents were given no direction or structure for the way they gave their answer to the questions asked. In this phase of the study a team from the USA also participated. In the case of the US survey the questions were reformatted as multiple choices from which students selected. This allowed the possibility of quantitative analysis of data and correlational expression of results if appropriate sampling techniques were employed.

Cultural distinctions mentioned above required adaptation of the original questionnaire to suit the local context. In the case of the US study a positivist research tradition led to the reformatting of the questionnaire to prescribed categories of responses amenable to quantification and correlation. The strictures this placed on student responses, however, interfered with comparability with the responses from other countries and the US data has not been used in the final analysis.

The questionnaire for the final stage of the multinational study explored six topics, again in open-ended format but this time asking for set numbers of responses. The responses sought were:

- three essential principles upon which the respondent made decisions with regard to the teaching and development of values in the curriculum programme;
- four classroom strategies (formal and informal) which the respondent employed in the areas of values development and teaching within the classroom context;
- five predominant cultural issues which the respondent perceived to exert major influence upon the values of dimension of curriculum;
- a comment on each of four sub-questions relating to values development and teaching in the respondent's context:
  whose knowledge forms the basis of the course
  how the knowledge is organized for learners
  how the knowledge is imparted to learners
  to whom the knowledge is made available;
- five most important elements which values teaching in schools and the values components of teacher education courses should address.

Interviews were loosely structured or semi-structured, addressing issues raised in the questionnaire. The interviews allowed responses which were unclear in the questionnaires to be clarified and for responses to be elaborated. In some cases the interviews brought out information not addressed in responses to the questionnaire; for example, teachers' unfamiliarity with the concept of values education became apparent through the interview process. Interviews were intended to be individual but in one case, England, a group interview was also conducted, providing the opportunity for more challenge to positions and more discursive responses.

REPORTING

In each country the local investigation team clustered the data, reviewing the data received to identify common types of response. In some cases the clustering process was computer-aided using Hyperqual, SPSS or Nudist software. In reporting, excerpts from open-ended questionnaire responses and from interviews have been used to illustrate typical responses or, in a few specified cases, atypical responses.

In interpreting the outcome of questionnaires in the final phase of the investigation, clustered responses were reviewed and reported against the four-category typology of approaches to values education based upon a typology devised by Hill (1991).

Categorization

The original categories of Hill's typology were consensus pluralism, religious monopolism and moral universalism. It was found necessary in the light of data emerging from the study to add a moral vacuum category. Consensus pluralism included approaches which emphasized tolerance and awareness of individual difference and tried to accommodate many values, possibly aiming at the development of critical thinking in analysis of value positions. Religious monopolism was associated with a view that the teaching of values should be or could only be addressed through religion. Moral universalism was based on the premise that there are values common to all cultures or values which are universally recognized. The moral vacuum category accommodated situations in which there was a loose collection of ideas about values in education rather than any particular structured approach; situations in which there was a lack of clear focus or direction.

Individual studies

The original study

The empirical component of the work reported in this book had its origins in an Australian study (Ling, Cooper and Burman, 1993) which examined teacher and student perceptions of the role of values in the school curriculum. The study surveyed 110 teacher education students from two universities preparing to teach in primary schools. The study employed a questionnaire which probed perceptions of the role of the teacher in the area of attitudes and values; problems in the teaching of attitudes and values; approaches which should be taken in teacher education; and the strengths of existing teacher education courses in this area.

It was apparent from the responses that teachers in Australia, which is a pluralist society, were conscious of the need to accommodate a range of attitude and value stances while at the same time they felt that the teacher had an obligation to act as a role model, which implies taking and inculcating a particular value position. The diversity of student cultural and religious backgrounds was perceived both as a given to be accommodated in values education and as a problem for curriculum design and for interactive class-room behaviours. Preferred approaches to the assessment of student work in the area of values education were soft focused. Observation of behaviour, art and drama activities, creative writing and anecdotal notes were mentioned as means by which to assess student values learning. The same theme ran through suggestions for teacher education with dilemmas, role-plays, problem-solving and the establishment of a caring environment being prominent in responses about appropriate activities for teacher education programmes in values education. Recognition and acceptance of individual differences was held by respondents to the survey to be a feature of teacher education, but there was room, according to respondents, for more attention to be given to values and attitudes in teacher education. A working group of the Association for Teacher Education in Europe, feeling that the issues raised needed to be addressed by teachers and teacher educators elsewhere, decided to pursue a similar investigation in a number of countries.

Multinational studies

The two-phase multinational study involved a refinement rather than a replication of the original study. A six-item questionnaire was devised to be administered in five countries, including Australia. The new questionnaire was administered in Australia as it contained questions additional to those of the original study. Complementary activities were undertaken in some of the sites to clarify meanings in responses to the questionnaire. Analysis of results from the surveys in the five countries led to the adoption of the typology previously mentioned for considering approaches to values education. In order to facilitate comparison between countries, the final-stage questionnaire was devised with a view to providing for the analysis of responses against the typology. The results reported in this publication are confined to those countries which participated in the final phase.

Australia, La Trobe University, Graduate School of Education and the University of Melbourne, Institute of Education

The final-stage questionnaire in Australia was administered to seventy-five pre-service teacher education students and to thirty-six experienced primary school teachers with a range of teaching experience. For each of the open-ended questions responses were analysed and grouped into clusters of concepts on an exclusive basis. The responses of student teachers were grouped separately from those of experienced teachers. Some distinctions between the two groups in the pattern of conceptual clusters emerged, particularly in terms of ideal approaches as against practical approaches.

As proved to be the case in the application of the questionnaire to other countries, some respondents had difficulty understanding the meaning of some questions, thus reducing the value their contribution could make to the clustering of concepts derived from the responses. There was also apparent difficulty in determining whether to respond in terms of espoused positions on values in education or in terms of the lived curriculum and practices.

Following the clustering of responses a commentary was provided interpreting the results against the agreed typology. This interpretation of the results was also informed by follow-up interviews with student teachers and experienced teachers. There was evidence of respondents adopting each of the positions provided for in the typology – religious monopolism, moral universalism and consensus pluralism – though not with equal force. In the Australian case, as in the Israeli experience, it proved necessary to add a category to the typology. In the case of Australia this category was styled the moral vacuum model. It was a classification which resonated with analysts from some other countries when reported at the 1995 ATEE conference and was taken into account in the final preparation of reports.

Ireland, University College Dublin, Education Department

The Irish study involved forty teachers, twenty practising primary teachers and twenty pre-service teacher education students. The gender balances of the two groups were reasonably representative of the teaching force.

The questionnaire of five open-ended questions employed in the original Australian study was administered to all forty participants. A content analysis of all questions was undertaken to divide responses into broad and narrow levels of abstraction. Further analysis and interpretation was carried out using SPSS software. The use of this package allowed observations to be made about relationships between clusters of respondents. It should be noted that this involves a different concept of clustering from that used elsewhere in this study. Clustering in the Irish responses relates to grouping of respondents according to their range of responses whereas clustering in the other cases refers to types or categories of responses, regardless of the other replies of the respondent. The use of the SPSS package also allowed the quantification of responses, which was not pursued in the original Australian study on the grounds that the study was descriptive rather than involving the identification of causal links and that sampling was non-systematic and analysis could not lead to probability statements about correlation or about cause.

The questionnaire was triangulated with informal discussions and semi-structured interviews and a small number of classroom observations.

In the Irish context values education has been treated as an integral component of religious education. This influences the ability to respond in terms of the values paradigm used in this study.

Israel, Tel Aviv University, Faculty of Humanities, School of Education

The agreed open-ended questionnaire devised for the final stage of the study was translated into Hebrew and applied to a sample of student teachers, practising teachers, pedagogical supervisors and teacher educators. Seventy-six returns were received. The questionnaire responses were analysed according to the model of Hill (1991) employed throughout this study. To suit Israel's situation and the responses received, an additional category – nationalism – was used to supplement Hill's categories of moral universalism, consensus pluralism and religious monopolism in encoding the data. Frequency of response for each category is noted. The respondent's ranking of value preferences was used as a means to indicate the intensity of responses.

The questionnaire was found to be problematic for some respondents who were uncertain of the intent of the questions, and was complemented by interviews and documented analysis of college course syllabuses.

The report distinguishes the results of interviews and document analysis from the results of the questionnaire. In reporting findings responses were categorized to distinguish discipline-based values training, particularly pertinent to the inculcation of nationalism, and more general values training. In relation to the latter, a distinction was made between religious schools and secular institutions, which were slightly over-represented in the survey. The views of Arab teacher educators in Israel were dealt with separately as they showed some distinctive characteristics.

Slovenia, University of Ljubljana, Faculty of Education

The study of the attitude of teachers to values education in Slovenia was informed by previous studies into values *per se* (Musek, 1993; Zupancic, 1991).

The agreed final-stage questionnaire of open-ended questions was translated into Slovene. The thrust of the questions and anticipated responses was discussed with the Australian team to produce the best fidelity of translation. The questionnaire was administered to twenty practising primary school teachers from different schools throughout Slovenia and to fifty-six primary pre-service second-year teacher education students.

In analysing the Slovenian responses a secondary tool for classification was employed. Eleven value orientations defined by Musek (1993) were used to categorize responses to the final question on the survey. No responses were found to fit two of Musek's categories. The values categories employed in this part of the analysis were sensual, status, patriotic, democratic, traditional moral, cultural, religious, conceptual, and self-actualization. For other questions, categories were constructed following review of responses. Responses were quantified.

Six second-year students were also interviewed about their own experiences of values teaching in schools. Interviews were individual. They were recorded and analysed.

Switzerland, Universität Bern, Forschungsstelle für Schulpädagogik und Fachdidaktik (University of Berne, Research Department for School Pedagogics and Subject Didactics)

The agreed six-item questionnaire, developed after the original Australian study, was administered in 1994 to secondary teachers who had completed their studies. Results were analysed and reported on at the Association for Teacher Education in Europe Conference of 1994. In 1995 the question-naire for the later phase of the study, which comprised the five agreed items, was administered to fifty-seven students and eighty-three secondary teaching graduates of the University of Berne selected at random.

The return rate was disappointing and a post-survey with a smaller ran-dom sample of students of a training institution as well as with practising teachers was conducted to find the reasons. Time pressures as well as uncertainty about questions raised in the survey were mentioned.

An analysis of responses was undertaken to cluster responses to the questions and to define the characteristics of a teacher influential in values education. The small number of returns allowed the detailed examination of responses by individual rather than by clustering of concepts and hence no correlations were reported, but patterns of response emerge in the concluding remarks. Observations include a differential between the con-fidence of older teachers and that of graduating student teachers in their capacity to transmit values or act as a role model. A summary of this is included as an appendix.

United Kingdom De Montfort University, Bedford, Department of Education

The questionnaire of five open-ended questions employed in the original Australian study was administered to forty-four final-year undergraduate primary students in 1994 and the agreed developed instrument for 1995 was completed by twenty practising primary school teachers working in state schools. The teachers were self-selected, though the schools were selected to give a spread of school size and social area. The age, sex and racial com-position of the respondent group reflects the position in English primary schools.

The questionnaire was triangulated with interviews and observations. Questionnaires were followed up with semi-structured interviews with fifteen teachers. One session was conducted in a group as an open dis-course allowing response to remarks of peers and the reformulation or re-expression of positions. The interviews were conducted with a cross-section of ages of teachers and types of school.

Observation sessions were conducted in three classrooms in separate schools selected to represent different social areas, school size and edu-cational methods. The observation sessions gave the opportunity to check impressions received from review of questionnaire and interview data against actual approaches to values education in the classroom, and against value stances indicated by teachers' classroom behaviours.

CHALLENGES

Cultural constraints in investigating the teaching of values

While a case could be made that there are some universally accepted values, values in education are culturally bound. No aspect of curriculum is taught in a cultural void, and the relationship of values education to cultural context throws up particular challenges in attempting an international study. Approaches to the teaching of mathematics may vary from one country to another but it has proved possible to come up with a single investigative instrument which can sensibly be applied internationally (Keeves, 1969). An international study of approaches to science teaching has also been undertaken (Comber and Keeves, 1973). To find a single tool or set of questions which are appropriate to the cultures and educational practices of the various countries participating in this study of values education is more difficult, and adaptation of the investigative tool has been necessary.

The role of religion in schooling varies between national system, with such fundamental implications for the relationship between schooling and values that a questionnaire devised for a multicultural society with a secular school system might have had no applicability to a school system based on one particular religion. In the event it was the pertinence of the questionnaire to their own situations which drew participants into the investigation.

Nevertheless some respondents apparently had difficulty with the meaning of some questions because of the inappropriateness of the questions to their situation. Questions shaped with the Australian school system in mind were not always applicable in other school systems. For instance, the distinction between formal and informal curriculum strategies for values education was not appreciated by English teachers.

A further difficulty was language. The questionnaire employed had to be translated from the original English in three cases, which, particularly given the subject matter, raised the possibility of altering meanings. In the Slovene language, for example, the expression for education implies moral and values education, making it difficult to isolate the role of values education in education. The potential for confusion is compounded by the subsequent need to retranslate reporting of clustered responses into English.

A further difficulty in international comparison is the fact that respondents may feel more or less familiar and comfortable with the processes involved, and more or less free to express their opinions.

Modes of investigation, particularly in the social studies arena, are also culturally bound. Research cultures differ. Following the initial survey conducted in Australia, some colleagues from the USA adapted the agreed multinational questionnaire devised with an open-ended structure to a closed-structure survey in order more readily to quantify results. The softly focused interpretative approach did not suit their research culture and they did not participate in the final survey. Those who did participate have sometimes referred to the survey as a qualitative investigation. Qualitative is often juxtaposed with quantitative. Several of the analysts in this investigation have utilized quantitative reporting forms as well as qualitative and all have made some reference, however oblique, to frequency of responses of particular types. It is more appropriate, therefore, to refer to the study as a whole as interpretative rather than qualitative in approach. That is, apart from the US survey mentioned above which was not included in the final study, all the tools employed by the various investigators – the agreed open-ended survey, interviews and observations – allowed open varied responses which required subsequent interpretation for clustering and for other forms of analysis. Comparability of results of the investigation is compromised in that in each case approaches to analysis of responses differed and in most cases supplementary tools were employed to assist interpretation of responses.

OBSERVATIONS

The basic tools used in the empirical component of the study of values education in the participating countries were developed and modified as the study progressed through its three phases. The investigation was an iterative process in which the thrust of the investigation remained constant but the elements to be explored and the tools for conducting the investigation were modified according to experience and adapted to suit changing focuses.

For educators working with values curriculum and others interested in the part that values inevitably play in education, questions asked in this investigation may be helpful in clarifying their own positions and the position of others around them. Value positions cannot be avoided in educational processes. The choice to be made is whether to operate with implicit values in ignorance of practice and possibilities, or to operate within an explicit values frame of reference, understanding one's own position and that of other agents in the education system and appreciating some of the alternatives which are available. Use of some of the investigative tools employed in this study can help in making a realistic assessment of constraints and choices in individual educational contexts. As was found in this study, the investigative tools need adaptation to new situations; the analysis of results can lead to the development of better instruments; new participants from different education systems bring new circumstances; and the focus of interest may change over time.

If we move from the tools to the analysis of result, the four-category typology employed in this study can assist with the interpretation of investigative results in a framework which has wide applicability. It also gives the possibility of comparison with the systems represented in this study. The framework can clarify one's own position and that of people with whom one works. In doing so it can contribute to the development of a coherent approach to the teaching of values.

REFERENCES

Comber, L.C. and Keeves, J.P. (1973) *Science Education in Nineteen Countries: An Empirical Study* (New York, Wiley).

Hill, B.V. (1991) *Values Education in Australian Schools* (Melbourne, ACER).

Keeves, J. (1969) *A Report on Australian Participation in the International Study of Educational Achievement in Mathematics in 1964* (Melbourne, ACER).

Ling, L., Cooper, M. and Burman, E. (1993) 'Values: Caught or Taught?' Paper presented at the Annual Conference for the Association for Teacher Education in Europe (Lisbon, Portugal).

Musek, Janek (1993) 'Value Crisis, Values and Psychology', *Horizons of Psychology*, 3/4, 123–41 (abstracts in English).

Zupancic, M. and Justin, J. (1991) *Otrok, pravila, vrednote* (Radovljica, Didakta).

Part II
PERSPECTIVES

3

THE AUSTRALIAN STUDY

Lorraine Ling, Eva Burman and Maxine Cooper

THE AUSTRALIAN CONTEXT OF EDUCATION

Australia has a population of approximately 18 million people, of whom over 3 million are school students. There are government and non-government schools in the Australian education system, thus a dual system operates. Approximately 74 per cent of students are enrolled in government schools. The non-government schools are frequently supported by a religious denomination but this is not always the case, as there are community schools, Montessori schools, Steiner schools and other alternative schools. Australia has a federal system of government and each of the six states and two territories is provided with an allocation of funding for education. Policy for the education system is constructed at three levels. At the macro or national level there are broad guidelines set down regarding the objectives and expected outcomes for education in Australia. This policy is then further specified at the meso or state level where curriculum frameworks and guidelines for the schools in the state are articulated and where the management system of government schools is decided. The third level of policy construction and decision making occurs at the micro or local level and involves the school community as a whole in decisions regarding curriculum and organization of the school. There are, then, three levels of policy with each level further refining and narrowing the policy directions so that it pertains to specific contexts of education.

The Australian education system has undergone almost continuous change for several decades. These changes have taken the form of structural changes, changes to methods of funding, construction and reconstruction of aims and goals of education, new staffing awards, curriculum change and innovation, and a reorientation in terms of the relationships which individual schools have with each other, the community in which they are placed, and the central educational bureaucracy. Much of the refocusing and reorienting which schools are experiencing centres around issues of accountability, self-management and school-based decision making. There has been a marked decentralization of administration and decision-making responsibilities to local sites, which has been viewed as having both advantages and disadvantages. The fact remains, however, that at a national level, the values which underpin education in Australian schools are articulated by the government of the day and are filtered through to local school sites.

Context of Victorian State education

Government schools in the Victorian State education system are the responsibility of the Victorian Minister of Education. Apart from a 'voluntary contribution' which parents are encouraged to pay, education in Victorian government schools is considered to be 'free'. In the non-government schools, parents pay fees but there is also some provision of funding from the government. There are approximately 1,941 schools in Victoria with a student enrolment of more than 535,000. There are approximately 39,000 teachers employed in the government school system. The Ministry of Education is responsible for the registration of non-government schools and teaching staff, but in other respects non-government schools are autonomous. It would be true to say, however, that the curriculum documents which direct the government school system set the dominant agenda for the curriculum of non-government schools. All students are required to attend school between the ages of 6 and 15 years but in general the majority of students begin school at 5 and remain until the completion of year 12 or approximately age 17 years.

Victorian schools are governed by school councils according to broad policy guidelines set down by the Department of Education (DOE). It is the principal's responsibility for ensuring that DOE policy is enacted.

TEACHER EDUCATION

Teachers in government primary schools must complete at least three years of tertiary education including the equivalent of at least one year of teacher training. The requirement is currently in the process of extension to a four-year qualification with conjecture that before the year 2000, the requirement will be for five years of tertiary education. Teachers in government secondary schools must obtain a first degree of at least three years' duration, followed by a Diploma of Education, which is a one-year course. All teacher education now takes place in universities following the amalgamation of the teachers' colleges with universities, thus altering the tertiary teacher education system from a dual system to a single system.

CURRICULUM

While there is currently not a National Curriculum, moves are afoot to instigate such a curriculum initiative. The federal government, however, sets down the key learning areas which must be part of the curriculum of all Australian schools. It is then the responsibility of each of the states and territories to provide broad curriculum guidelines to the government schools to ensure that the key learning areas are taught. The curriculum guidelines are typically referred to as being 'non-prescriptive' and are designed to allow for flexible interpretation and for idiosyncrasies of specific contexts to be accommodated. The key learning areas (KLAs) which are to be the core of all curriculum in Australian schools are:

English
Mathematics
Science
Health and Physical Education
Languages Other Than English (LOTE)
Studies of Society and the Environment
Technology
The Arts

It is important to note, especially in the context of values in education, that the Australian government and the Victorian Department of Education strongly support the teaching of Languages Other Than English. In a statement issued by the Directorate of School Education in a report to the Minister for Education (1994) it is claimed that:

> The study of languages is an intrinsically and extrinsically worthwhile activity. It contributes to the development of skills essential to the worlds of study and work, as well as to meaningful participation in the life of society. It can develop the creative imagination, intellectual rigour, the critical faculty, an awareness of cultural contexts and the tolerance of diversity.
>
> (Directorate of School Education, 1994: 14)

The languages which have been designated as the eight key languages in Australian schools in the area of 'Languages Other Than English' are Chinese, French, German, Indonesian, Italian, Japanese, Modern Greek, Vietnamese. This represents a balance between the European and Asian languages and may show the link between the recent moves to join the Asian Pacific Basin as a trading nation and the past connections with Europe.

Over the past decade and a half in Australia it has been clear that the agenda which is driving the curriculum documents and policy is one of economic rationalism. In the 1970s in Australia the dominant discourse of educational policy was that of social justice. In the mid-1980s a transition occurred when the agenda shifted from one of social justice to one of economic rationalism with its accompanying strategies of micro-economic reform. This has heralded an era in education in Australia where schools have been exhorted to produce more with less. Resources have been reduced at the same time as the expectations of schools to produce better outcomes have increased. Schools have thus undergone dramatic restructures, as has the education system as a whole. Teachers have responded with feelings of alienation and confusion in many cases, and staff morale has been at a low ebb. Despite this, however, it is clear that the central concern for the teachers is the learning of their students and they remain committed to this. Thus, the curriculum directions which are outlined by the state government have been addressed at a local level, and schools have seriously devised school policies which are in line with the guidelines and which address the needs and expectations of the local community in which they are set.

There is, therefore, a range of responses to the area of values and values teaching within the curriculum and this will be addressed later in the chapter by means of an examination of the Curriculum and Standards Framework (1995), which constitutes the current curriculum guideline in Victorian schools. The teaching staff of the school determines the curriculum content and teaching and learning methods. There is currently greater responsibility being devolved to local schools under the banner of a movement termed 'Schools of the Future'. This is portrayed as being a movement towards self-managing schools and a greater devolution of power and control to local sites and away from the central bureaucratic level. Each school is required to enter into a contract with the central bureaucracy which ensures that schools are kept accountable for the curriculum and for the outcomes which are achieved. This contract is designated with the title of 'The School Charter' and forms the platform upon which a school is able to 'market itself'. No apology is made for the fact that the 'Schools of the Future' movement is about 'the market economy of schooling' and thus is directing the operations of educational institutions to market forces and towards competition for scarce resources. Schools are urged to seek corporate sponsorship in order to gain a competitive edge and also in order to 'top up' the funding which is provided from the government. Critics of this movement suggest that this kind of competitive and corporate ethos will further entrench inequality in the education system and serve to ensure that the advantaged are still further advantaged, and the disadvantaged fall even further behind the field. It is expected in social, political and economic systems that there will be a tension between the centre and the periphery of the system, but this tension has been exacerbated over the last decade or so by the constant restructures and dislocations which have occurred in Victoria.

It is almost inevitable when dealing with social systems and social processes such as education that there will be inherent tensions between the centre and the periphery of the system. It is clear that in education there will be a range of values and interests rubbing against each other continually, thus giving rise to a state of constant transformation and reconstruction.

The values upon which the curriculum is founded, then, will be an area of contest and struggle as groups vie with each other to have their agenda included in the curriculum. This leads to a situation where there is a plethora of agendas operating within the one curriculum and also highlights the danger of a curriculum becoming overcrowded with subjects and activities which are about social process rather than about the knowledge upon which society is founded. The overshadowing of content (knowledge) with process learning has been a feature of the curriculum in Victoria over the past two decades or so. This has led to a situation where the curriculum resembles a 'Pandora's Box' with teachers being exhorted to cover such subject areas as drug education, bike education, peace education, environmental education and driver education. It is clear that a curriculum cannot be continually added to without the loss of other areas. In the case of Victorian schools, it has often been the bodies of pure knowledge that have suffered in the name of 'integrated curriculum' and process approaches.

Behind the notion of an integrated curriculum is a premise that learners learn best when concepts are related to each other in a real-life context. Links do need to be made for learners, and interrelationships between bodies of knowledge are crucial. This, however, does not imply that knowledge should become a blurred conglomeration of concepts without allowing learners to experience or have access to the pure bodies of knowledge upon which society from the time of the ancient Greeks has been founded. Thus, in the name of 'relevance' and 'access and success' we run the risk of entrenching existing disadvantage by only allowing the privileged classes, who can afford to send their children to private schools where the pure bodies of knowledge are still taught, to gain the kind of elite knowledge which society still values above other knowledge. When it comes to gaining entry to the elite courses such as Law, Medicine, Engineering and Science in universities, it is pure bodies of knowledge which constitute the prerequisites, not an amorphous mass of concepts which are not easily unpacked into their appropriate modes of inquiry of ways of knowing.

It is critical for curriculum designers, developers and implementers to consider the values which underpin the curriculum and also to consider the effect of the curriculum upon the life chances of all learners. In the name of a 'relevant' curriculum, much harm may be done to the chances of disadvantaged groups to move beyond their current class status. Curriculum has the potential effectively to lock people into their existing social strata, and thus is an efficient means of social control. If this hegemonic value underpins the choice educators make regarding the way curriculum is organized and implemented, existing social inequalities will be perpetuated and further increased.

Integral to the notion of values is the concept of power and empowerment. In the current era where the ideology of economic rationalism prevails and predominates, skills and competencies are the basis for potential social power. Ryan (1993: 23) states:

> In the innovative economy and society, higher levels of facility in the basic educational competencies are now nominated as both the knowledge and the currency of power: in providing the basis of 'learning how to learn' they would provide a springboard at a time of rapid socio-cultural change, for continuous and substantial developments in cultural identity and job skills. The new curricular emphasis, in short, in aiming to sustain both living better and working more efficiently, promises a resolution of the historical liberal dilemma. Nevertheless, I reject the new agenda for Australian education as being both culturally restrictive and elitist. The current preoccupation with basic skills and knowledge cannot reasonably be seen as providing the necessary foundations for the pursuit of broader cultural and social ends.

Ryan continues by observing that it is in the area of higher-order understandings that curriculum policy in Australia has failed and that this represents a 'conservative assessment of educability in terms of class origins and likely school destinies' (ibid.).

The curriculum of schooling is thus one of the most powerful tools available to bring about social control and to promote the narrow ideologies of economic rationalism and competency movements which serve to value already privileged discourses, individuals and social groups. Within the hegemonic system, however, educators in Australia currently tend towards a moral vacuum model when it comes to the teaching of values in the classroom. It has been the role of teachers to make decisions about teaching and learning methods and about the kinds of evaluation strategies which will be employed in the curriculum at a classroom level. Teachers are set an almost impossible task of attempting to accommodate an irreconcilable array of values, interests, motivations and discourses. This goes beyond pluralism of values to an almost anarchic situation where intellectual logic and reason is suffocated by an agenda of pragmatism, rationalism and structural functionalism. The confusing part for teachers is that at the same time as this situation is operating, the policy rhetoric or ideal which is being highlighted creates a cultural logic where self-management, independence and autonomy are supposedly valued.

As an example of the difficulty in finding common values upon which to base a classroom curriculum programme, the area of individual and group rights with the concurrent concerns for self-discipline may be cited. Ryan addresses these dimensions of values.

> Given a schooling system that increasingly denies real culture and opportunity to most, there would be no viable grounds for promoting

a policy commitment to self-discipline, one that would be based upon understanding of individual needs and group rights, nor . . . does any concept of values education have a significant place in the new-skills-based agenda. . . . What is more, since the standardization of basic schooling priorities and practices involves the key elements of personal and social identity, it follows that, increasingly, most children would be denied a systematic understanding of their place in the world and its relationship to what they are taught. . . . In terms of everyday class-room relationships we need more negotiation and co-operation if the distinctive educational needs of different social groups are to be met and if some basis for future social solidarity and empathy is to be cultivated.

(Ryan, 1993: 27 and 30)

With the almost total preoccupation with the economic agenda and the use of the schooling system as a tool for micro-economic reform, the teaching of values in the curriculum in Australian schools is a contested and contentious field of activity or, in some cases, inactivity. The values of the era of social justice and equity no longer apply and thus many of the traditional approaches to the teaching of values in classrooms are no longer appropriate or relevant. It is crucial, therefore, to hold up to rigor-ous critique recent curriculum documents which purport to set guidelines for the values dimension of curriculum. Teachers are required to approach the reading of curriculum documents critically and reflectively so as to become aware of the agenda, hidden or overt, which directs values educa-tion in the current era in Australian schools. It is significant to note that in the latest Victorian curriculum documents (Curriculum and Standards Framework 1995) each curriculum area is divided into a number of levels, which reflects the strong competency-based thrust of the curriculum. A critique of the Victorian curriculum documents, in the area of values education, follows.

As stated earlier in this chapter the federal government has set down the key learning areas which form the basis for curriculum development in Victoria. The policy documents which provide the curriculum framework for each of these key learning areas are the Curriculum and Standards Framework (1995) documents.

The Curriculum and Standards Framework documents were issued in 1995 and supersede the previous document called the Curriculum Frame-work (1987–9). The 1995 curriculum documents appear to have implicitly incorporated many of the ideas and concepts described in the Framework documents of 1987–9. The 1987–9 Framework documents will therefore be examined in some detail before curriculum policy is explored.

The Framework documents

The Framework documents published by the Curriculum Branch of the Ministry of Education (Victorian Schools Division) were implemented in schools in Victoria from 1987. The documents were developed to help teachers to plan, develop and assess their programmes more effectively. They were not aimed at presenting teachers with prescriptive directives for curriculum planning but rather constituted a framework for curriculum design and development. Between 1987 and 1989 Curriculum Framework documents were published for the curriculum areas of the Arts, Commerce, English, Languages Other Than English (LOTE), Mathematics, Social Education, Personal Development and Technology.

An examination of these documents published 1987–9 indicates that there is little explicit reference made to values or values teaching in the documents, apart from the one relating to Social Education. Overall the 1987–9 Framework documents for Mathematics, English, Commerce, Science and LOTE are content- and process-oriented and concentrate on the acquisition of skills and knowledge and the integration of specific disciplines into the school curriculum. The Science and LOTE Frameworks do, however, make some reference to values in the curriculum.

In the Science Framework links between Personal Development and Science are described. In this document it is stated that 'Science is . . . valuing, caring, being responsible, making decisions and taking action' (Ministry of Education, 1987b: 8) This document also contains a description of the importance of the acquisition of knowledge and skills through the science curriculum. It is stated in Science Framework (1987) that students will 'gain value from their studies' valuable content, valuable experiences, wide range of teaching strategies and problem solving activities' (ibid.: 10). It is left to the reader's interpretation to decide what is meant by the word 'valuable' and thus the clarity of the concept of value is left unresolved.

The LOTE Framework document makes reference to values education in a section outlining government policy statements. Reference to values is made in the section relating to Curriculum Development Planning in Victoria (Ministerial Paper no. 6, 1984: 11); this includes the attainment of a number of socio-cultural goals, one of which is that 'Language studies help the learner to . . . respect the rights of others to hold different points of view and to maintain their own belief and value systems' (ibid.: 12). The focus here is on values education being seen as an integral part of the attainment of one of the goals outlined in the introduction to the 1987 Framework document; that is, in the context of the socio-cultural dimension of schooling.

The Personal Development Framework (Ministry of Education, 1989) provides close links between the development of values in students and the development of effective decision-making and problem-solving skills. This link between values education and decision making is also made in a number of the other Framework (1987–9) documents including Science and Social Education.

In the Social Education Framework document (Ministry of Education, 1987c) it is suggested that one of the responsibilities of schooling is to develop in students broad understandings about society. The document contains a statement that there are two major goals of Australian society, one of which is that students need to acquire the knowledge and develop the skills, attitudes and values to participate effectively in society. Within the four critical dimensions of knowledge, skills, values and attitudes which underpin the Social Education Framework, the document provides a brief overview of how schools may reflect on and identify values, incorporate these values into the school curriculum and link values teaching to the other three dimensions.

The Social Education Framework document also contains statements to the effect that values can be learnt and that individuals learn values by being a member of a group such as a family or a school. Although individual values vary greatly both in the types of values held and the strength with which they are held, the document contains a statement that 'There are aspects of our culture and society which are highly valued and which should be shared, maintained, and strengthened (ibid.: 8). These cultural aspects relate to universal values, such as justice and fairness, which are commonly held across cultures. It is suggested in the document that in order that students may gain a 'better understanding of other cultures or values' (ibid.: 57), teachers should incorporate a range of perspectives into the teaching of Social Education including an Australian, global, social justice, environmental and futures perspective.

In relating the values dimension of curriculum to the teaching of values, this Framework document distinguishes between procedural and substantive values and suggests that as we develop and mature, our value systems become more complex. 'In studying substantive values, students need to understand the processes, institutions and rules by which conflicts of values can be resolved in a democratic society' (ibid.: 13). The Framework document highlights the need for students to develop decision-making and problem-solving skills as preparation for democratic citizenship.

In the Social Education Framework document the inquiry method is seen as a means by which students can develop skills for effective participation in a democratic society. The link between the values dimension and the inquiry process is seen as one where students can be encouraged to reflect upon both individual and societal values so that they may effectively develop their own individual value systems. In this document it is stated that it may be difficult for teachers to set goals relating to the teaching or development of values, and thus it may also be difficult to assess values teaching. The document provides a description of a number of methods and processes for the teaching of values which include:

43

- the promotion in the classroom of a set of procedural values that enhance inquiry and model responsible social participation;
- the exploration of the attitudes and values of other groups and individuals, including an understanding of how these influence social processes; and
- helping students to refine and extend a personal system of values through discussion and reflection.

(ibid.: 46)

These methods and processes are linked and may be assessed using a number of procedures and processes outlined in the documents. Other Framework documents, such as Science, Technology, Economics and LOTE, also outline the need for students to develop these skills within their specific curriculum areas. In each of the 1987–9 Framework documents the development of a positive classroom climate is encouraged so that students are able to express freely their values, develop decision making and questioning skill, and take responsibility for their actions. Consistent questioning in relation to values is also encouraged so that students reflect on their personal and societal values, consider a range of options, and become more sensitive to issues of diversity.

An extensive discussion of the 1987–9 Framework documents has been undertaken here in order to provide a picture of the changes which have occurred in less than a decade in the policy which drives curriculum policy and practice. Whereas some of the 1987–9 documents explicitly contained direct coverage of the values dimension of curriculum and were objectives- and process-based, the 1995 documents are less explicit about values and are outcomes- and product-based. What follows is an examination of the 1995 Curriculum and Standards Frameworks documents.

Curriculum and Standards Framework documents

The Curriculum and Standards Framework (CSF) documents (1995) provide outlines of the major learning areas to be covered by schools from Prep (age 4–5) to year 10 (age 14) and aim at providing a framework for curriculum development as well as assessment and reporting procedures. Using the documents as a guide, schools are responsible for detailed curriculum development at a school level.

It is stated in the 1995 curriculum documents that one purpose of these curriculum guidelines is to cater more effectively for individual students by meeting their various developmental needs through the implementation of a balanced and sequentially presented curriculum. The documents also provide outlines of a number of key principles, including principles of gender equity and equal opportunity, of which teachers need to be aware when designing and developing the curriculum. In the introduction to each of the CSF documents there is a section which outlines the need for teachers to

> be aware of the importance of inclusiveness in the development of their teaching and learning programmes . . . in particular the principles of gender equity and equal opportunity for students from all ethnic, socio-economic and cultural backgrounds.
>
> (Board of Studies, 1995e: 5)

Curriculum developers are provided with guidelines for developing curriculum for students with disabilities and impairments. This section of the Mathematics CSF outlines elements which are common to all forms of curriculum development, such as the need for curriculum to be 'relevant to the student's physical, intellectual, social and emotional needs' (ibid.: 5), and also describes ways in which curriculum may be adapted for students with special needs, such as the use of various forms of verbal and non-verbal communication and audio-visual aids. Previously, the 1987 Framework documents focused on the aims and objectives of individual curriculum areas without providing curriculum developers with comprehensive guidelines relating to issues such as inclusiveness and equity. This explicit focus on gender and disability may reflect the impact on current social processes such as education of new social movements and interest groups. This is a feature of the new era and is an illustration of the mobilization of previously marginalized groups within society and of the influence such groups may exert on policy.

In each of the eight key learning areas, curriculum content and classroom processes are organized into strands. For example, the key learning area of SOSE (Studies of Society and Environment) is divided into five strands, namely: time, continuity and change; place and space; culture; resources; and natural and social systems. The number of strands varies with each of the curriculum areas, and each learning area provides a rationale for its strand structure. Within each strand there is a statement which details the curriculum focus or the material to be covered and standards which relate to the outcomes students are expected to attain in a particular curriculum area.

Each of the documents is organized into seven levels, each of which is linked to levels of student achievement and years of schooling – for example Level 1 (end of preparatory year to 5 years of age), Level 2 (end of year 2 to 7 years of age) and Level 3 (end of year 4 to 9 years of age). The levels are organized into two-year blocks and continue to level 6 to end of year 10. These levels are aimed at providing schools with clear guidelines for student achievement and progress. Reporting and assessment procedures are clearly linked with the organization of strands and levels in that they relate to the skills and knowledge upon which the strands are based.

The 1995 Curriculum and Standards Framework documents are outcomes-based in that they focus on the acquisition of knowledge and skills which are closely linked to learning outcomes. As well as the emphasis on curriculum focuses and outcomes, in each of the subject disciplines a number of learning processes are highlighted. The documents provide an outline of goals, curriculum focuses and learning outcomes and then key processes which are integral to a specific discipline are specified. For example, the development of the skills of investigation, design, production and evaluation represents the four key phases which make up the technology process as outlined in the Technology C and SF (Board of Studies, 1995h), while the development of scientific investigation, reasoning and analysis is a key element in the development of the Science C and SF (Board of Studies, 1995f).

In a number of areas of the Health and Physical Education document the development of values is described, as both a curriculum focus and a learning outcome. For example, as a curriculum focus at level 6 (14 years) the document suggests that students 'discuss their own values, attitudes and behaviour and how these can be maintained when dealing with people who hold different views'. The learning outcome outlined for this level suggests that students should 'analyse how different contexts and situations influence personal values, attitudes, beliefs and behaviour'. In other sections of this same document curriculum focuses include a discussion of 'universal values' where students are encouraged to 'describe a range of values that diverse groups of people share (honesty, truthfulness, justice, reverence for life)' (Board of Studies, 1995c: 59), or are asked to 'identify and analyse the relationships between values and beliefs of various cultural groups in Australia' (ibid.: 51).

Within the Arts document (1995a) the emphasis is upon recognizing and valuing the traditions and cultural forms which provide the basis for our cultural and artistic heritage.

The Studies of Society and Environment (SOSE) document (1995g), unlike the Social Education Curriculum Frameworks (Ministry of Education, 1987b), does not explicitly address the issues of values development, transmission and assessment in its introduction and does not attempt to define terms or processes relating to values education which may be used to integrate the teaching of values in the curriculum. The SOSE document does, however, implicitly integrate aspects of values education into its curriculum focuses and outcomes. For example, at level 6 (age 14) the curriculum focus is on students examining 'the cohesion in a community or a society. Students analyse the contribution of core values and beliefs to the cohesion in that society.' The learning outcome at this level requires students to explore 'the core values of Australian society' (1995g: 49). At other levels students examine the values which underpin Australian culture and analyse some effects of major values and beliefs in world affairs. It may appear that personal values could be seen to have been subsumed into a concern for national and global values in the curriculum. This may reflect the concern to make Australia more competitive and influential as a global trading nation. The emphasis

46

placed on the learning of Asian languages illustrates the drive for Australia to be regarded as a major trading nation in the Asia Pacific Basin. In the SOSE document the connection which will be made between issues, ideas and themes such as multiculturalism, diversity, relationships, the environment (e.g. social, political, economic), gender, technology and change, and the study and transmission of values in the curriculum, is an underlying expectation.

The inquiry-based approach to learning underpins the SOSE curriculum document with a focus on students developing the skills of investigation, communication and participation. In this document, as with its predecessor, the need for students to 'develop knowledge, skills and values that enable them to participate as active and informed citizens in a democratic society' (ibid.: 9) is explicit.

The foregoing comparison between the earlier Framework documents (1987–9) which directed curriculum in Victorian schools until the intro-duction of the Curriculum and Standards Framework documents (1995) highlights the shift in the educational policy agenda during the late 1980s and into the 1990s. The transition from a social justice agenda which prevailed throughout the 1970s and until the early 1980s to an economic rationalist agenda which has become the dominant one in the 1990s is evident. During the mid-1980s Australian educational policy concurrently reflected both a social justice and an economic rationalist agenda, with the result that a num-ber of dualisms were apparent in curriculum policy documents. Examples of such dualisms are devolution and decentralization, co-operation and com-petition, diversity and standardization, access and success. In each of these examples the two words were used alongside each other in the policy docu-ments, in a way which implied that they were compatible and congruent. Curriculum development in the mid-1980s, then, appeared to be directed at meeting two agendas simultaneously. The later curriculum documents, Cur-riculum and Standards Frameworks (1995), however, unequivocally adopt an economic rationalist discourse. The documents are premised upon the pre-dominance of outcomes, accountability, competencies, generic skills, market forces and the creation of a multi-skilled workforce. The dominant values from which curriculum policy proceeds have moved from social to politico-economic ones. This signals a shift from what is perceived to be the under-lying purpose of formal schooling.

Through the comparison of the 1987–9 and 1995 curriculum documents, the area of values, within the economic rationalist climate of the 1990s, is seen to have undergone a change. This change stems largely from the dis-course of policy, which is underpinned by the need to employ the process of schooling in its capacity to bring about micro-economic reform. In this regard, the current documents are effectively transmitting, entrenching and legitimizing the government agenda of economic rationalism and the Hawke Prime Ministerial exhortation to make Australia 'the clever country'.

Extrapolated to the micro-context of schools and classrooms, the economic rationalist policy agenda may be seen to have altered the focus of the teaching of values in the curriculum and also to have changed the values which underpin curriculum development. One of the most obvious changes with regard to values teaching and learning in the current 1995 documents is that values are less explicitly addressed and that the focus is upon skills, knowledge and competencies.

The following section of this chapter constitutes a summary of the Australian findings, based upon research conducted between 1993 and 1995.

THE AUSTRALIAN RESEARCH: SCOPE OF THE RESEARCH

This study into values in the curriculum and the teaching of values in schools began in 1993 with an Australian study of teacher education students' understandings about values and values education. In order to demonstrate the sequence of the research, which began in the Australian context and was then expanded to an international context, the three distinct phases into which the research falls will be described here.

Phase 1

The curriculum in schools and the teacher education curriculum were both initial areas of concern within the study. Crucial to such a study is the recognition of diversity and change in Australian schools and society. The values and beliefs of all members of the school community, changing government policies in relation to school organization and curriculum in the areas of values education, and the teaching of values in educational contexts constitute central concerns for exploration.

> Every curriculum is also an expression of values ... where particular values are clearly understood and supported, they can provide a firm basis for curriculum planning: where they are not clear or not publicly recognized, decisions about curriculum are likely to be controversial, arbitrary or trivial.
>
> (Ministerial Paper no. 6, 1984: 8)

From a teacher educator perspective it is clear that there are frequent differences and disjunctions between the policies of schools and the lived practices of schools. The actions educators perform within educational settings all arise from, or tend to reflect, a particular value or set of values. Crucial questions are 'How do we choose those values and how are those values constructed?' Curriculum is an expression of values, and in implementing educational policies educators possess a powerful tool to impose or to exert particular values and meanings upon those with whom they interact. It was asserted in the paper resulting from phase 1 of this study (Ling, Cooper and Burman, 1993) that the choices which are made regarding curriculum content, teaching and learning methods, and evaluation strategies have far-reaching ramifications for the life chances of particular individuals and groups within society.

The four questions upon which the initial study was based were:

1 What do you believe is the role of a teacher in the area of attitudes and values in the classroom?
2 What problems or issues do you expect to experience in classrooms with regard to the teaching of values and attitudes?
3 What approaches should teacher education courses adopt for their role in the teaching of attitudes and values in the classroom?
4 What do you consider are the strengths of your teacher education course in preparing you as a future teacher to address values and attitudes in the classroom?

In responding to these questions in the first phase (1993) of the study, teacher education students reported that they experienced problems with regard to the teaching of values and in relation to the conflict of values which exist in school communities. The student teachers were aware that in pluralist societies, such as Australia, with a multitude of different ethnic groups and myriad values operating, ongoing negotiation and accommodation will be required. With diverse groups a plethora of diverse values is available and classroom programmes and teaching and learning strategies need to take account of this diversity. Student peer pressure was seen as having the potential to diminish the effectiveness of the teachers' efforts in the area of values education. The teacher education students also emphasized that they needed the time and encouragement to reflect upon the teaching of values in the classroom and that they also required time and an appropriate environment in which to begin to clarify their own values as individuals living in the last decade of the twentieth century. The students in the study identified the strengths they saw in their teacher education course with regard to values in education. Examples of such strengths included developing the recognition and acceptance of individual differences and development of respect for the opinions of other group members, being allowed time to clarify personal values, having access to appropriate role models, being exposed to current thinking and the latest developments and trends in values education, creating awareness of policy directions in values teaching and learning, and promoting an understanding of the broader social context of values and attitudes.

The message which emerged from this first phase of the study was that:

> there is a need to be open to a range of values and to support this with a range of teaching and learning approaches. In addition the teaching

of values is regarded as being an integral and inextricable component of all other areas of study and thus should not be artificially separated or divorced from them. All bodies of knowledge involve values and attitudes and teachers in classrooms and in teacher education programmes are responsible for presenting a balanced, holistic and well-rounded approach which is consonant with the context within which the programme is implemented.

(Ling, Cooper and Burman, 1993: 22)

Phase 2

Phase 2 of the international research project, which was conducted in 1994, involved a 'replication' of the 1993 research study. The questionnaire, designed in Australia, was translated where necessary and administered to pre-service teacher education students in Australia, Slovenia, Switzerland, the UK and the USA. While the study was loosely called a 'replication' study it may be more accurate to call it an extension of phase 1. The questionnaire which was administered in each of the contexts was as follows.

1 What do you believe is the role of a teacher in the area of attitudes and values in the classroom?
2 What problems or issues do you expect to experience in classrooms with regard to the teaching of values and attitudes?
3 What approaches should teacher education courses adopt for their role in the teaching of attitudes and values in the classroom?
4 What do you consider are the strengths of your teacher education course in preparing you as a future teacher to address values and attitudes in the classroom?
5 When deciding upon the content to be included in or excluded from school curricula, which three main factors do you perceive it is important to take into account?
6 Comment upon what you believe is the place of socially relevant topics, such as environmental education and peace studies, in school curricula.

In addition interviews were conducted as a means to follow up the questionnaire.

The major conceptual clusters which emerged from the data collected in this Australian part of the research related to the teacher's role in relation to values education. The attitudes that teacher education students perceived to be the most necessary for teachers included: respect for individuals' values and beliefs regardless of cultural background; fairness; honesty; even-handedness; non-bias; critical reflection; a non-judgemental approach; and sensitivity to issues of race and gender. As in the study of 1993, the respondents endorsed the importance of the role of the teacher in relation to the teaching of values and mentioned teacher roles such as: facilitator;

50

guide; leader; imparter of knowledge; supporter and developer of a positive learning environment. It was acknowledged that conflicts will occur between people whose values do not coincide. Different religious, socio-economic and ethnic backgrounds may influence family and community values. Having identified conflicts, the respondents saw it as the task of the teacher to develop strategies for themselves and the students to cope with the plurality of values and beliefs. The multicultural dimension is a central feature of Australian society.

The respondents in the study (1994) stated that they saw it as necessary for teachers to facilitate and initiate discussion in classrooms where student opinions are able to be freely aired. As in the previous phase the need to allow students to develop strategies to cope with peer pressure was seen as important. The critical dimension was also seen as important as a means to provide students with the environment and opportunity to inquire, problem-solve and to make informed choices and decisions. The need to respect and acknowledge the individuality of students and to allow for a range of ideas and approaches to decisions and problems was seen as crucial.

Respondents stated that values teaching was best accomplished in an open and balanced way and approached through an integrated curriculum. It was claimed that an integrated curriculum takes account of the interests and backgrounds of the learners, is relevant to their lives and makes links between concepts which have the potential to empower the learners. Respondents perceived a need to balance the requirements of the community with those of the individual. Opportunities for learners to strike this balance should be provided in the classroom. The centrality of incorporating environmental concepts in teaching, along with preparing students to cope positively with future change, was stressed. A number of respondents stated that teachers have a responsibility to allow students to develop a perception of themselves and their role as members of a local, national and global community.

When the Australian findings for this phase of the study were compared with other participant countries it was noted that

> There is a noticeable commonality in the findings from each of the countries which were involved in the study in terms of the major issues which are seen as important with regards to values education. Nevertheless, there are also context specific features which may be discerned and which are seen as important in curriculum decision making for each setting.
>
> (Ling, Cooper, Burman *et al.*, 1994: 11)

The Australian context-specific findings for phases where international co-operation was further extended will be discussed in the remainder of this chapter.

51

Phase 3

The third phase of this study (1995) involved extension of the study to explore the perceptions of both experienced teachers and pre-service teacher education students regarding the basis on which the values dimension of the school curriculum is founded. The point of departure in the third phase, as compared with phases 1 and 2, was the inclusion of experienced teachers as respondents in the study as a means to compare and contrast the perceptions of pre-service and experienced teachers regarding education. The questions were asked through the administration of an open-ended questionnaire and subsequent interviews. The same questionnaire was administered in each of the national contexts and translated as necessary. It is included as Appendix II.

AUSTRALIAN FINDINGS

In reporting the Australian findings for the study into values in education, a composite picture which has emerged at the end of the study will be presented rather than a detailed report for each of the phases. There is no attempt made in reporting the findings to quantify or tabulate the data in any way. To do this is in fact contrary to the spirit of the qualitative methodology which was the basis of each phase. An effort was made to eschew the quantitative element as, where values and attitudes are concerned, quantification potentially leads to trivialization and simplification of complex dialectical elements which are not susceptible to measurement. It has been an unexpected facet of this study that research methodology has a cultural context in that researchers in each study site reported the data in different ways. This has meant that while the questionnaires which were administered in each context of the research were identical, the method of treating the responses was culturally specific. This has been an important side issue in terms of research methodology and its culturally bound nature in the area of values. In our reporting of the Australian findings, the conceptual clusters into which the responses were seen to fall, form the basis for the report here.

Principles upon which curriculum decisions are made

Responses from experienced teachers demonstrated that the principles which were seen to be of most importance as the basis for decisions regarding the values dimension of the curriculum and the classroom programmes were: tolerance and respect for individual and cultural issues; the right of every person to an effective education; school mission and vision statements; personal beliefs and values; and equal opportunity and equity. There was not a strong response in terms of the part which religious beliefs play as providing the principles for the decisions teachers make about values education, though it was mentioned by a small number of respondents.

The responses of student teachers to the question seeking perceptions of the principles upon which decisions are made regarding the values education dimension of the curriculum, stressed the elements of mutual respect and respect for the individual; tolerance, honesty, fairness and justice; student background; freedom of speech and beliefs; moral values; equality; the right of every person to an effective basic education; the need for values which reflect the core issues of the society; consistency with the values of the teacher; and care for the independent learning of students.

Classroom strategies in the area of values development

When reporting the findings regarding the strategies which teachers use in the classroom, the responses which were provided for the question referring to the way knowledge is imparted in classrooms were so inextricably inter-woven with descriptions of strategies that it is seen to create an artificial and unnecessarily pedantic barrier to separate them here. The responses of the experienced and pre-service teachers were congruent in addressing this issue and thus will be reported here as a common set of responses. The major strategies which were seen to be effective for teaching values in classrooms were: discussion; role-play; simulation games; values clarification exercises and activities; conflict resolution activities; moral dilemmas; co-operative learning. In addressing the strategies which teachers may apply there was a concentration upon the process skills area of values education. Processes which were mentioned in terms of their relevance and applicability in values education programmes included: co-operative learning; class meetings; development of class rules; teacher role modelling; active listening; integrated and inclusive curriculum; equal rights; and awareness of universal values.

Five predominant cultural issues which exert a major influence upon the values dimension of curriculum

In addressing this question, many of the respondents had difficulty grasping the concept of the influence which the broader socio-cultural context may exert on the school or classroom curriculum. This was one point which exemplified the problem some educators experience in having any clear broad basis for the consideration of values education. Educators are fre-quently able to discuss what happens in a micro-context such as a school, or a classroom, but they are less comfortable about attempting to anchor or ground those perceptions in a broader socio-cultural context. This is considered by the Australian researchers to reflect the difficulty which some people experience in understanding the dialectical relationship which exists between the global, macro, meso and micro domains within which social processes occur. Thus to consider only the micro-context without relating it to the influences which are exerted upon that context by each of the other domains provides a limited perspective. Nevertheless, some respondents were able to extrapolate the issue of values in education to the broader social context.

In many instances the responses of the experienced teachers and the pre-service teacher education students were consonant. The consonances are able to be distinguished in responses which dealt with the cultural influence of concepts which society in the broader sense exhorts such as: equality and social justice; value for ethnicity and cultural diversity; awareness and action in the areas of gender equity and access and participation in social processes for all individuals and groups; freedom of and tolerance for a range of religious and spiritual beliefs; changing family structure, influence of parents and aspirations of parents.

In the case of the responses by pre-service teacher education students some additional elements emerged which were not apparent in the responses from experienced teachers. The pre-service teacher education students referred to broader socio-cultural factors which may influence the values curriculum in terms of: impact of government policies; democratic rights; rise and mobilization of new social movements; changing social customs and beliefs; environmental issues; social attitudes to the work ethic; economic and financial changes. This difference which has been identified here between the concerns of the pre-service students and those of the experienced teachers is illuminating. It underscores the changing focus of students who are about to enter the workforce in the current era of micro-economic reform and transition. It is the socio-economic and socio-political issues about which the students express concerns rather than the more traditional socio-cultural perspective which had been the dominant discourse of the 1970s and up until the mid-1980s in the Australian context and which remains as the discourse for teachers in the school system.

Whose knowledge forms the basis of values education curriculum?

The Australian researchers consider that this question provides insights into the question of the curriculum as a social control mechanism. It may be argued that in any curriculum area it is the knowledge of the dominant social class which forms the basis of the knowledge that is considered to be valuable. Responses to this question from both the experienced and the pre-service teacher education students were too similar to warrant separation in this report.

The teacher's knowledge was seen to be the most important source of values curriculum knowledge. This, of course, carries with it the implication that the teacher has critically reflected upon his/her own values system and has a theorized and informed basis for the actions which they take as human beings. The Department of Education, which employs the teachers surveyed, was seen to be an influential source of curriculum knowledge. This stems from the fact that policy and documentation which concern the school curriculum emanate from this point. The politicians and those individuals and groups with access to political power were also seen to exert influence over knowledge choices for the values curriculum. Teacher education students perceived that the theories addressed by and the practices of university lecturers exerted an influence. In a few cases religious elements were seen to provide the basis for choices of curriculum content.

Values curriculum organization

This question addressed the issue of how to organize curriculum content and methods, having decided upon the knowledge to be included. In almost all cases the respondents, experienced teachers and students alike, perceived that values education should be integrated within other subject areas. It is self-evident that no body of knowledge or method of teaching or learning is value-free, and thus it is impossible not to integrate values throughout all other areas of the curriculum. It was seen by some respondents, however, that there is a need for there to be a discrete subject area which addresses values. This was seen to be necessary because of the need to develop and foster the ability of learners to clarify and critically reflect upon their own values and those of others. If the Kohlberg philosophy is considered, values education is seen as a distinctive cognitive area and thus must be addressed in its own right as a discrete area of the curriculum.

Accessibility of values education to all

While many respondents perceived that values education was freely and readily available to all students, some respondents claimed that values education was less accessible to some individuals and social groups. Those for whom values education is less accessible were seen to be those from non-English-speaking backgrounds, learners with disabilities and lower socio-economic groups. Student teachers commented that the influence of political pressure groups and power groups was evident in terms of providing access for some groups while denying it to others. Experienced teachers in the education system generally did not perceive this political element.

Five elements which values education in schools and teacher education should address

In this question the views of the respondents were sought in order to provide a basis for review and redevelopment of values curricula. In the current era, there are new demands on educators in all knowledge areas, but it may be seen that in the area of values education, the challenges and demands are even more acute. In an era of transformation, values will be in a state of dynamic creation and re-creation so that the traditional values are replaced by those which herald a non-traditional era.

In the Australian context, then, in a non-traditional era, the following elements were considered to warrant consideration and action by educators and curriculum developers. Respondents perceived that the elements of tolerance for others and respect for self and others were crucial. Equal opportunity was also seen as an important element to be addressed. Linked with this is the issue of gender inclusiveness. These elements may reflect a feature which is apparent in the current era, of the rise of marginalized groups or individuals as new social movements which bring into creation new social discourses. Consonant with the concerns for rights and opinions of others was a perception that students were required to develop social survival skills and independence. This concept was seen to run parallel with the desire to promote a concern for the environment and for human rights on a global scale. Student teachers displayed an awareness, not previously highlighted in responses, of the interaction of the four domains of social process – global, macro, meso and micro.

For teacher educators, it may provide some comfort that the student teachers' responses appeared to reflect a critical awareness of and reflection upon the challenges of the current era. This does not, however, exonerate teacher educators from some personal and group reflection about the needs of teacher education courses to provide prospective teachers with a means to theorize critically and intelligently their own values, and to use this as the basis for their informed and empowered action as teachers in the area of values curriculum and education. There is also a need to provide for experienced teachers a means to confront their own existing practices and understandings critically and to approach the activities and programmes in values education as problematic.

In Australia, the respondents demonstrated concern for the diversity of values and about the selection of appropriate strategies for the teaching of values in the classroom. This concern may have resulted in what appeared to be a reluctance to make definitive comments and in a hypersensitivity to the need to accommodate and take account of a wide diversity of values. There was a tendency for the pre-service teacher education students to emphasize the 'ideal' situation while the experienced teachers emphasized the 'practical' context and referred to the situation as it is currently 'lived' in classrooms. There was an apparent disjunction between the intended curriculum and the lived curriculum in the values dimension. The values which were espoused in the rhetoric of policy or curriculum documents were not necessarily those which were lived in the practical classroom context.

Teacher educators in Australia, the Irish Republic, Israel, Slovenia, Switzerland and the United Kingdom were involved in this international

56

comparative study. It became increasingly apparent that the issue of values education was one about which there was little or no shared meaning among educators at various levels of the system in the national contexts in which the study was undertaken. For the purposes of providing a theoretical and interpretative framework for the findings of this study at this stage of the research, four models for examining values and for interpreting the ways individuals conceive of them were employed. These models were religious monopolism, moral universalism, consensus pluralism (Hill, 1991) and the moral vacuum model (Ling *et al.,* 1995: 3). This framework is discussed in detail in Chapter 2.

Interpretation of Australian findings

In interpreting the Australian data in the light of the four models mentioned above, it was apparent that there was not a strong element of religious monopolism within the Australian responses. The respondents in general did not appear to consider that values or morals should be taught only in a religious framework. There were, however, some respondents from specific religious groups who stated that values should be taught in conjunction with religion and through religion. In the Australian findings there was an emphasis upon the need for religious tolerance and openness. For those respondents who did emphasize the need to teach values through religion, religious values were seen as the basis for all other life values, and thus for these respondents there was no other legitimate way to address this area in the curriculum.

If it is accepted that, for most students, the diversity of religious beliefs renders religion an inappropriate basis for moral education, then the model of moral universalism (Hill, 1991), which rests upon the belief that common or universal values should form the basis for moral education, may be considered. Common values were itemized by Australian respondents who referred to principles of social justice and inalienable rights of human beings which could be construed as falling within this theme of moral universalism. Specific universal values which were mentioned included tolerance, respect, independence, self-respect, sensitivity, honesty, courtesy and consistency. The repeated citing by respondents of these universal values indicates that there is an explicit element of moral universalism which forms the basis for thinking in the area of the teaching of values in the curriculum within the Australian context.

Consensus pluralism (Hill, 1991), which emphasizes the need to develop awareness of the diversity and plurality of values, and the need to foster critical awareness of the values domain and to take personal responsibility for espoused values, was the theme that appeared most frequently within the Australian responses. Both the teacher education students and the experienced teachers emphasized the need for tolerance and awareness of individual differences, and the necessity for teachers to recognize the diverse backgrounds and environments of learners. Respondents also emphasized the need for students to take responsibility for their own learning in the area of values, the desirability of learners developing the ability to make choices, and the need for teachers to take account of the learners' beliefs and ideas and to show respect for these. Importance was placed upon the prior knowledge of students and teachers with respect to values. Respondents stated that young children can be critical thinkers and that the development of critical literacy skills is an important element of the teacher's role as a curriculum implementer.

The apparent reliance upon the model of consensus pluralism in the Australian context as the basis for the teaching of values may explain the difficulty of respondents in answering some of the questions. In an effort to be open and non-judgemental, respondents have found it hard to make any clear statements about values teaching. It may follow, then, that when the society is diverse and is based upon the concept of consensus pluralism, there is a greater difficulty in identifying any clear structure or framework for values teaching. The risk here may lie in the values dimension of the curriculum becoming so sensitive and contested that it is ignored or avoided or, alternatively, becomes so bland and colourless as to be ineffective. Consensus pluralism, in this context, appears on the surface to be democratic and open, but in practice may lead to ambivalence, avoidance, confusion and even a rejection of the need to address formally the values dimension of curriculum in classrooms.

An extreme example of consensus pluralism could lead to the moral vacuum model. Such a situation may occur when, in an effort to take all values on board in the curriculum, a loose collection of ideas rather than a coherent philosophy emerges. This may be the state Australian education is approaching, given the lack of clear direction or focus which seemed to be evident in the way respondents reacted to the questionnaire. While we may not be at the stage of a total vacuum, devoid of matter, unless teacher education courses at the pre-service and in-service levels take action to avoid this situation, the vacuous nature of values will predominate over those value positions which are valid in the curriculum of values teaching in Australian schools.

Conclusions resulting from interpretations

Teachers do not seem to delineate clearly the difference between the philosophical basis for the teaching of values and the practical implications for values teaching. Within the Australian findings, there was a blurring of the distinction between the principles on which the curriculum is based and the strategies for classroom practice in this area. The disjunctions between intended curriculum and lived curriculum were not appreciated by respondents in the study.

The responses from teachers within the Australian context suggest that some teachers are hesitant to make a public commitment regarding their own opinions and perceptions about values education and have an equivocal and ambivalent attitude towards presenting their ideas about values education for public or research scrutiny.

RECOMMENDATIONS

In both pre-service and in-service teacher education courses it would appear that there needs to be a more structured and reflective basis for the values dimension of the curriculum. Teachers and student teachers require a structure which will provide them with the ability to reflect upon the teaching of values in education and with models against which they may confront their own value system and attempt to equate it with one based upon a recognized theoretical framework. Teachers need to explore their own value systems and to develop a clear direction to assist them in selection of content and strategies to teach values in the school curriculum. (See Chapter 8 for strategies in values education.)

Teacher education courses need to address values education explicitly in two distinct, yet interrelated, aspects:

- the principles upon which values education may be based in the current era;
- the strategies for the implementation of the values curriculum in education.

Since the philosophy and the strategies of values education are dialectically interrelated and continuously make and remake each other, it is not legitimate to conceive of one without the other.

The issues of classroom management, discipline and behaviour are linked with the concept of values. The rights, responsibilities and rules which form the basis for the practices and activities of classroom environments will depend upon particular values educators hold about the world and their relationship with it, and about the rights and power relationships which exist between people. Thus it is necessary to interrelate the decisions about classroom management and discipline with the theoretical and practical understandings teachers should have about the teaching of values in the curriculum.

Within the Australian findings one predominant opinion which emerged from the respondents was that it is the teacher's knowledge which forms the basis of the curriculum for the teaching of values. This assumption appears to overlook other influences which are exerted upon the kinds of values which are privileged in any specific social context. These influences would include context-specific meanings which are commonly held within a particular social context. These meanings may pertain, for example, to class stratification and notions of equality, economic and political imperatives as articulated in government policies, the history of the cultural context in question and the relationship between different groups and individuals within society. Such meanings will not rely simply upon what teachers as individuals perceive about values given that a teacher's values system is, in most instances, likely to be a reflection of the particular social context within which he or she lives and a composition of the socially constructed meanings about values which exist within that context.

REFERENCES

Board of Studies (1995a) *Arts Curriculum and Standards Framework* (Victoria, Carlton).

Board of Studies (1995b) *English Curriculum and Standards Framework* (Victoria, Carlton).

Board of Studies (1995c) *Health and Physical Education Curriculum and Standards Framework* (Victoria, Carlton).

Board of Studies (1995d) *Languages Other Than English (LOTE) Curriculum and Standards Framework* (Victoria, Carlton).

Board of Studies (1995e) *Mathematics Curriculum and Standards Framework* (Victoria, Carlton).

Board of Studies (1995f) *Science Curriculum and Standards Framework* (Victoria, Carlton).

Board of Studies (1995g) *Studies of Society and Environment (SOSE) Curriculum and Standards Framework* (Victoria, Carlton).

Board of Studies (1995h) *Technology Curriculum and Standards Framework* (Victoria, Carlton).

Directorate of School Education (1994) LOTE. Ministerial Advisory Council on Languages Other Than English: Report to the Minister for Education (Victoria, DSE).

Hill, B.V. (1991) *Values Education in Australian Schools* (Melbourne, ACER).

Ling, L., Cooper, M. and Burman, E. (1993) 'Values: Caught or Taught?' Paper presented at the Annual Conference of the Association for Teacher Education in Europe (Lisbon, Portugal).

Ling, L., Cooper, M., Burman, E., Killeavy, M., Razdevsek-Pucko, C., Polak, A., Grunder, H. and Stephenson, J. (1995) 'Values Valid or Vacuous?' Paper presented at the Annual Conference of the Association for Teacher Education in Europe (Oslo, Norway).

Ling, L., Cooper, M., Burman, E., Killeavy, M., Zuzovsky, R., Yakir, R., Gottlieb, E. and Stephenson, J. (1996) 'International Partnerships: Reflections, Recollections and Relationships'. Paper presented at the Annual Conference of the Association for Teacher Education in Europe (Glasgow, Scotland).

Ling, L., Cooper, M., Burman, E., Razdevsek-Pucko, C., Polak, A., Peter, W., Beard, P. and Stephenson, J. (1994) 'Values for a Changing Context: A Global Perspective'. Paper presented at the Annual Conference of the Association for Teacher Education in Europe (Prague, Czech Republic).

Ministerial Paper no. 6 (1984) Government of Victoria.

Ministry of Education (Schools Division) (1987b) *Social Education Framework*, 10.

Ministry of Education (Schools Division) (1987d) *Science Framework*, 10.

Ministry of Education (Schools Division) (1989) *Personal Development Framework*, 10.

Ryan, W. (1993) 'Schooling for Relevance – Whose Agenda?' in A. Reid and B. Johnson (eds) *Critical Issues in Australian Education in the 1990s* (Adelaide, Painters Prints).

4

THE IRISH CONTEXT

Maureen Killeavy

INTRODUCTION

The Republic of Ireland is a small island country of just over three and a half million people on the western fringe of Europe. It has been a self-governing state since 1922 and it is a member of the European Community. Ireland has a younger population than most other European states with half the population under 25 years of age (OECD, 1991). Emigration has historically been a necessity for many Irish people who were forced to seek employment in other lands, notably the USA, Britain and Australia. While the rate of emigration decreased noticeably during the prosperous years of the 1960s and 1970s it has escalated again in the early 1990s because of increasing unemployment and lack of opportunity for young people at home.

Ireland, according to the OECD Report of 1991, is overwhelmingly a Roman Catholic country with 90 per cent of the population belonging to the major religious denomination in the state. Because of this, and despite a rapid growth in the rate of economic development since the 1960s, Ireland has preserved many of the attributes of its distinctive national culture and identity, such as the Irish language, and a distinctive Celtic identity in literature and the arts. However, the country is undergoing some cultural and social changes with the accompanying problems faced by most Western societies. These changes in Irish life include the effects of declining employment in agriculture and the consequent growth in urbanization, the decision in a recent referendum to legalize divorce, the increase in foreign travel, the rise in the number of single-parent families, the impact of new technology and mass access to world media, and the growth in social problems associated with inner-city poverty, in particular drug abuse and related crime. As a result, society has become more pluralist, there is increasing dissent and a growing focus on individual rights, and there is a heightened awareness of social class, gender and minority inequalities and the beginnings of multiculturalism. It is in this context that Irish teachers concern themselves with the education and development of pupils in their care.

Values education as a specific subject does not form part of the curriculum in the Irish education system. However, 'values' both explicit and implicit are a pivotal element in the curriculum of Irish schools, particularly at primary level. This stems from the involvement of the Roman Catholic and Protestant churches in the various educational provisions of the state at first and second level. Unlike in many Western liberal democracies, denominational and state-organized education in Ireland are not separate. As a result of this, the vast majority of Irish students at first level and most students at second level receive formal Religious Instruction in school. It is necessary to point out, however, that it is not compulsory for any student to take part in Religious Instruction and no attempt may be made to interfere with the religious tenets of any pupil.

Primary or first-level state schools in Ireland are organized on a national basis and they provide education for children from the ages of 4 to 11 or 12 years. The Roman Catholic and Protestant churches and the state Department of Education play complementary roles in the provision and organization of primary schooling. The ultimate responsibility for each primary school lies with the 'patron', usually the bishop of the relevant denomination, who delegates authority to a school board (OECD, 1991). The responsibility for the day-to-day management of the school, the appointment of teachers and the application of the rules laid down by the Minister for Education rests with the school board.

Nearly all primary schools are denominational in their intake and management and their location and organization are parish-based (OECD, 1991). However, parents may send their children to any school of their choice where a place is available, regardless of their religion. A small number of schools do not conform to this pattern. These include a Jewish school and a Muslim school together with eight recently established multi-denominational schools to which Catholic, Protestant and other children have equal right of access.

Religious education has traditionally been accorded the highest priority in the Irish primary school. The revised *Primary School Curriculum* issued by the Department of Education in 1971 suggests that:

> Of all the parts of the school curriculum Religious Instruction is by far the most important, as its subject-matter, God's honour and service, includes the proper use of all man's faculties, and affords the most powerful inducement to their proper use. Religious Instruction is, therefore, a most fundamental part of the school course, and a religious spirit should inform and vivify the whole work of the school.
>
> (Department of Education, 1971: 23)

Most teachers in primary schools in Ireland take responsibility for the religious education of their own class. However, the prescribing of the subject matter of Religious Instruction, the examination of it, and the supervision of its teaching have been, up to the present time, acknowledged as being outside the competence of the Department of Education and are a matter for the relevant church authorities.

In the past Religious Instruction in Ireland has not been regarded as a separate subject in a compartmentalized sense. The revised primary curriculum of 1971 proposed that the values underlying the religion of the school should permeate the teaching of all subjects regardless of the curriculum area in which they occur.

> The teacher should constantly inculcate the practice of charity, justice, truth, purity, patience, temperance, obedience to lawful authority, and all the other moral virtues. In this way he [*sic*] will fulfil the primary duty of an educator, the moulding to perfect form of his pupils' character, habituating them to observe, in their relations with God and with their neighbour, the laws which God, both directly through the dictates of natural reason and through Revelation, and indirectly through the ordinance of lawful authority, imposes on mankind.
>
> (Department of Education, 1971: 23)

Other areas of the curriculum, particularly History and Civics, were similarly regarded as of special significance in the teaching of values. It was suggested that illustrations of History should not be confined to sublime examples of patriotism, courage and noble ideals lest the lessons that the subject conveys for the conduct of ordinary life be overlooked. Similarly, Civics was proposed as a means of developing acceptable social habits and heightening awareness through a study of the social problems which directly affect the children.

The most recent indications of government policy on primary education contained in *Charting Our Education Future* suggest that the expected revised curriculum will reiterate the rights of schools, in accordance with their religious ethos, to provide denominational religious instruction to their students while underpinning the constitutional rights of parents to withdraw their children from religious instruction (Department of Education, 1995). However, the lack of reference in the White Paper to the pervasive influence of religion to inform and vivify the whole work of the school would seem to indicate a changing emphasis in relation to policy in this regard. This change is evident in the values which are inherent in the philosophy of the proposed developments in curriculum which are currently under discussion by the National Council for Curriculum and Assessment (discussions with officers of the National Council for Curriculum and Assessment, 1996). It is suggested that in the future History should promote a critical appreciation of all the peoples who have contributed to the development of Ireland.

Similarly, it is envisaged that Geography will promote a valuing of a wide diversity of people who make up a community and it is suggested that pupils' vision should be extended beyond a Eurocentric view of the world.

These aspirations suggest that policy makers view curriculum as important in engendering values appropriate to a pluralist and multicultural society.

Among the most important curriculum changes proposed in terms of the willingness of the state to assume responsibility for an area heretofore regarded as falling solely within the remit of Religious Instruction is the introduction of the subject areas 'Social Personal and Health Education' (SPHE) and 'Social Environmental and Scientific Education' (SESE).

The first component of SPHE, entitled Relationships and Sexuality Education, which is currently in the process of preparation by the National Council for Curriculum and Assessment, deals with questions of morality which heretofore were regarded as falling solely within the jurisdiction of the religious authorities in the state.

Second-level education

Second-level or post-primary school in Ireland extends over a five- or six-year cycle and includes five types of school: secondary, vocational, comprehensive, community school and community college. Secondary schools, which comprise about two-thirds of all schools at second level, are privately owned and managed, usually by religious orders (OECD, 1991). These schools, most of which provide free education, are in receipt of state funding and they belong to the classical grammar school tradition. Vocational schools were established originally to provide technical education but their role has been expanded to cover all areas of the second-level curriculum. Comprehensive schools were set up to meet the needs of areas without second-level education and they offer a broad curriculum including both academic and technical areas. Community schools, which offer the same type of broad curriculum as comprehensive schools, were designed to serve as cultural and educational centres in their neighbourhoods. Community colleges arose from the vocational tradition and are similar to community schools but the curriculum they offer is more extensive and they often cater for older students.

The rules of the Department of Education require second-level schools to provide Religious Instruction, which is frequently given by a specialist catechetical teacher (Coolahan, 1981). A conscience clause similar to that existing for pupils at first level, allowing for the withdrawal of pupils from Religious Instruction at the request of parents, applies. It is important to note that Religious Instruction in Irish schools up to the present has been based upon the study of the teachings of a particular denomination as opposed to a comparative study of different religions. However, there are indications that this situation may soon undergo fundamental changes if curriculum developments currently being considered come to fruition. These changes concern proposals to develop Religious Education as a subject area which would conform to the general syllabus structures and which

64

would be examinable in public state examinations for students at second level.

This new subject would constitute an attempt to give students a critical appreciation of religious views and beliefs and an understanding of the role of religion in society. Unlike in Religious Instruction the emphasis would be on theology rather than the study of doctrine or catechism. If the current discussions come to fruition a school may offer either Religious Instruction, as heretofore, or Religious Education as an ordinary examinable subject or both. It should be noted that these discussions concerning the development of Religious Education as a new subject at second level are at an early stage and definite policy decisions have yet to be taken in this matter. Special legislation will be required to allow for the incorporation of Religious Education as an examinable subject into the timetable of second-level schools in Ireland. This is currently prohibited by legislation dating from 1878.

Teachers at second level in Ireland are subject specialists rather than class- or form-based teachers as is the case at primary level, and the majority of these teachers are not responsible for the teaching of religion. Further, unlike schools at first level, not all schools at second level are denomination-ally based. At second level the church's power to influence the curriculum is not enshrined in any rule or regulation laid down by the state with the exception of the rule giving each denomination control of the teaching of its own religion in all schools. However, as Drudy and Lynch (1993) point out, the churches, particularly the Catholic Church because of its strong repre-sentation on policy-making bodies, can have a considerable influence on curriculum development.

The general thrust of the proposals of the National Council for Curriculum and Assessment in relation to the values underlying the various curriculum areas at second level, however, is similar to the new pro-posals for primary education. This is evident in such proposed new subjects as 'Civic Social and Political Education' which are to a consider-able extent 'values driven' and the new programmes in the sciences which are being designed with an increased emphasis on critical thinking and inquiry.

These developments point to a lessening of the influence traditionally wielded by the religious denominations in the state with regard to the teach-ing of values. Together with this, the decrease in numbers entering religious orders and the consequent growing numbers of lay or non-religious teachers in the profession, and more importantly in school principalships, have resulted in increased secular control of the education process. These changes, however, have not fundamentally changed the values dimension of education in Ireland. This is because the historically strong religious element in Irish society provides a coherence of beliefs and attitudinal dispositions which permeates the education process in the state.

THE DATA COLLECTION PROCESS

The population surveyed in the Irish study comprised forty teachers, twenty of whom were qualified practising primary teachers and the remaining twenty were pre-service teacher education students. The group of primary teachers was taking part in a degree programme leading to a Master's in Education at University College, Dublin. The student teacher group was studying for the Higher Diploma in Education, which is a year-long university-based course for graduates leading to a professional qualification for teachers at second level. The gender balance of the sample, 70 per cent (n = 28) female and 30 per cent (n = 12) male, reflects fairly closely the gender balance of the primary teaching profession nationally and that of pre-service second-level teachers. Ninety per cent of the primary teachers surveyed had been awarded a B.Ed. degree and the remainder had degrees in Arts. All of these first-level teachers had an honours qualification. The qualifications of the pre-service teacher education students included degrees in Arts, Science, Social Science, Commerce and Agriculture. Over three-quarters of the pre-service teachers sampled had been awarded their degrees at honours level, the majority (70 per cent) having reached a second-class honours standard.

Over 50 per cent of the sample had some additional qualifications ranging from certificates and diplomas acquired on education-based in-service courses to qualifications in subject specialisms. All of the primary teachers surveyed were undertaking studies for a Master's degree in Education and two members of this group had already completed a degree at master's level in another subject area. Three of the pre-service teacher education students had completed master's degrees and one student in this group had successfully completed a Ph.D.

The pre-service teachers group (75 per cent of whom were under 25 years of age) tended to be younger than the primary teachers, who were required to have at least five years' professional experience prior to beginning their master's programme. In all, 77.5 per cent of the entire group was under 35 years of age and only 10 per cent or four students were 45 years or over. All the respondents were domiciled in the greater Dublin area during the time the survey was carried out. However, the areas of origin of more than half the group were in the farm lands and small towns of rural Ireland.

The M.Ed. degree undertaken by the primary teachers group on a part-time basis was financed by the students and this endeavour necessitated financial borrowings on the part of many of these individuals. The course demanded a considerable time commitment over a three-year period both in terms of course work and continuous assessment and examinations. Because of these considerations it seems reasonable to assume a degree of commitment to professional enhancement and career advancement on the part of the group in excess of that of the average primary teacher.

THE RESEARCH METHODOLOGY

The research methodology of the study was primarily qualitative, and a triangulation approach involving a questionnaire, semi-structured interviews and classroom observation was used. Triangulation is a multi-method approach in which the existence of certain phenomena and the veracity of individual accounts are investigated by cross-checking data gathered from a number of informants and a number of sources in order to produce as full and balanced a study as possible (Open University, 1988). The questionnaire, comprising five open-ended softly focused questions, was administered to the forty teachers. A content analysis of all the answers to each question was undertaken prior to computer analysis. This provided a basis for the categorization of the responses at two different levels of abstraction, broad and narrow. These categories were subsequently used in the cluster analysis. All the data were then entered in the computer program SPSS (Statistical Package for the Social Sciences) and analysis and interpretation was carried out (Earl and Halley, 1995; Norusis, 1990). Meanwhile informal discussions and semi-structured interviews were undertaken with respondents and classroom observations of a small number of teachers were carried out.

The content-specific nature of the process

Some aspects of the analysis are specific to the Irish situation and as such should be treated with caution in any comparative context. Values education as a formal subject area has not formed part of the curriculum in Irish schools up to the present time. The Irish state-funded education system, particularly at primary level, has always been seen as falling within the remit of religious influence. Traditionally primary teachers in Ireland have taken responsibility for the religious instruction of their pupils and the preparation of their classes for First Communion and Confirmation. These are key events in initiating students into the practice and value system of the particular religion to which they belong.

Certain fundamental changes which will affect the values aspect of Irish education are envisaged with the development of the new curriculum areas which are being introduced. These changes are evident in the growing concern on the part of the state to take responsibility for the delineation of the values which are inherent in the new subject areas of the curriculum. Certainly, a more secular basis for decisions, which heretofore would have been seen as falling exclusively within the province of church authority, is being developed.

Many of the teachers in the cohort studied here, particularly the primary teachers who were all experienced professionals, were cognizant of the changes in the political culture of the state and were striving to accommodate more traditional perspectives to the often changing attitudes and outlooks which their pupils bring from their homes. They all believed values education (although they were not familiar with thinking about values education as a separate entity) to be a very important aspect of their role as educators. This lack of familiarity with the concept of values education on the part of Irish teachers, who nevertheless are deeply concerned with the development of values in the pupils they teach, proved to be problematic in adhering to the common interpretative model.

Because of the unique aspects of the Irish situation in the intermingling of religious and values education in the education system of the state, it was decided to categorize respondents' answers into groupings which would reflect their perceptions as faithfully as possible. The categorization of the cohort's responses to the completed questions was based on subsequent group discussions with one-third of the teachers involved. It was considered necessary to explicate and amplify the intended meanings of respondents' answers because of their lack of familiarity with the conception of 'values education' as understood in state-provided secular education systems.

INTERPRETATION OF DATA CONCERNING TEACHERS' ATTITUDINAL DISPOSITIONS TO THE VALUES DIMENSIONS OF TEACHING AND THEIR ACTUAL PRACTICE WITH REGARD TO VALUES EDUCATION

Any attempt to analyse the findings of the Irish study in accordance with the common interpretative model which is presented in Chapter 2 must take cognizance of tradition and practice in education in the Irish system. The teachers surveyed tended to see religion and morality as closely linked and would not necessarily subscribe to Hill's (1991) suggestion that they should be regarded as conceptually separate curriculum domains. Further, the study of religion in Ireland has, up to the present, involved training in the tenets and practice of particular denominations rather than the study of comparative religion as advocated by Hill (1991). It is necessary, therefore, to analyse the Irish findings with reference to their unique context, and to align this analysis with the common interpretative model adopted in this research study, where this is appropriate.

In this section the most frequently suggested answers to the main questions posed to respondents are presented in rank order of frequency of response and examined in the light of teachers' opinions expressed during discussions and interview and in the practices observed in their classrooms. Following this a cluster analysis of the individual teachers sampled based on the various categories of their responses to the main questions is presented. For this purpose it was necessary to group teachers' responses into broad categories based on a content analysis of their answers to each question. These broad categories, which were devised in consultation with respondents, are presented in the key included in each figure depicting each cluster. A table outlining the gender, age range and teaching level of the individuals in each cluster identified in the analysis is presented.

Table 4.1 presents the nine most frequently stated essential principles upon which respondents reported making decisions with regard to the teaching and development of values in the curriculum programme. Democratic values, suggested by one-third of all respondents, was the most frequently stated suggestion, receiving considerably more mention than any of the other principles. The general tenor of the items ranked in this table relates to principles centring on the obligation of individuals as members of society. Such principles as honesty, equality, respect and care for others, fairness and tolerance seem to indicate that teachers place considerable importance on the societal duties and responsibility of the individual.

From an initial examination of this data it seems that moral universalism is to a certain extent demonstrated in respondents' answers. Consensus pluralism, however, seems to be the dominant feature of most of the answers. The principles suggested by the majority of respondents highlight concern for democratic principles which would guarantee the individual in society equality, respect, care and tolerance. Interestingly, religious principles as such rank a mere joint fourth in terms of respondents' assessment of their importance as a basis for decision making with regard to the teaching and development of values. This suggests that religious monopolism is not a distinctive or important feature in this regard. However, this interpretation must be viewed with a degree of caution. For many teachers those values grounded in their religious beliefs and those they would see as universal or humanitarian values are inextricably linked.

The grouping of teachers' responses into categories, which was done in consultation with respondents, highlights the distinctive nature of values education in the Irish context. The first category decided upon was entitled

Table 4.1 The most frequently cited principles which teachers consider essential in making decisions regarding the teaching and development of values

Most frequently stated principles	Rank	%	Number
Democratic values	1	32.5	(n = 13)
Honesty/truth/integrity	=2	20.0	(n = 8)
Equality/equity	=2	20.0	(n = 8)
Care for others	=4	17.5	(n = 7)
Respect for others	=4	17.5	(n = 7)
Religious values	=4	17.5	(n = 7)
Children's needs	=4	17.5	(n = 7)
Fairness	=8	15.0	(n = 6)
Liberal values/tolerance	=8	15.0	(n = 6)

ethical principles. This grouping includes the universal ethical notions or convictions in the abstract such as justice and truth which permeate all civilized
human society. The consensus of teachers concerning this category would
suggest that religious monopolism is not a feature of respondents' attitudinal
dispositions in that such values were seen as not the prerogative of one
religion. However, the degree to which this would indicate either moral
universalism or consensus pluralism is not at all clear. The second category,
care for others, encompassed practical aspects of consideration, sharing and
respect for others. *Religious and moral principles* was the third category identified
and this includes values pertaining specifically to a particular religious
denomination. The fourth category selected, *socio-political principles,* concerns
issues, ideals and values related to aspects of the current political culture such
as gender equity, pollution and unemployment, with particular reference to the
means of resolving problems of this nature in a Western liberal democracy.
The fifth grouping identified, *curriculum-centred principles,* involves issues related
to the curriculum and textbooks and learning materials. The sixth category,
entitled *pupil-centred principles,* encompasses principles related to the development of pupils' self-confidence and their attitudes to study and the provision
of learning activities suitable to pupils' age and level of understanding.

Figure 4.1 presents the clusters based on the data derived from the broad
categorization of respondents' answers to Question 1. This analysis identified
four separate clusters of teacher attitude regarding essential principles underlying decisions in values education. These are presented in Figure 4.1,
together with the number of teachers in each cluster and a key to the categories of attitude involved. Cluster 2, to which 50 per cent of the respondents
belong, is characterized by an almost equal valuing of ethical principles and
care for others and a somewhat lesser importance accorded to socio-political
and pupil-centred principles. This cluster is typified by a greater balance of

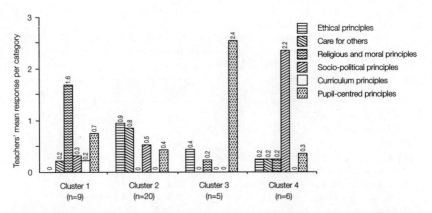

Figure 4.1 The four clusters of teachers based on respondents' attitudes concerning
the essential principles underlying decision making and development of values

attitude than any of the other three clusters. Interestingly, none of the individuals identified in this cluster considers the religious and moral principles specifically associated with one particular religious denomination as essential in their decision making in the teaching and development of values. This is a strong indication that religious monopolism in not a major force in this regard.

Teachers belonging to cluster 1, who comprised just under one-quarter of the sample, accorded most importance to the religious and moral principles pertaining to a particular religious denomination. This would seem to suggest that religious monopolism was a major feature of this group. Respondents belonging to cluster 3 are typified by a high valuing of universal ethical principles and those belonging to cluster 4 accord a high value to socio-political principles. This would seem to suggest an adherence to the values underpinning consensus pluralism among the individuals identified in the third and fourth cluster.

Table 4.2 illustrates the results of an examination of the gender, teaching level and age range of the members of each of the four clusters respectively. Cluster 1, which is distinguished by the high adherence to religious and moral principles and without the reference to abstract ethical ideals which characterized religious monopolism, is marked by a high level of males. Cluster 2, on the other hand, with a slightly greater proportion of female members, is characterized by high adherence to ethical principles and ideals, and none to religious and moral ideals. Clusters 3 and 4, which are predominantly female, are characterized by regard for pupil-centred and socio-political principles respectively.

An examination of column 3 reveals little or no difference in cluster membership attributable to the educational level of the teachers concerned.

Table 4.2 The gender, school level and age range of the members of each of the four clusters of teachers based on respondents' attitudes concerning the essential principles underlying decision making in the teaching and development of values

	Gender		Level		Age range			
	Male (n = 12)	Female (n = 28)	First (n = 20)	Second (n = 20)	<25 (n = 15)	26–35 (n = 16)	36–45 (n = 5)	over 45 (n = 4)
Cluster 1 (n = 9)	6	3	5	4	4	3	1	1
Cluster 2 (n = 20)	5	15	9	11	5	8	4	3
Cluster 3 (n = 5)	0	5	4	1	2	3	0	0
Cluster 4 (n = 6)	1	5	2	4	4	2	0	0

Similarly, column 4, which outlines the age range of respondents, indicates that membership of clusters 1 and 2 is not differentiated by the age range of respondents. It is of interest, however, that membership of cluster 3 and cluster 4 is restricted to the two younger groups in the sample. In respect of cluster 3, this may be an indication that younger female primary teachers place high significance on child-centred principles in the development of values. The analysis relating to cluster 4 suggests that young female teachers at second level place a considerable importance on socio-political principles. Discussions with respondents revealed that these teachers believe a high degree of political involvement to be desirable as a means of improving the functioning of society. Consequently, they considered that the school had a duty to instil a questioning attitude in the system and to make students aware of their responsibilities and their power to influence change in a democracy.

In general terms it seems that religious monopolism is only a minor feature among teachers, and its adherents tend to be younger male teachers. There are indications that the majority of teachers would favour the approach of moral universalism although this would seem to be tempered with many features of consensus pluralism. This is evident in the importance accorded to care and respect for others and values such as tolerance and the autonomy of the individual. Perhaps the fact that universal values seem to be so linked with religion for many Irish people makes it difficult to ascertain the extent to which each of the two models of consensus pluralism and moral universalism is applicable here.

It is now proposed to examine informal strategies which the teachers employ in the area of values development.

Table 4.3 outlines the eight most frequently suggested informal strategies which the teachers employ in the area of values development. Over half the group sampled stated that they employed such flexible methods as debates,

Table 4.3 The eight most frequently suggested informal strategies which teachers report using in the area of values development in the classroom context

Informal strategies	Rank	%	Number
Flexible teaching methods (debates, quizzes, discussions, projects and discovery learning)	1	57.5	(n = 23)
Drama, story-telling and role-play	= 2	22.5	(n = 9)
Strategies involving teacher's example (treating children equally – respecting their opinions)	= 2	22.5	(n = 9)
Strategies for co-operation	= 4	15.0	(n = 6)
Code of behaviour concerning peers, fair play	= 4	15.0	(n = 6)
Explaining and questioning	6	12.5	(n = 5)
Religious education	= 7	10.0	(n = 4)
Individualized work by students	= 7	10.0	(n = 4)

discussions and quizzes in this regard. During discussions with the respondents it emerged that these strategies were favoured because of their flexibility, which allowed for the inclusion of topical subjects and matters of public interest as they arose. Primary teachers in particular found the imaginative activities involved in storytelling, drama and role play to be very useful in regard to the development of values and rated them equally in terms of their use. Equal importance was accorded by respondents to the teacher's example as a strategy in the development of values. Strategies for co-operation and fair play were accorded equal importance in terms of their use by respondents. Teachers suggesting these strategies accorded considerable importance to the formalization of structures in both of the areas.

In view of the important place of Religious Education in the curriculum of state schools in Ireland it may seem surprising that this subject is ranked equal seventh in the list of strategies employed in values education. However, it emerged in discussions that respondents, particularly those teaching at the primary level, considered this relatively low ranking to be indicative of the central place of values development in Religious Education. They asserted that the ethos of the school and the underpinning of all values in the curriculum were informed by the beliefs of the particular religion taught in the school. Here again the particular context of the Irish study must be borne in mind. The centrality of religion was particularly evident in the first-level classroom observation which was carried out during the four weeks prior to Christmas. Both the curriculum and the actual classrooms and incidental activities at all levels in the primary schools were indicative of the coming Christian feast. A typical classroom was decorated with a large crib and picture of Bethlehem and a collage depicting the Christmas story. In addition, the art work of all pupils completed during the month, including individual paintings of the nativity scene at Bethlehem and Christmas decorations made by the remainder of the pupils, were displayed. However, it would be an error to consider this an example of religious monopolism; rather the situation was used by the teacher to discuss such issues as social inequality, care for others, tolerance, and respect for minorities. Interestingly, these were not presented with reference to religious pronouncements but rather as desirable aspects of community for which all members should develop responsibility.

The information requested in relation to the teacher's use of formal strategies is presented in Table 4.4. The most striking aspect of this table is the almost complete similarity between it and the previous table outlining suggested informal strategies. Discussions with respondents indicated that this similarity is a reflection of their views on the situation. The only difference in relation to the suggested informal and formal strategies occurs in relation to the use of texts as a formal approach in this regard. Respondents suggested that the analysis of characters and of situations in textual material could usefully be employed in the area of values development. Not

Table 4.4 The eight most frequently suggested formal strategies which teachers report using in the area of values development in the classroom context

Formal strategies	Rank	%	Number
Flexible teaching methods (debates, quizzes, discussions, projects and discovery learning)	1	57.5	(n = 23)
Drama, story-telling and role-play	2	22.5	(n = 9)
Teacher's example (treating children equally – respecting their opinions)	2	22.5	(n = 9)
Strategies for co-operation	= 4	15.0	(n = 6)
Code of behaviour concerning peers, fair play	= 4	15.0	(n = 6)
Positive reinforcement	6	12.5	(n = 5)
Religious education	= 7	10.0	(n = 4)
Using texts for character analysis, etc.	= 7	10.0	(n = 4)

surprisingly, this was particularly true of teachers of the arts and humanities at second level.

Respondents' motivation for using the various strategies employed in the areas of values development was investigated during discussions. All of the teachers without exception stated that their commitment to methods exemplifying democratic practice, mutual co-operation and fairness was based on the belief that this was the best way of preparing their pupils for adulthood. Most of the teachers perceived that codes of discipline in schools should be built on consensus if at all possible. These beliefs underlying the practical strategies which teachers employ in the area of values point to an underlying conviction indicative of a consensus pluralism model as a basis for values teaching in schools. However, these teachers were unfamiliar with the idea of values education in any formal academic sense, and consequently did not present their views with reference to any of the four models presented in the interpretative analysis.

Table 4.5 presents the eleven most frequently suggested predominant cultural issues which teachers assessed as exerting a major influence upon the values dimension of curriculum. Over half of the group considered that inequality, in all its forms, exerted a major influence on this area of curriculum. In discussion with respondents it emerged that teachers' responses to this question were, to a large extent, influenced by the socio-economic level of the school in which they were teaching. Teachers from schools in under-privileged inner-city areas, and from suburban schools with a high concentration of unemployment within the school community, were likely to view inequality (together with associated social and financial deprivation) and unemployment (although this was regarded as a separate issue and not only a problem in poor or disadvantaged areas) as exerting a major influence on the values dimension of curriculum in their particular contexts. In the interviews with respondents it emerged that teachers' interest in these issues was

Table 4.5 Teachers' assessments of the predominant cultural issues perceived as exerting major influence upon the values dimension of curriculum

Most frequently stated cultural issues	*Rank*	*%*	*Number*
Social and financial inequality, deprivation and poverty	1	52.5	(n = 21)
Religious issues	2	45.0	(n = 18)
Unemployment	=3	35.0	(n = 14)
Modernization, new technology, enterprise culture, multinationals and media culture	=3	35.0	(n = 14)
Political issues	5	32.5	(n = 13)
Irish language, culture and tradition	6	30.0	(n = 12)
Equality, minority rights, gender equity, travellers' rights	7	27.5	(n = 11)
Students' personal problems, family stability, exam pressure, learning disability	8	25.0	(n = 10)
Modernization, divorce, child abuse, changing attitudes to sexual matters	=9	22.5	(n = 9)
Environment	=9	22.5	(n = 9)
Consideration for the less privileged in society	=9	22.5	(n = 9)

predicated on a concern for those in need, and a belief in the necessity to foster in pupils a feeling of caring and responsibility for the problems caused by inequality in society. It seems that consensus pluralism is the approach evident here in the importance accorded to concern for the weak, justice for the oppressed and active benevolence. These issues were all suggested by teachers without reference to religious underpinnings or justification.

Religious issues were second in order of importance in answers to Question 3, which focused upon teachers' assessments of the predominant cultural issues perceived as exerting major influence upon the values dimension of curriculum. In discussions it emerged that current problems such as divorce, child sexual abuse, abortion and problems in the major churches, which in recent times have become the focus of much media attention, have had to be dealt with by teachers in the classroom context. In the past such issues, in so far as they arose, were dealt with in a theoretical and doctrinal manner within Religious Instruction. More recently, the consideration of both the theoretical and the practical aspects of these problems in schools has become unavoidable. In discussions it emerged that changing moral mores, and what teachers termed more secular standards of behaviour in society, required particular sensitivity in the classroom context. Teachers considered it most important that the matters dealt with in Religious Instruction should not cause any pupil to feel less respect for his or her parents because their lives did not conform to religious teaching.

At a practical level, recent innovations such as the *Stay Safe Programme* (Department of Education, 1991) which was introduced in primary schools in an effort to deal with the problem of child physical and sexual abuse, have not been without problems. This programme or teaching package consists of a video for children, two separate curricula for junior and senior cycles and an educational component for parents. It was developed by the Department of Education and the Eastern Health Board and produced by the Department of Health. While all the respondents interviewed attested to the value of the *Stay Safe Programme* some misgivings were expressed. For a small number of teachers expressing more traditional views, there was some unease about removing the area of sexuality education from Religious Instruction. Other teachers were not always comfortable with the increased personal nature of their relationship with pupils, which involvement in the programme brought about. However, the view of most of the group was that teachers as carers would inevitably have to take increasing responsibility for developing values relating to issues in areas where traditionally Religious Instruction had been the arbiter of right and wrong. The model of religious monopolism would feature strongly for less than one-third of the teachers interviewed. However, the majority of the group exhibited aspects of moral universalism and consensus pluralism regarding issues relating to sexual morality. These teachers were strongly of the opinion that personal responsibility, tolerance, respect for others and the autonomy of the individual were the values which should underpin sexuality education and moral development in schools.

Most of the other predominant cultural issues which are perceived by respondents as exerting major influence upon the values dimension of curriculum may be of concern to teachers in all countries. These issues include the problems of modernization and recent technological advances, changing values in society, the care of the environment and consideration for the less privileged in society. In the interviews with respondents it was made clear that the focus of teachers' concern was that dignity and respect for the individual should not be lessened by pressures of modernization or change. Certainly, shades of consensus pluralism seem implicit here in that teachers are seeking to accommodate independence of thought and individual differences.

However, the importance of the national language, culture and tradition is particular to Ireland and seems to be of increasing concern to teachers. Successive governments since the foundation of the state more than seventy years ago have set the education system the task of restoring the Irish language through ensuring that all students have bi-lingual competence in Irish and in English. This endeavour has not been a complete success and teachers' lack of results in this regard, particularly with underprivileged students, have been disheartening even for the most committed professional.

The predominant cultural issues perceived as exerting major influence upon the values dimension of curriculum in the Irish context were categorized (in consultation with respondents) into six broad groupings or conceptual clusters The first category or cluster identified, entitled *ethical values issues*, encompasses theoretical values involving moral and civic duty, such as respect for authority, co-operation and respect for the environment. The second grouping, entitled *national issues*, encompasses the areas of national identity, the Irish language, culture and tradition. The third category identified, *religious issues*, concerns religious practice and observance and the religious ethos of the school. *Modernization issues*, involving problems relating to divorce, abortion, child abuse, and the problems ascribed to new technology, enterprise culture, multinationals and 'media culture', comprise the fourth grouping of issues. The fifth category, entitled *societal and socio-economic issues*, involves social inequality, poverty, emigration, unemployment and minority rights. *Student-centred issues*, the sixth grouping identified, concerns exam pressure, bullying, drug abuse, alienation and low self-esteem.

The four clusters of teachers based on the broad categorization of the data derived from their answers to Question 3, which are presented in Figure 4.2, are of considerable interest. Cluster 1 is typified by the high degree of importance accorded by its members to values related to ethical issues in an abstract sense. Members of this group do not consider student-related issues to be of influence. Teachers identified in this group are concerned with the ethical nature of the issues which exert major influences on values. In discussions it was ascertained that respondents believed that these values should be obtained through community negotiation and consensus. This seems to suggest that the consensus pluralism model features strongly with this group of teachers.

Cluster 2, to which fourteen respondents belong, is characterized by a relatively similar rating of all six types of issues in terms of their influence on the values dimension of curriculum. Respondents in this cluster accord considerable importance to religious and national issues which traditionally have been seen as an important feature of the political culture of the state. This

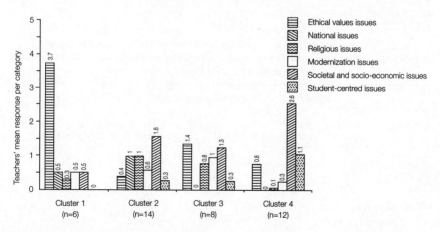

Figure 4.2 The four clusters of teachers based on respondents' perceptions of predominant cultural issues which exert major influence upon the values dimension of curriculum

seems to indicate the existence of aspects of religious monopolism among members of this cluster. A factor common to teachers belonging to both cluster 3 and cluster 4 is the lack of importance they accord to national issues in terms of their influence in the values dimension of curriculum. At one level this may be interpreted as indications of a growing tendency towards moral universalism or indeed consensus pluralism. Certainly, teachers in Ireland have traditionally been characterized by their adherence to religious principles combined with a strong belief in the promotion of cultural identity and the national language. Respondents in cluster 4 consider societal and socio-economic problem issues to exert major influence upon the values dimension of curriculum. During the subsequent interviews it was ascertained that the teachers here were concerned that the curriculum should represent values with which pupils could identify. Concern was expressed regarding the alienation of disadvantaged students if the values dimension of curriculum did not reflect their environment, their concerns and their interests.

Table 4.6 examines the gender, teaching level and age range of the members of each of the four clusters which are presented in Figure 4.3 (p. 82). Cluster 1, which is distinguished by the high adherence to ethical values indicating consensus, is made up of female members only. This is surprising, particularly as student-centred issues are not mentioned by this group. Cluster 2, which seems to indicate a degree of moral universalism and somewhat less religious monopolism, is not differentiated by any of the demographic measures presented, except the teaching level of respondents. Almost twice as many primary teachers as those teaching in second-level schools belong to this cluster. Teachers belonging to both cluster 3 and cluster 4 do not consider national issues influential in the values dimension of curriculum while those respondents in cluster 4 consider societal and socio-economic problem

Table 4.6 The gender, school level and age range of the members of each of the four clusters of teachers based on respondents' perceptions of predominant cultural issues which exert major influence upon the values dimension of curriculum

	Gender		Level		Age range			
	Male (n = 12)	*Female* (n = 28)	*First* (n = 20)	*Second* (n = 20)	*<25* (n = 15)	*26–35* (n = 16)	*36–45* (n = 5)	*over 45* (n = 4)
Cluster 1 (n = 6)	0	6	3	3	2	3	1	0
Cluster 2 (n = 14)	7	7	9	5	4	6	2	2
Cluster 3 (n = 8)	2	6	3	5	5	1	1	1
Cluster 4 (n = 12)	3	9	5	7	4	6	1	1

issues to exert major influence upon the values dimension of curriculum. Younger teachers are more numerous in these two clusters than their older colleagues. Cluster 4, which indicated a concern for consensus pluralism, is marked by a high proportion of female, second-level and younger teachers among its membership.

Table 4.7 outlines teachers' rankings of the most frequently stated sources of knowledge relating to values development. A feature of the data presented in this table is the importance accorded by 67.5 per cent of respondents to the teacher's own knowledge and life experience as a basis for values education. This is in excess of any of the other suggested sources of knowledge and would seem to suggest a form of 'self-referencing' by the teachers involved. In fact the respondents who did not mention the teacher's knowledge and experience in this regard were all from among the pre-service group which had not yet acquired professional classroom experience. This group cited textbooks and the Department of Education as providing the knowledge basis for values education. There is little evidence of religious monopolism to be found in responses to this question, with a mere 10 per cent of teachers citing religion in answer to the question posed. However, it is not possible to discern the relative importance of moral universalism and consensus pluralism in the responses cited. Subsequent discussions with teachers identified two opposing points of view. One group of teachers considered that universal human values should form the basis for values education, indicating a basis in moral universalism, while the other group was adamant that students should be helped to develop a system of values through a process of critical analysis based on respect, tolerance and care for all the individuals who make up society. This latter approach is close to the notion of consensus pluralism as described by Hill (1991).

Table 4.8 outlines teachers' rankings of their methods of organizing the knowledge relating to values development. The most striking fact which emerges from the data in this table is the extent to which teachers use an integrated approach (wholly or in part) in the teaching of values. A mere 20 per cent (n = 8) of the sample report using a discrete approach to organizational methods in values education. This finding is not surprising for

Table 4.7 Teachers' views on whose knowledge forms the basis of the course

Most frequently stated sources of knowledge	Rank	%	Number
Teacher's knowledge and life experience	1	67.5	(n = 27)
Interaction with pupils	2	30.0	(n = 12)
Texts	3	20.0	(n = 8)
Curriculum	4	17.5	(n = 7)
Department of Education	5	15.0	(n = 6)
Religion	= 6	10.0	(n = 4)
Store of human knowledge	= 6	10.0	(n = 4)

Table 4.8 Teachers' assessments of how the knowledge is organized for the learners

Most frequently stated organizational methods	Rank	%	Number
Integrated and discrete	1	50.0	(n = 20)
Integrated	= 2	20.0	(n = 8)
Discrete	= 2	20.0	(n = 8)
Integrated in Religious Education	4	10.0	(n = 4)

respondents who are involved in first-level education. Teachers in Irish primary schools have been teaching an integrated curriculum for the past twenty-five years. It is of interest, however, that teachers at second level, who are all subject specialist teachers, also favour an integrated approach in this regard.

Table 4.9 outlines teachers' rankings of the most frequently used teaching methods in the area of values education. An examination of this table reveals that over three-quarters of respondents employ conventional teaching methods to impart knowledge relating to values development. This is in contrast to the strategies suggested in response to Question 2, which were predominantly informal (to both sections of the question) and tended to be flexible in nature. It is to be hoped that this distinction is due to teachers' differentiating between 'classroom strategies' and 'teaching methods' in the areas of values education. Certainly, there were indications both in the subsequent interviews and in the classroom observations that teachers were strongly committed to the use of informal classroom strategies in values education.

It is obvious from Table 4.10 that most teachers consider that the knowledge pertaining to the values dimension of the curriculum is available to all students. In subsequent discussions it emerged that teachers in first-level education were more likely to hold this view than teachers in second-level schools. Secondary teachers tended to point to the extra private tuition and enriching experiences enjoyed by students from affluent backgrounds. Teachers expressing these views accepted that these advantages did not

Table 4.9 Teachers' views on the teaching methods used to impart knowledge relating to values

Most frequently suggested formal strategies	Rank	%	Number
Conventional instruction	1	77.5	(n = 31)
Discussion methods	2	60.0	(n = 24)
Activity-based learning, drama, role-play	3	22.5	(n = 21)
Guided discovery	4	37.5	(n = 9)
AV methods, overhead projector, blackboard	5	15.0	(n = 6)
Explanations and answering questions	= 6	12.5	(n = 5)
Demonstration/example	= 6	12.5	(n = 5)

Table 4.10 Teachers' views as to which individuals or groups of learners is the knowledge pertaining to the values dimension of curriculum available

Suggested groups	Rank	%	Number
All	1	60.0	(n = 24)
The academically advantaged	2	15.0	(n = 6)
The financially advantaged	= 3	12.5	(n = 5)
The academically and financially advantaged	= 3	12.5	(n = 5)

necessarily mean increased availability in relation to the values dimension of the curriculum. However, they suggested that groups loosely described as 'the have-nots' often became alienated, embittered and antagonistic to society and its values. This may well indicate that what teachers are pinpointing here are features of the moral vacuum model. However, the evidence is too tenuous to make any firm suggestions in this regard.

The two sections of Question 5 elicited the most coherent responses from teachers concerning aspects of values education. Table 4.11 presents teachers' rankings of the most important elements which values teaching in the schools should address. The nature of elements in values teaching as identified in the data include the individual's responsibility to care for others, tolerance, honesty, fairness and the ability to co-operate. These elements are somewhat similar to the principles suggested in response to Question 1, although care for others is accorded more importance in this case, while democracy (or a related area) does not feature here. However, they are quite dissimilar from the influences on values education cited in response to Question 3. This would suggest that the respondents are drawing a clear distinction between, on the one hand, the current cultural influences on values education which, in general terms, seemed to suggest that moral universalism prevails at present, and, on the other, the elements values teaching

Table 4.11 The most frequently cited elements which values teaching in the schools should address

Most frequently suggested elements	Rank	%	Number
Care for others/kindness	1	70.0	(n = 28)
Tolerance	2	37.5	(n = 15)
Honesty	3	30.0	(n = 12)
Fairness	= 4	27.5	(n = 11)
Ability to co-operate	= 4	27.5	(n = 11)
Pride in oneself/self-respect	= 6	25.0	(n = 10)
Encouragement/positive reinforcement	= 6	25.0	(n = 10)
Understanding of children	8	22.5	(n = 9)
Independence of thought	= 9	20.0	(n = 8)
Current social and political issues	= 9	27.5	(n = 8)

should address, which indicate a specific preference for an approach featuring aspects of consensus pluralism.

Figure 4.3 presents four clusters of teachers based on respondents' assessment of the most important elements which values teaching in schools should address. Five categories of elements were decided upon in consultation with the respondents. *Ethical concerns* comprises such items as tolerance, fairness and honesty, and *socio-political problems* involves current social and political issues, gender equity and social justice. The grouping *family and school concerns* involves parental values and the ethos of the school. The fourth category, *the social and personal development of pupils*, concerns the development of pupils' self-respect and their ability to co-operate, and the fifth grouping, entitled *the learning experience of pupils*, concerns pupils' academic development.

Members of cluster 1, which includes 40 per cent of respondents, place the highest value on ethical concerns such as tolerance, fairness and honesty. In discussions with respondents it was revealed that adherents to these views were strongly of the opinion that these elements should be addressed both in theory and in practice by educators. They believed that it was essential to provide pupils with participative learning experiences of the suggested elements. Respondents in this cluster were also concerned with socio-political problems in society. They were of the opinion that it was important to ensure that pupils acquire an awareness of the problems faced by various disadvantaged groups in society and that they develop an active concern for those less fortunate than themselves. This suggests that members of cluster 1 demonstrate features of both moral universalism and consensus pluralism. Because of the lack of familiarity with the concept of values education on the part of respondents it was not possible to elicit any more interpretative information in this regard.

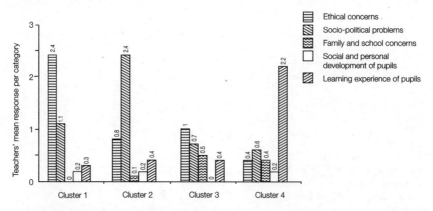

Figure 4.3 The four clusters of teachers based on respondents' assessments of the most important elements which values teaching in schools should address

Cluster 2, comprising twelve respondents, is characterized by the concern of those teachers for members of society suffering from what were termed socio-political problems. This group was of the opinion that such problems should figure prominently in relation to the teaching of values. These problems do not figure to any great extent in the rank order of elements presented in Table 4.11 because the problems suggested by respondents were both diverse and large. However, the common aspect presented by all of these problems was teachers' suggestions that pupils should be encouraged to develop an active concern for less privileged groups in society and for those who were marginalized, discriminated against or disadvantaged.

Teachers in cluster 3 are characterized by an almost equal valuing of four of the five categories of elements suggested by respondents; however, the social and personal development of pupils is not considered important by members of this cluster. Teachers comprising cluster 4 place by far the greatest importance on the learning experience of pupils and an almost similar value on the other four categories of elements used here. It is not possible to ascertain from the profile of teachers in these two clusters the attitudinal dispositions of respondents concerning the elements which values education in schools should address.

Table 4.12 examines the gender, teaching level and age range of the members of each of the four clusters respectively, based on teachers' assessments of the most important elements which influence values teaching in schools. The most interesting facet of this table is the lack of any significant pattern of association between cluster membership and either the gender, level of teaching or age range of the members. There is a slight indication that teachers at second level are more likely to be members of clusters 1 and 3 while teachers at first level are more likely to be members of the other two clusters. However, this pattern of association is too tenuous to warrant comment.

Table 4.12 The gender, school level and age range of the members of each of the four clusters of teachers based on respondents' assessments of the most important elements which values teaching in shools should address

	Gender		Level		Age range			
	Male (n = 12)	Female (n = 28)	First (n = 20)	Second (n = 20)	<25 (n = 15)	26–35 (n = 16)	36–45 (n = 5)	over 45 (n = 4)
Cluster 1 (n = 6)	5	11	7	9	7	7	1	1
Cluster 2 (n = 12)	4	8	8	4	3	7	1	1
Cluster 3 (n = 7)	1	6	2	5	4	0	2	1
Cluster 4 (n = 5)	2	3	3	2	1	2	1	1

Table 4.13 outlines in rank order teachers' assessments of the most important elements which values education components of teacher education courses should address. The views of respondents as expressed here are indicative of teachers' assessment of deficiencies in teacher education courses or of areas to which more attention should be given. Some of the elements seem to be more closely connected with the pedagogical aspects of teacher training than to values education. This stems in part from the concerns of the 'pre-service' group and their current concerns with both teaching practice and examination-related problems. It is also due to respondents' lack of familiarity with the concept of values education.

An examination of Table 4.13 reveals that tolerance, the element ranked first, was suggested by almost half of the group sampled. Ethics or moral standards was the element which was ranked second by teachers. The respondents were at pains to suggest the importance of basing these standards on ethical principles on which full discussions should be carried out with students rather than on a set of unexplained rules. Many of the respondents suggesting the inclusion of this particular element in teacher education courses were strongly of the opinion that future teachers should be made aware of the importance of all pupils experiencing a school system in which standards of behaviour were based on ethical principles. These two elements which are ranked first and second in order of importance here are indicative of features of both moral universalism and consensus pluralism.

A number of elements suggested here, such as principles of child development, organizational skills, child-centredness and communication skills, demonstrate once again a lack of familiarity with values education on the part of respondents. These elements relate to Psychology and the Teaching Studies areas of teacher education courses rather than to values education. However, the concern of respondents indicates these are of interest in that

Table 4.13 The most frequently cited elements which the values components of teacher education courses should address

Most frequently suggested elements	Rank	%	Number
Tolerance	1	47.5	(n = 19)
Ethics, moral standards of behaviour	2	45.0	(n = 18)
Principles of child development	3	40.0	(n = 16)
Organizational skills, resourcefulness	4	35.0	(n = 14)
Equality	= 5	32.5	(n = 13)
Respect for children	= 5	32.5	(n = 13)
Child-centredness	7	27.2	(n = 11)
Coping skills concerning bullying, sexual issues, depression, health issues, social problems, etc.	= 8	20.0	(n = 8)
Communication skills	= 8	20.0	(n = 8)

they are indicative of a valuing of childhood and the provision of learning experiences appropriate to particular ages in the child's development. An important concern of respondents is evident in their suggestion that future teachers be equipped with coping skills appropriate to dealing with such problems as bullying, sexual abuse, depression, health issues and social problems. Teachers seem to be of the opinion that family and community support systems and resources are no longer sufficient to cope with such problems effectively. This may indicate that teachers are aware of certain growing tendencies which may well indicate the emergence of a moral vacuum model in Ireland. However, there is little overall indication that this model exists to any marked extent in the country. A possible explanation for this may be the historically strong religious element within Irish society.

Figure 4.4 presents the four clusters of teachers based on respondents' assessments of the most important elements which values teaching in teacher education courses should address. The six categories of elements were devised in discussions with the respondents to this question. The first category, entitled *socio-economic concerns*, includes unemployment, poor housing, emigration, financial hardship, inequality and social deprivation. Although none of these separate elements features individually in the first nine factors ranked in Table 4.13, subsequent discussions revealed that respondents considered them important as a grouping. It was considered important by many of the teachers sampled that a social conscience be developed among student teachers in relation to problems of a socio-economic nature. The objective of this strategy was that these students would in the future pass on a sense of responsibility to their pupils in schools. The second category, entitled *moral standards*, refers primarily to the regulations and ethics associated with the various religious denominations in the state. The teachers

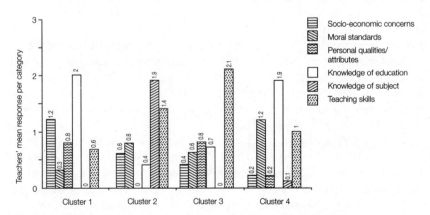

Figure 4.4 The four clusters of teachers based on respondents' assessments of the most important elements which values teaching in teacher education courses should address

sampled suggested the existence of common universal moral principles and did not conceive of any major area of diversity of belief in this regard. This strongly and explicitly indicates features of moral universalism on the part of respondents. The remaining groupings are for the most part concerned with the practical and theoretical aspects of teacher training rather than values education. This, once again, points to the lack of familiarity with values education on the part of teachers in Ireland.

The four clusters of teachers identified in Figure 4.4 are not particularly indicative of typologies of teachers based on respondents' replies to the important elements which values teaching in teacher education courses should address. This is due to a lack of familiarity with the notion of values education and the consequent inclusion of general aspects of teacher education in responses to this question already noted. Members of cluster 1 are characterized by a high valuing of theoretical knowledge of the components of education courses together with socio-economic concerns in teacher education. Teachers in cluster 2 consider knowledge of the academic subject to be taught in schools and teaching skills as the most important elements of a student teachers' course. Respondents in cluster 3 place a very high value on teaching skills and consider the personal qualities of the teacher such as patience to be important, while members of cluster 4 believe knowledge of education together with moral standards and teaching skills to be important.

An examination of the most important concerns suggested by the members forming each of the four clusters is not revealing regarding these teachers' views as to the most important elements which the values education component in teacher education should address. However, the fact that the category entitled 'moral standards' features in all the clusters is a significant factor. The inclusion of moral standards in each of the four clusters which comprise the responses of all of the respondents is the strongest suggestion encountered up to this point in the analysis, that moral universalism is a distinct feature of the attitudinal dispositions of teachers in Ireland. It is also clear that this inclusion of moral standards here is not indicative of religious monopolism. None of the teachers considered that values should be taught within the framework of religious studies. Further, they were of the opinion that the moral principles which they would advocate were all ones which would command universal agreement regardless of the particular religion to which individuals belonged.

As noted earlier, however, the attitude of teachers as expressed here must be seen in the context of Irish society. The population is made up largely of Roman Catholics with about 5 per cent belonging to other Christian religions and less than 1 per cent adhering to non-Christian traditions. While some lessening of religious observance has been evident over recent years, over 95 per cent of parents at the current time opt to have their children receive formal religious instruction in the tenets of one particular religion as part of their schooling at primary level. It is evident, therefore, that Irish society does not accommodate a diverse range of religious, racial or cultural differences. Application of the model of moral universalism or, more particularly, that of consensus pluralism, in such a society has a limited currency.

Table 4.14 examines the gender, teaching level and age range of the members of each of the four clusters based on respondents' assessments of the most important elements which values in teacher education courses should address. For the most part no obvious patterns of association between cluster membership and the three demographic factors, the gender and age range of respondents and the level at which they were teaching, presented in this table emerge. One exception to this is found in the high proportion of female members in cluster 1. This would seem to indicate a somewhat more marked tendency on the part of females to consider knowledge of education and socio-economic concerns as important elements of values teaching in courses for future teachers. However, the main interest of Table 4.14 is that it suggests that respondents' attitudinal dispositions to values teaching in teacher education courses are not differentiated in any major way by gender, age range or the level at which they teach.

APPROACHES WITHIN THE CLASSROOM

The classroom approaches of teachers relating to the values dimension of education which were perceived during observations in schools and which were enunciated by respondents during semi-structured interviews are considered in this section of the chapter. These practical approaches of teachers are examined with reference to the practice of respondents as outlined in their answers to the questionnaire which is reported in the previous section of this chapter. Observations of teaching sessions in primary school with

Table 4.14 The gender, school level and age range of the members of each of the four clusters of teachers, based on respondents' assessments of the most important elements which values teaching in teaching education courses should address

	Gender		Level		Age range			
	Male (n = 12)	Female (n = 28)	First (n = 20)	Second (n = 20)	<25 (n = 15)	26–35 (n = 16)	36–45 (n = 5)	over 45 (n = 4)
Cluster 1 (n = 9)	1	8	5	4	4	3	0	2
Cluster 2 (n = 8)	3	5	3	5	4	4	0	0
Cluster 3 (n = 11)	4	7	6	5	1	6	4	0
Cluster 4 (n = 12)	4	8	6	6	6	3	1	2

pupils from 10 to 11 years and in a second-level school with 16-year-old pupils were carried out subsequent to the administration of the question-naire. The schools visited were located in a suburban area of south Dublin and their student populations came from both middle-income and lower-income families.

The sixth-grade class of boys and girls at primary level was organized in mixed ability groups in a bright and cheerful classroom which had been specially decorated for the Christmas season. The English language lesson was based on a Scandinavian legend in which the heroic rescue of a ship-wrecked fisherman by a young boy is recounted. The story was read by the teacher, who paused at intervals to check for comprehension and to explain any difficulties encountered by the pupils. An informal approach was adopted by the teacher in discussions, and associations were made to related subject areas such as History and Geography as appropriate.

The manner in which the teacher interacted with pupils was very support-ive and positively reinforcing. Constant awareness of pupils' needs and problems, and concern for their self-esteem, underpinned all teacher–pupil interaction in the classroom. The teacher moved freely around the working groups and was close to each individual at some point during the lesson. She used both gestural and verbal reinforcement and all her interaction with the class conveyed awareness and positive regard. Her comments such as 'Well imagine! I didn't know that', and 'Anne gave us a very good idea a few minutes ago', brought smiles of pride to the pupils in question.

The behaviour code or agreed set of rules which was in operation in this class was based on democratic principles most of which had been negotiated with the class. These rules were invoked by the teacher at points during the lesson when pupils' enthusiasm to answer questions threatened to become disruptive. In every instance in which a rule was invoked the justification for having the particular rule was mentioned, in most cases by the teacher, and in others by the pupils themselves. In this classroom both the example of the teacher and the classroom rules demonstrated an attempt to operate a demo-cratic code in order to maintain a fair and congenial classroom environment. This commitment to teaching methods in which democratic interaction is practised is a clear indication that aspects of consensus pluralism were a feature of this Irish primary school classroom.

The second-level History lesson was more focused on specific subject content than the lessons observed in the primary school classroom and the proximity of examinations seemed to be a major motivating force for the class group. The relationship between the teacher and this class of 16-year-old students was quite friendly; however, it was more formal than the teacher–pupil relationship observed in the primary school. These second-level students were accorded the responsibility for their own learning by the teacher and they seemed familiar with this type of approach. The students themselves were keenly aware of the immediacy of examinations and the teacher was forced at various points in the lesson to intervene in order to curtail their enthusiasm for speedy progress in an effort to allow time for the less able among the class group to formulate an answer or a query.

The minor breaches in the code of behaviour which occurred during the History lesson were occasioned by students' eagerness to 'cover the material' and their impatience at delays caused by the teacher's endeavours to ensure that the whole class understood. In these cases the teacher's reference to the agreed code relating to fairness and respect for others brought an immediate response. The rationale underlying these interventions was not always made explicit by the teacher. However, students themselves made reference both to what had been agreed and to the principle of fairness at times during the lesson. This suggests that aspects of consensus pluralism are a feature of classroom practice in this second-level school with regard to the agreed code of behaviour and the justification underpinning school rules.

The subject matter content of the History lesson was not related to any aspect of values education and no ethical or moral principle was adverted to in the course of the lesson. It seems that this was due to the proximity of examinations for this class of academically ambitious students. Their priority at this particular point in the year was efficient revision of subject matter, and this utilitarian approach took precedence over any other consideration. For this reason it is not possible to discern whether any of the four models which have been used as an interpretative basis apply to the manner in which subject matter content was handled in the History lesson.

As far as it was possible to discern there was no perceptible difference in the manner in which boys and girls were treated by the teacher at first or second level. Male primary school pupils were far more forthcoming in response to the teacher's questions and they seemed more anxious to be called on to answer than their female counterparts. However, the teacher requested contributions in equal number from both boys and girls. An interesting aspect of primary school pupils' attitudes become evident in the ensuing discussion about deeds of valour. The examples of bravery suggested by both male and female students were all perpetrated by men and most of the deeds of valour suggested related to men who were prominent in the area of sports. This seems to suggest that bravery is not perceived as an attribute of women and it may well indicate a lack of female role models for pupils of both genders at primary school. However, the teacher was at pains to avoid gender role stereotyping in this regard by directing the discussion to women's achievements both in other subjects studied recently and in the area of sports.

At second level there was no perceptible difference between the manner in which male and female students were treated by the teacher. Pupils of both genders were given equal opportunity to contribute and the class was arranged in mixed gender groups. However, unlike the pupils at first level, the male and female 16-year-old students seemed somewhat wary and shy of performing individually and they had a tendency to tease each other. This may have been due, at least in part, to the presence of an observer in their classroom. Pupils at first level seemed to forget the presence of a stranger almost immediately; however, the second-level students remained conscious of the presence of an observer right throughout the class period.

The approach of Christmas was particularly important in the learning environment of pupils in the primary school, which was visited in the month of December. While this is partly attributable to the younger age range of pupils at first level it also reflects the religious ethos of the primary school. The main areas of the school and individual classrooms were decorated both in general festive terms and with religious displays relating to the Nativity. The class discussions in which reference was made to Christmas did not give any indication for the presence of religious monopolism. Rather, the values which were highlighted in these discussions, in particular caring and compassion, demonstrate support for the concept of moral universalism.

The second-level school on the other hand had much less seasonal decoration and few obvious religious symbols relating to Christmas. Classrooms were well furnished and comfortable but the emphasis was on utility and efficiency rather than on promoting a sense of belonging on the part of students. An exception to this was the furniture in the school hall in which the students ate lunch. This furniture had been made by students at woodwork classes. Interestingly, these students displayed a considerable pride in this achievement and, despite the fact that over 500 students used the facility each day, the furniture remained in pristine condition.

The classroom observations indicated that the reported classroom practices of teachers are closely related to their theoretical perspective with regard to the values dimension of teaching. This was true of the explicit and implicit values which were promoted by teachers and also of the teaching methods and the classroom management techniques used in values education. In the primary school the values promoted explicitly by the teacher such as kindness and care for others tend to reflect strong features of moral universalism. These specific values may have been focused upon because of the particular lesson topics and because of the relevance of these values to the Christmas story.

In broad terms it may be said that the codes of behaviour which were negotiated between teachers and pupils, and the rules implicit in the classroom management techniques used by the teachers, strongly indicate features of consensus pluralism. These were based on democratic principles and are in broad agreement with teachers' responses relating to their most frequently used classroom strategy in the area of values development. Teachers suggested that flexible methods, strategies for co-operation, codes of discipline, explaining and the example of treating all children equally were important in this regard.

Semi-structured interviews with three groups, comprising sixteen of the respondents in total, were held after the administration of the questionnaire and the classroom observations. Each of these interviews began with teachers, particularly those teaching at primary level, endeavouring to separate the notion of values education from Religious Instruction or Religious Education. The class teacher in the Irish primary school usually teaches Religious Instruction, while at second level schools have a specialist Religion teacher. Sixth grade or final year in primary school is very significant for pupils in terms of their religious development. At this time the class teacher traditionally prepares pupils for the examination in Religious Instruction prior to their Confirmation, which symbolizes the initiation into adulthood of boys and girls. Further discussion revealed that religious education, the moral development of pupils, the engendering of acceptable behaviour patterns, and the development of values were inextricably linked for primary teachers. They believed that the primary school was the environment most amenable to this approach, culminating in sixth class with the preparation of pupils for Confirmation, in which one-third of the teachers interviewed had been involved. This group commented, 'The Confirmation programme is not about religious doctrine but it is full of values, valuing yourself, valuing other people and valuing the difference between people.'

While both the first- and the second-level teachers considered Religious Instruction to be very important, their convictions in this regard are not indicative of religious monopolism. This is evident in their considered opinion of the curriculum materials for the Religion programme in Roman Catholic schools, the *Children of God* series for students at first level. The teachers were unanimous that the textbooks in this programme were a good basis for teaching values. However, all of the teachers reported that these texts 'must not be taken as Gospel'. Further, they suggested that 'once you do not pay too much attention to the very religious bits you're all right and the main parts are very good'. Many of the group paid tribute to the religious authorities for their response to the needs of teachers with regard to course materials. 'Twenty-five years ago there was a little blue catechism and the answer to every question was learned off by heart. Since then the programme has been revised three times. No other area of the curriculum has received this sort of attention.' This view of the textbook materials in the *Children of God* series was held by teachers regardless of the denomination to which they belonged. 'It's not about what the Catholic Church says and I don't bother with all this Bible stuff and Covenants and the like. I take from it what I want from it.' Another teacher suggested that 'often it is absolutely necessary when using a very good lesson that applies to humanity generally to leave out a tacky little bit at the end. A bit that was dragged in to highlight a Catholic perspective.'

Teachers were of the opinion that the religious influence in Irish education particularly at first level was welcomed by the vast majority of parents. However, some of the teachers interviewed expressed certain doubts about the sincerity of the motives of some parents in this regard. It was suggested by a number of the teachers that some middle-class parents, particularly those who were very ambitious for their children, valued Religious Instruction for utilitarian reasons rather than from any spiritual or religious conviction. Some of the teachers suggested that 'it may be because it gives children civilized values, and develops a sense of responsibility and good work habits'.

The principles of fairness and respect were common themes relating to values for all of the fifteen first- and second-level teachers who took part in the interviews. This was echoed in the classroom practice of the teachers in relation both to the curriculum aspects of their teaching and to the codes of behaviour they favoured. As reported above, all of the teachers interviewed were strongly of the opinion that it was essential for all aspects of relationships in the classroom to be based on democratic principles of fair play. There was agreement among the teachers that it was only through experience of these principles in action that the pupils of today would develop into the 'body politic of a caring, fair, tolerant democracy'. A number of these teachers took the ideals advocated in the UN Charter along with 'suitably diluted religious doctrine' as a basis for their teaching values. Respect for others was an important element of the code of behaviour for teachers at both first and second levels. In the second-level school visited this included such practices as using a title when addressing all adults regardless of their position and many other similar forms of courtesy. This strongly indicates that features of consensus pluralism and, to a lesser extent, moral universalism operate in Irish education.

A number of the respondents interviewed who were teaching in schools in deprived areas were very concerned about the degree of alienation in poor communities with high unemployment levels, drug abuse and many other associated problems. These teachers considered that there was no point in teaching the old version of the Catholic religion in such schools. 'It would not get any support from the parents.' 'A teacher would be hard pressed to get across a simple code of behaviour, some basic manners and a few simple Christian values.' They suggested that for many of their pupils 'Confirmation, like marriage, is something that happens in church. It has little or nothing to do with religion, they buy expensive clothes that they can't afford, and have a good day out.' These views support the responses of teachers to Question 4 noted in the previous section indicating that 'the have-nots' often become embittered and antagonistic. This may well be an indication of the applicability of the moral vacuum model in this regard.

All of the teachers interviewed suggested that tolerance was one of the most important principles that values teaching should address. However, it was generally considered that the attitudes of the home predominate in this area regardless of what is taught in the school. One respondent who had taken part in a development education programme found the learning of pupils in the section on racism to have been very superficial with little transfer or retention of the learning concerning the values related to tolerance. The other teachers in the group reported similar experiences. They considered that one of the most intractable problems experienced recently in certain schools concerned the integration of pupils from the travelling community into the ordinary classroom. While pupils from the settled community will work with pupils from the travelling community in the context of the classroom, they will not be persuaded to associate in playground activities. These pupils have adopted the attitudes of their parents, many of whom were openly hostile to the settlement of travellers in local communities. This suggests that while teachers seek to promote values of tolerance indicating an acceptance of consensus pluralism and moral universalism, they are aware of the disregard for such values in the communities in which they teach.

Religious beliefs, values and dispositions in Ireland have undergone considerable changes in recent years and such changes have become the matter of public discussion in a manner heretofore unknown in the country. This situation has had an effect on classrooms in relation both to Religious Instruction and to more general curriculum areas. During interviews it was established that many of the teachers had found themselves in a moral dilemma in situations where the official teaching of the Roman Catholic Church was at variance with parental norms. Many problems of this nature surfaced in relation to the public discussions concerning the referendum to allow for legal divorce in the Irish Republic which took place in November 1995. The teachers interviewed all agreed that their primary duty was to their pupils and they would not wish to violate the relationship between children and parents by any suggestions that the views of parents were in error. They considered that this duty to their pupils superseded any official religious or personal beliefs they might hold in the area of moral values.

The interviews and classroom observations conducted in connection with this study provide some indication of the relevance of the religious monopolism model to the teaching of values in Irish schools. However, aspects of both the moral universalism model and consensus pluralism are more strongly evident than religious monopolism in the values dimension of education in Ireland. This is in broad agreement with the findings of the questionnaire. It is not possible to discern the relative applicability of these two models of consensus pluralism and moral universalism to the teaching of values in Irish schools.

CONCLUSIONS

1 The Christian religion, particularly the Roman Catholic Church, is deeply enmeshed in the social fabric of Irish society and it is an important feature of the political culture of the country. Because of this, religious

values and general social values have traditionally been considered as synonymous.

2 Teachers in Ireland are unfamiliar with the concept of values education as a separate curriculum area.

3 Religious Instruction is the subject area in which the formal teaching of values occurs most usually in Irish schools.

4 One-third of respondents considered moral religious principles to be a basis for teaching values in schools. This suggests features of the religious monopolism model.

5 Teachers who taught Religion Instruction as a subject were at pains to assert that they used curriculum materials and texts from the approved curriculum materials in a selective manner and in accordance with 'universal human values' or 'civilized values'.

6 A number of respondents were of the opinion that parental approval of and involvement in values education programmes is necessary if democratic values are to be encouraged.

7 Moral universalism appears to exert a strong basis for values teaching in Irish schools. Universal values such as honesty, fairness and care for others were suggested as a foundation for values education.

8 Consensus pluralism seems to exert considerable influence in the framework within which Irish teachers view values education. Respondents accorded considerable importance to tolerance, independence of thought, the autonomy of the individual, co-operation and self-respect in this regard.

9 Irish teachers demonstrate a considerable degree of support for consensus pluralism in the manner in which they approach classroom management, particularly in regard to the democratic negotiation of codes of behaviour.

10 All teachers asserted strongly that practices adhered to in the school classroom should be based on a democratic model in order that pupils develop in a context of democratic interaction. This is indicative of consensus pluralism underpinning classroom management practice in Irish schools.

11 Only slight support is evident for the moral vacuum model in Irish education. The concerns of teachers for the alienated sections of society, for the problems of drug abuse, bullying, sexual abuse, depression and other social problems, indicate the emergence of aspects of the model.

REFERENCES

Coolahan, J. (1981) *Irish Education History and Structure* (Dublin, IPA).

Department of Education (1971) *Primary School Curriculum*, Teachers' Handbook Part 1 (Dublin, Department of Education).

Department of Education (1991) *The Stay Safe Programme* (Dublin, Health Promotion Unit, Department of Health and Department of Education).

Department of Education (1995) *Charting Our Education Future: White Paper on Education* (Dublin, The Stationery Office).

Dometrius, N.C. (1992) *Social Statistics Using SPSS* (New York, HarperCollins Publishers Inc.).

Drudy, S. and Lynch, K. (1993) *Schools and Society in Ireland* (Dublin, Gill & Macmillan).

Earl, B.R. and Halley, F. (1995) *Adventure in Social Research Using SPSS for Windows* (London, Pine Forge Press).

Hill, B.V. (1991) *Values Education in Australian Schools* (Melbourne, ACER).

Miles, M.B. and Huberman, A.M. (1984) *Qualitative Data Analysis* (California, Sage).

Norusis, M.J. (1990) *SPSS Advanced Statistics User's Guide* (Chicago, SPSS Inc.).

OECD (1991) *Review of National Policies for Education, Ireland* (Paris, OECD).

Open University (1988) Course E811, *Educational Evaluation* (Milton Keynes, Open University Educational Enterprises).

5

ISRAEL

Ruth Zuzovsky, Ruth Yakir and Esther Gottlieb

INTRODUCTION

Two metaphors have dominated the discourse about teachers and provided the backdrop for teacher education in Israeli society. One is based on the idea of the teacher as the bearer of a vision of national rebirth and social liberation – as the educator of new generations in a period of social and national transformation. The other image of the teacher is of the transmitter of objective scientific knowledge, which has traditionally been considered value-free. These two images of the teacher created a dichotomous, seemingly contradictory definition of the teacher role: educator as opposed to subject-matter specialist.

In the early days of the Zionist venture and in the first decade of statehood, the majority of the population received education at the elementary level. Completing secondary matriculation and continuing on to university was for the privileged few. Waves of immigration of Jews from many countries, speaking many languages, emphasized the importance of formal and informal educational frameworks in creating a consensus national identity. 'Veteran' immigrants and their children became the teachers of the newcomers. As is often the case in immigrant societies, children and their parents learned Hebrew simultaneously, as they assimilated the new ways of Israeli society. In this milieu of societal construction the image of teacher as educator and bearer of culture was dominant, especially at the elementary level and as provider of basic education for immigrant adults.

The ethnic groups which formed Israeli society did not come from 'no-man's land'. Each group brought with it a cultural heritage which shared some commonalities with other groups but was also different in many ways. Not all of them 'melted' easily and painlessly into the 'pot' of Israeli cultural evolution. It is important to note that this 'melting pot' into which newcomers were required to assimilate was not itself monolithic in nature. It was characterized by deep-rooted social cleavages defined by attitudes towards religious observance, social outlook and political identities. 'Absorption centres for new immigrants' were set up in religious and in secular

96

communities, in kibbutzim and in towns, under Labour auspices and under Liberal auspices, and by various World Zionist bodies. Each interest group fought for its 'share' of the right to influence newcomers to its special values and ideas, even as it made its everyday contribution to the process of nation-building.

Private school 'systems' were created by these groups before the establishment of the State of Israel, to educate their children and absorb newcomers. The Labour movement maintained a relatively large system which was disbanded in the early 1950s as its schools were incorporated into the 'general trend'. Vestiges of the 'Labour trend' are still visible in federations of agricultural schools and kibbutz schools, which continue to function in many ways as distinct entities, though officially they are a part of the 'general trend'. Many religious groups also established and maintained their own 'system', of which two remain today – the 'religious trend' as a sub-division of the general national system and the 'independent trend' which comprises extreme orthodox religious schools (Eisenstadt, 1985; Elboim-Dror, 1990). In addition, the Ministry of Education maintains separate schools for the Arab minority, in which Arabic is the first language. Some Arab children attend Jewish schools, especially in the larger cities, but the majority are affiliated with the Arab sub-system.

Many of these 'trends' established and maintained colleges to prepare teachers who shared the group values to teach in their 'system'. These forerunners of colleges of education were 'owned' and maintained by political, social or religious groups whose values defined their mission. Though most of the colleges of education have since been incorporated into the national system and are budgeted by the Ministry of Education, many of them are bound to their historical missions by tradition and present affiliations. Ties to religious groups, to the Labour organizations and the kibbutz movement, and to the more general liberal orientations, are still manifest.

Today student teachers are educated in a variety of institutional settings the most important of which are schools of education in universities and state colleges of education (Ben-Peretz, 1990). Secondary school teachers usually acquire extensive subject-matter preparation in the departments of arts and sciences in the universities; schools of education take responsibility for their professional training. All of the universities have as their primary focus academic research, and their teacher education programmes accommodate this approach. The one exception is the religiously oriented university, which requires of all students a large number of hours in Jewish studies regardless of their disciplinary majors.

Teachers for the elementary and primary schools study in teachers' colleges which integrate subject-matter knowledge, pedagogy and field experience. During the last two decades, teachers' colleges have upgraded academically, lengthening their programmes to four years and granting a first academic degree in addition to teaching certification. More rigorous academic standards in the subject matter specializations, and added emphasis on the educational sciences, characterized the curricular changes effected in the upgrading process. Despite the changes pushing in the 'academic' direction, most of the colleges jealously guard their traditional values orientations as well as the integrated model of teacher education with its focus of practice, which is common to all of them.

In recent years the sharp distinctions and strong boundaries between the teacher education programmes in the two types of institutional settings seem to be fading as the programmes become more similar. This study focuses on the college model of teacher training. In line with their traditions, most of the colleges view values education as part of their mission. A suggested programme for civics education prepared by a committee from one of the colleges and published by the Ministry of Education (Aden, 1990) provides an example of their common approach to values education. The proposed curriculum is directed to classroom teachers of the elementary grades.

A reading of the programme conveys the importance which teacher educators in the colleges attach to values education and the convictions of the curriculum committee. The description of the goals of values education includes a categorization reminiscent of Hill's models of values in a secular democracy (Hill, 1991). Humanistic values (moral universalism) head the list, followed by good citizenship in a democratic society (consensus pluralism). Other categories included in the list are nationalism, values connected with the life-cycle, and aesthetic values. Implementation of informal methods in the formal framework is seen as an important strategy for values education. The frameworks (class, cohort, school, community) and the activities (newspaper, social hour, sports day, etc.) are treated in great detail. An outline of a course for student teachers is suggested to ensure that the future teacher will be prepared for his or her role as an 'educator' of citizens in a democratic society.

THE RESEARCH PROGRAMME

The aim of this research was to present an Israeli perspective on the place of values in teacher education. Several questions were addressed. The first question related to content and attempted to delineate the values and ideologies which students and teachers of education wished to transmit. The second question related to the teaching strategies and methods of presentation they use and deem most effective.

The instruments used to collect the data included an open-ended questionnaire adapted from the international study and translated into Hebrew, content analysis of college course syllabuses whose titles indicated that they might provide relevant material, and interviews with some of the respondents to gain deeper insight into and understanding of their replies to the questionnaires.

The questions were addressed to a sample of student teachers, practising teachers, pedagogical supervisors and teacher educators. The data here places the main focus on pre-service teacher education students and their teachers. The various institutions from which participants were selected are identified in Israel with prevalent ideologies: a leftist humanistic ideology which is characteristic of the kibbutz movement; the general, liberal orientation characteristic of most of the schools in Israel; and the religious ideology that distinguishes religious schools.

The first part of the account will summarize the results of the questionnaire addressed to all the respondents. The second part will treat the data collected from the syllabuses and the interviews with teacher educators.

Which values belong in the curriculum?

First we will analyse the responses to the question of which values are important and should be transmitted via the school curriculum. The responses of 76 student teachers, practising teachers, pedagogical supervisors and teacher educators were recorded.

Table 5.1 presents the distribution of respondents according to their status and the type of institution they come from. We note that colleges with left-wing traditions are slightly over-represented and religious institutions under-represented. Practising teachers are not distributed over the types of institutions and are concentrated in religious frameworks. Teacher educators are not classified by institution, though they were the only group that represented all the institutional types. Since this study was of an exploratory nature, the samples are small and chosen for convenience rather than representativeness. The project as a whole can be seen as a qualitative one which can provide insights for future research.

During the administration of the questionnaire, several responses which deserved attention were noticed. For many student participants, the questions seemed unclear and they had difficulty in responding even after verbal explanations. Many of them claimed that the questions demanded a lot of thought. Some made comments on the gap existing between the rhetoric

Table 5.1 Distribution of population by status and institution

Institution	Student teachers	Practising teachers	Pedagogical supervisors	Teacher educators	Total
Religious	0	9	0	0	9
Liberal	14	0	2	0	16
Left-wing	38	0	5	0	43
Other	0	0	0	8	8
Total	52	9	7	8	76

which is used in regard to values education and the actual teaching related to it. In retrospect, it can be seen that this vagueness contributed to the variety of responses that emerged. On the other hand, the same questions seemed clear to the teacher educators and elicited quite extensive replies.

One of the important issues raised in the data deals with the values which participants consider to be those that should be treated in the Israeli educational context, both in the schools and in teacher education institutes. Participants' responses to this issue were categorized using Hill's (1991) broad categories: religious monopolism, moral universalism and consensus pluralism. This categorization was consistent with the one used in the international study. In the analysis of the Israeli data a fourth category was defined to enable the classification of a group of responses which did not fit into the Hill framework. This category, labelled 'nationalism', represented national values which co-existed with religious values, and seemed important in the Israeli context because of the unique national character of the Jewish religion.

Following are examples of categorized responses for each of the four categories. From the examples we can get the feeling for the rhetoric used in the descriptions. However, the listing does not represent the frequency for each category since there is more repetition in some categories than in others. Responses categorized under the heading 'moral universalism' are most frequent and may be sub-categorized as human relationships, character attributes, individualism, and environmental or 'green' values. Two sorts of measures were derived from the analysis of the coded data: frequency of each category of responses for the whole sample and for sub-populations (student teacher, practising teachers, pedagogical supervisors, and teacher educators), and a measure of the intensity of the preferred value which took into account not only the appearance of a categorized response, but also whether respondents tended to emphasize this type of value over and over in their statements.

Moral universalism

Concern for your neighbour's
  property
The value of giving
Mutual relationships
Mutual respect
Altruism
Human relationships
Helping others
Co-operation
Mutual assistance
Tolerance

Patience, diligence
Good manners
Openness
Being disciplined
Civil behaviour
Critical thinking
Intellectual integrity
Culture of proper speech
The value of life
Concern for human resources
The value of self-esteem

The value of personal uniqueness
The value of the beauty of nature
Protecting nature
Keeping the environment clean and
  unpolluted

Consensus pluralism
Pluralism
Democracy
Freedom of speech
Equal rights, equality
The rights of everyone to a good life
Accepting the different (ethnic,
  socio-economic, racial, the
  exceptional, the newcomers)
Peace for its own sake as a value

Religious monopolism
Love of religion
Love of the Bible

The values of the Bible
Commandments and religious
  covenants between God and man
Jewish tradition
Love of the people of Israel
Love of the Jewish people
Love of Judaism
Biblical laws and humanitarian
  behaviour
The eternal triad: the Bible, the land
  of Israel and the people of Israel
Belief in God – the creator

Nationalism
Love of country
Love of motherland
Love of the people and the land
Patriotism
Zionism
The belief in 'Greater Israel'

Table 5.2 presents the total frequencies of categorized responses. Two categories of values seem to be mentioned equally by most respondents: pluralistic values and universal, moral ones. Next in popularity are the national values, which are mentioned by almost half of the sample. Religious values are mentioned least of all, by only 5 per cent of the sample. This order changes somewhat if the measure is the percentage of total responses assigned to the category. Moral universalism receives the highest score – 43 per cent of all the responses. Consensus pluralism is second with 36 per cent of the total responses; nationalism and religious monopolism comprise 16 per cent and 5 per cent of the total responses respectively. Using intensity (number of responses in the category/number of respondents selecting the category) as the ordering criterion, we note that again moral universalism is

Table 5.2 Frequencies of responses by values category

Values category	Respondents		Responses		Intensity
	N	%	N	%	
Moral universalism	62	82	137	43	2.21
Consensus pluralism	62	82	117	36	1.89
Nationalism	36	47	51	16	1.42
Religious monopolism	9	12	17	5	1.89
Total	76		322	100	

at the top of the list. This result supports the order apparent in the list of responses by category. This picture repeats itself to some extent when looking at the sub-populations. Table 5.3 shows the percentage of responses and the intensity of responses for each sub-population.

The moral universalism items are mentioned most frequently by most of the groups. Pluralistic values receive a high rating in all the groups with the exception of practising teachers, who are all religious in this sample. The two other categories are less frequently mentioned.

The picture changes somewhat when intensity is used as the ordering criterion. Both practising teachers and teacher educators seem to view Jewish religious values as dominant. This result can best be understood in the light of the fact that all the practising teachers in the sample are religious. In the group of teacher educators, the responses in this category were also supplied by teachers from religious colleges. Moral universalism and consensus pluralism are strongly emphasized by student teachers, teacher educators and pedagogical supervisors. The exceptionally high score of teacher educators on the moral universalism category is worth noting. In general, teacher educators seem to have higher intensity scores than others. The level of intensity reflects to some extent the level of commitment. In this sense the teacher educators seem to be the most committed. However, their high score may also have resulted from their tendency to be more 'wordy' than other groups.

We can safely say that moral universalism and consensus pluralism are the dominant themes for all the respondents. Religious monopolism and nationalism are secondary. However, in the sub-population of religious teachers, moral universalism and nationalism dominate. The attention given to religious monopolism on the part of religious people is somewhat surprising and may indicate the problematic nature of the sample.

Table 5.3 Frequency distribution of values categories by sub-populations

Values category	Student teachers $n = 52$		Practising teachers $n = 9$		Pedagogical supervisors $n = 7$		Teacher educators $n = 8$	
	% response	Intensity	% response	Intensity	% response	Intensity	% response	Intensity
Consensus pluralism	84.6	2.11	44.4	1.75	100	2.29	87.5	2.14
Moral universalism	76.9	2.02	88.9	1.75	100	1.86	87.5	4.14
Nationalism	40.3	1.52	88.9	1.25	42.9	1.67	50.0	1.0
Religious monopolism	7.7	0	33.3	2.3	0	0	25.0	3.0

Values in the curriculum of teacher education: views of teacher educators

Now we turn to the views of teacher educators as they revealed themselves in the descriptions of a representative sample of courses for prospective teachers, whose stated objective is to address value-laden issues. The descriptions are based on reports of the teachers of the courses and represent an attempt to elicit their intentions and motivations for teaching the courses. The data was collected with the aid of an open questionnaire intended to gain insight into the underlying attitudes of teachers of courses offered in various types of teacher education frameworks.

Several classification categories were used in analysing and formulating the results. The responses in each of the categories were analysed as to descriptions of course content as well as teaching strategies and methods of presentation. Titles of exemplary courses in each category as they appear in the syllabuses are included in an attempt to illustrate the context.

The first level of categorization involved assigning the courses to disciplinary categories or considering them as being related to education and values in general. Most of the courses reported belonged to the latter category and some of them, seemingly disciplinary, could not be adequately assigned to a discipline because not enough information was given about the manner and framework of presentation. However, it is clear that subject-matter knowledge is seldom value-free and the most 'objective' paradigmatic scientific disciplines are value-laden, though the social values they bear are rarely explicated clearly. Post-modernist and constructivist theories of knowledge have yet to permeate the vast expanses of scientific knowledge transmission, especially in the natural sciences. The biologists, chemists and mathematicians have been slow to claim their ownership rights to 'multi-cultural mathematics' (Nelson *et al.*, 1993) or the social and environmental effects of technology applications. They have until now allowed these cultural artefacts to be claimed by the sociologists, the philosophers and the educators. So it is no surprise that in our sample where clear disciplinary ownership can be assigned to explicitly value-laden courses it is almost invariably in the humanities and social sciences. However, we can expect that in the future many of the disciplines will claim control and ownership of at least some of the value-laden knowledge they create. In the present study we have chosen some history courses described by the teachers as representative of this disciplinary category.

The second level of categorization related to all the reported courses that did not fit disciplinary categories. Since this group was relatively large, sub-categories were based on the type of institutional affiliation of the teacher. First a distinction was made between religious and secular institutions; this classification is recognized by the Ministry of Education as stated above and is parallel to the official affiliation of elementary and secondary schools in the system. In the group of secular institutions, a sub-category of left-wing orientation represents institutions with traditional and present-day connections to labour and social movements. Thus the courses separated by institutional affiliation of the teacher could be separated into three groups: religious, secular with a liberal orientation, and secular with a left-wing orientation. A fourth category is represented by teachers from Arab teacher colleges.

Values education through the disciplines: history

The content of the courses sampled encompassed several themes. One of these themes, which repeated again and again, was exploration of Jewish national history (Zionism) and cultural heritage (memorial and festive days) in relation to universal values. It is claimed that studying Jewish history builds national values such as solidarity, patriotism and national rebirth, at the same time as it addresses the universal ones such as social justice, democracy, peace and human rights. Courses about the Holocaust were seen as teaching anti-racism, tolerance and the sacredness of human life rather than being attuned to Jewish national values exclusively.

Many of the course syllabuses sampled addressed current events, local and world-wide, though the title of the course implied that it dealt with past historical events. Some examples mentioned in syllabuses included Nobel Prize awards, violation of human rights in various parts of the world, the fall of autocratic regimes, and the peace process in the Middle East.

Several of the courses described were actually interdisciplinary as they tried to link examples from literature and the arts with historical material. One mentioned dealing with linkage between myth and history.

Teaching strategies aimed at learning the rules of democratic participation in decision making and discussion. Also mentioned were values clarification techniques for revealing value preferences in the classroom context, and simulations to achieve tolerance in the classroom as preparation for active citizenship in the future. Examples of history courses in colleges of education whose value-laden nature is reported by the faculty who teach them are:

- history and teaching civics in the junior high school;
- Jewish history in modern times;
- Jewish national values and secular democracy;
- development of American democracy from the seventeenth to the nineteenth centuries.

Values education as the main justification for separate religious schooling: view of religious teacher educators

Religious educators stress that the values content that should be taught in religious institutions is Jewish values as expressed in the written and spoken

Torah (body of religious law), and in Jewish philosophic and ethics literature. These values deal with matters between man and his creator, and between man and his fellow man, far and near. They also involve issues faced by individuals in relation to their people and country, as well as issues which confront them in relation to the physical and natural environment, such as care for animals, preservation of nature, and regard for public property. Since some of these values are contradictory a priority scale should also be offered.

Another formulation of value sets presented by a religious educator mentioned 'believing' as a value, love of country, helping one another, and democracy, in that order.

Religious teacher educators felt that underlying tensions between the concepts of education and indoctrination related mainly to teaching strategies. One teacher expressed his awareness of this tension and acknowledged the difficulty in educating toward a heterogeneous set of values in a pluralistic society. One solution relates to the possibility that students will accept such values as part of an autonomous process, despite their absolute and predetermined source. It would seem that some of the values of pluralism and secular democracy have penetrated the religious community at least as strategies of legitimization. Another question raised by these educators relates to the socializing agents who should legitimately be involved in values education. Religious educators cannot ignore the role of parents in the process. It is clear that religious teacher educators have spent much time and energy in trying to solve tensions inherent in values education and that they see the values element in the curriculum as the main justification for their existence as a unique trend in the national educational system. Reading the responses of these teachers highlights their deep personal involvement and commitment.

An important remark of one of the religious teacher educators in regard to the process of teaching values education relates to his perception of constantly having to educate himself through this process. Another typical remark is that values education involves practical aspects and that it is important to live by one's values; values education is essentially formative rather than informative. Values education should be embedded in all fields of study; an example of values embedded in physical education was given by one of the religious respondents. Topics required for term papers in one of the courses had individual values as their titles (mutual aid, integrating the special child in the regular classroom, integrating new immigrants, believing in God, love of country, democracy, viewing television) with suggested school curricula and lesson plans as the content.

Examples of courses in religious colleges of education whose value-laden nature is reported by the faculty who teach them are:

- values education in non-formal frameworks;
- educating towards Jewish values;
- values education.

Views of teacher educators from liberal secular teachers' colleges

Descriptions of the content of the courses distinguish between concrete, specific values, labelled informative, and a second type of values, labelled formative. According to one teacher informative values include honesty, fidelity, love of country as examples; the teacher is not sure that he has the right to educate towards them. Most certainly not all of them are to be included in teacher education curricula. He would include humanism in its broadest sense, viewing humanism as an end in itself and not as a means to other ends. He would also include democracy as an agreed-upon framework for social existence. Formative values include certain mental faculties and dispositions that are best described as social awareness and willingness to act in the interest of national identity, local and international societal problems, and political goals – active citizenship.

The discussion of teaching strategies is based on the assumption and belief that the main 'working instrument' of a teacher is his personality. Values education is aimed to shape this personality and thus it is perceived as the goal of all teaching that occurs in teacher education settings. Special emphasis is given to the role of the individual teacher.

Examples of courses in secular liberal colleges of education whose value-laden nature is reported by the faculty who teach them are:

- television, the family, and the school;
- teaching Civics.

Views of teacher educators from left-wing colleges

Descriptions of course content based on syllabuses and responses of teacher educators delineate three broad themes: personal, interpersonal and social. The first theme includes values such as responsibility, independence and diligence. The second theme includes consideration for others, mutual aid, acceptance of 'the other', and refraining from violence and exploitation in interpersonal relations. The third theme includes the social, Jewish–Zionist and universal value sets and includes democracy, equality, humanistic values, love of country and striving for peace. These teachers place special emphasis on values of democracy, freedom, equality, non-violence. Two of the teacher educators in these institutions distinguish between core values which define normative behavioural rules and other values which are secondary.

Some of the teacher educators are aware of contradictions between values and the dynamic, self-constructed and adaptive nature of a 'value approach', which they contrast with a fixed 'value system'.

In formulating teaching strategies, many of the teacher educators are aware of the limitations of formal education as well as the problem of legitimacy of teacher educators to educate towards values that are not in the general consensus. They point out that 'meaningful' values education can take place only in a climate of experiential learning, 'touching' the learner in his/her entirety – cognition, emotion and behaviour – and oppose both indoctrination and values neutrality. It is deemed important to expose different points of view, but also 'to take a stand' on controversial issues (Varom, 1993). The definition of core values helps the distinctions between which values should be intentionally fostered and which should be presented for consideration. The need in such cases to develop critical rationality is stressed. Values education should be treated in a cognitive, emotional and practical way. In this respect, it should be practised in the life of students, both in the colleges of education and in their field experiences.

Examples of courses offered in left-wing colleges of education whose value-laden nature is reported by the faculty who teach them are:

- values education and formal education;
- internalizing a 'values approach';
- values socialization in the school framework;
- education for living in a democratic society.

Views of Arab teacher educators

The content of courses stressed in the Arab colleges relates to democracy, equality, tolerance, and acceptance of 'the other' – which is regarded as very important.

A categorization mentioned by one teacher delineates five values sets:

- vital – values directed towards life maintenance such as health;
- aesthetic values which bear on all domains of life including dressing, eating and other rituals;
- moral values especially characteristic of Arabic society;
- personal and social values such as good manners and good interpersonal relationships;
- cognitive values leading to logical and critical thinking.

Very little mention is made of national values and then only as moral values unique to Arab society. Teaching strategies emphasize the example set by a 'democratic teacher' as manifested in his classroom practice. Again we note the method as it relates to content.

Examples of courses in an Arab college of education whose value-laden nature is reported by the faculty who teach them are:

- education for democracy;
- conservative and progressive education;
- discipline.

Commonalities

Values education is considered by all teacher educators as a very important component in the curriculum of teacher education and the majority of them think it should be incorporated in all subject areas and especially in the practical component of teacher education. A need to apply cognitive, problem-solving strategies which involve a values clarification is highlighted.

FINAL REMARKS

One of the questions we should address in conclusion is to what extent the views of teacher educators, student teachers and practising teachers in Israel reflect the values prevalent in the general public? Values education does not occur in a vacuum. We can assume that values prevalent in Israeli society will impact on the values held by educators and prospective educators.

The general picture which emerges from the present study highlights the importance of items related to moral universalism for all population groups. In most of the groups studied, items related to consensus pluralism receive preference in frequency and intensity as compared to items related to nationalism and religious values. Among religious people, nationalism takes preference over consensus pluralism.

Nationalist values, which are not specifically mentioned in Hill's classification, are important for a large part of the sample in this study. It seems that national issues are on the agenda of all Israeli citizens regardless of their political ideologies. A longitudinal study of values preferences evident in Israeli public opinion polls (Shamir and Shamir, 1995) reveals four major values preferences that characterize political cleavages in Israeli society: Israel as a state with a Jewish majority, peace, Israel as a democratic society, and retaining the expanded borders of Greater Israel. In the present study these cleavages seem to lead to a dichotomy between consensus pluralism and nationalism.

Polarization in Israeli society today is indicated by the level of commitment to nationalistic values on the one hand and those associated with pluralism, democracy and humanism on the other hand. Which sets of values are more dominant – the humanistic ones or the nationalistic ones? Recent events, as well as responses in the present study, demonstrate that all sections of the community are divided on these issues.

REFERENCES

Aden, S. (1990) *Preparing Classroom Teachers as Educators* (Jerusalem, Mofet Foundation, Ministry of Education) (Hebrew).
Ben-Peretz, M. (1990) 'Studies of Teacher Education in Israel: Topics, Methods and Findings', *Dapim*, 10: 24–9 (Hebrew).

Darom, D. (1993) 'Values Education in a Democratic Society'. Workshop presented at the International Conference on Education for a Democracy in a Multicultural Society (Jerusalem).

Eisenstadt, S.N. (1985) *The Transformation of Israeli Society* (London, Weidenfeld & Nicolson).

Elboim-Dror, R. (1990) *Hebrew Education in Eretz Israel* (Jerusalem, Yad Izhak Ben-Zvi Institute).

Hill, B.V. (1991) *Values Education in Australian Schools* (Melbourne, ACER).

Nelson, D., Joseph, G. and Williams, J. (1993) *Multicultural Mathematics* (New York, Oxford University Press).

Shamir, M. and Shamir, J. (1995) *Values Preferences Evident in Israeli Public Opinion Polls* (Megamot).

6

THE SLOVENIAN CONTEXT

Cveta Razdevsek-Pucko and Alenka Polak

INTRODUCTION

Slovenia, a new European state which was granted independence on 25 June 1991 and was internationally recognized in January 1992, lies at the crossroads of diverse influences, in the geopolitical, ethnic and cultural sense.

Geographical context

Slovenia covers an area of 20,250 square km, and has nearly 2 million inhabitants, of whom approximately 86 per cent are Slovenes by ethnic origin. The prevailing religious affiliation is Roman Catholic.

Historical context

Until 1918 Slovenian territory was part of the Austro-Hungarian Empire. After 1918 the larger part of the territory was incorporated into the first Yugoslavia (Kingdom of Serbs, Croats and Slovenes). After the Second World War, during which the majority of Slovenes joined the Resistance Movement, Slovenia became one of the federal republics within the Socialistic Federative Republic of Yugoslavia. In 1948 Yugoslavia seceded from the Soviet (Eastern) bloc and the Yugoslav government gradually introduced a self-management system which incorporated some humanistic elements, but centralism and unsolved nationalist issues were ongoing problems.

The act of independence and the transition from a one-party (communist) system to a parliamentary democracy in Slovenia are currently proceeding relatively smoothly. Since 1990 attention has been directed towards establishing a pluralistic and democratic society which stresses respect for human rights, tolerance and other universal values, and which facilitates the development of a market economy, thus establishing international relations on a new basis.

110

Economic context

Slovenia appears to have already recovered from the shock of losing the Yugoslav market, but in comparison to countries in Western Europe can still be considered an under-developed country. In 1989 the GNP per capita was $5,869, while in 1993 it was $6,366.

The transition to a free-market economy has been accompanied by increasing unemployment and with growing tendencies towards a more socially and economically stratified society. The total unemployment rate for 1994 was 9 per cent (8.4 per cent for women); the employment (activity) rate of women for the same year was 51.5 per cent and is among the highest in the world (more than 46 per cent of all employed persons are women) (data from *Statistical Yearbook*, Republic of Slovenia, 1995).

The high rate of female employment in Slovenia has influenced the education system, especially at the pre-school level. Equal access to all levels of schooling for both sexes appears to have been attained, but women are still under-represented in leadership positions in the economy and in the political arena.

Cultural context

A strong emphasis has been placed on the Slovene language and culture in order to ensure its survival against the pressure of dominant neighbours and/or prevailing political strength (German, Italian, Serbo-Croatian). In Slovenia, education has been generally regarded as a way of promoting national identity and the Slovene language. Those who are regarded as a most important source for the creation of Slovene identity are poets and writers (not scientists, political or military leaders). The constitution strongly advocates education in the Slovene language and culture for all, which includes Slovene children living abroad. Equal concern and respect are demonstrated for the educational needs of the Italian and Hungarian minorities in Slovenia (summary of data from Marentic-Pozarnik, 1993).

Historical events and problems arising from the transitional period have had and continue to exert an important impact on the value system which operates within society and especially within the educational system in Slovenia.

Political context

Slovenia is regarded as a Central European country in a period of transition. It may appear unusual that no major changes have occurred in educational policy since the end of the socialist system (the end of Yugoslavia) and the beginning of an independent democratic society. The absence of revolutionary changes does not mean that no changes at all have taken place. The most

111

obvious change was the withdrawal of some ideologically based subjects from the curriculum. For example, 'self-management and the fundamentals of Marxism' was withdrawn from the curriculum of secondary schools and 'military education' from the university curriculum. Within the primary school curriculum a new subject called 'ethics and society' was substituted for 'social and moral education'; compulsory Serbo-Croatian first became a part of the elective curriculum and was later withdrawn altogether. Previously, in geography and history the study of Yugoslavia had been over-dominant; now, topics from the geography and history of Slovenia, previously under-represented, have been put in their place. Themes which centre on beliefs and especially religion were gradually but increasingly included in the programmes and textbooks of existing curriculum subjects.

VALUES EDUCATION IN THE SLOVENIAN CONTEXT

Dilemmas concerning value (moral) education in Slovenia

One of the perennial problems in the field of moral education is the relationship between religion and public education; this is one of the issues which, from time to time, become the subject of public and/or political debate. In order to address this issue, and to give insights into the Slovenian context, a brief history of religious education in Slovenia follows.

A problem arose after the Second World War, when the church (Roman Catholic) was strictly separated from state affairs, and religious education (catechism) was withdrawn from schools. In 1952, an extra school subject, 'social and moral education', was introduced into primary and secondary education with the aim that this subject become a substitute for a religious education.

The goal of social and moral education was

> the education in the spirit of socialist society moral values in correspondence to the development of science and socialist consciousness. The socialist society demands from its members the highest level of moral consciousness, which cannot be obtained with religious instruction.
>
> (Kodelja, 1995: 164)

According to this perspective, a consequence of withdrawing the ideological subject 'social and moral education' would be the re-introduction of religion as a school subject. However, the standpoint of the Ministry of Education concerning the new school legislation is:

> Religious instruction (catechism) will not be organized in state schools, but the basics of religions and churches will be introduced in individual subjects within the curriculum.

The introduction of an optional subject dealing with different religions and churches is also proposed within the third educational level (the last three years) of primary education.

Organized religious instruction will be available in private schools and within church institutions.

(Ministry of Education and Sport, 1992: 35)

The debate regarding Religious Education continues. According to the opinion of the Minister Elect of Education and Sport, Dr Gaber, 'in the field of education, the state must be neutral in its relation to religions and should not introduce religious instruction (catechism) as a subject of the school curriculum' (Gaber, 1990: 17). In an interview five years later, Dr Gaber (now Minister of Education) still insists that the

> public school must be legally neutral. This does not mean that there are no values within the school. The school must represent and educate those values which are acceptable for all citizens, regardless of their beliefs. Within the subject of Ethics and Society everybody should learn about the universal values commonly accepted in modern European society: tolerance, democracy, human rights, non-violence . . .
>
> (Gaber, 1995)

Moral, ethical, religious or civic education?

Recently, especially in connection with the debate about new school legislation, there has been on-going discussion about the introduction of a compulsory new subject which would cover moral education.

Some authors in the fields of philosophy, sociology and theory of education oppose the introduction of a special ethical subject in the educational system, regardless of whether the subject would be planned and implemented as religious, moral or political (civic) education (Zadnikar, 1994; Kanduc, 1994). On the other hand, the necessity of special civic education or education (instruction) in human rights is strongly advocated (Pecek, 1994) with an awareness of the risk that civic education may merely replace past ideological indoctrination (Zadnikar, 1994). According to Zadnikar, the task of public education is to provide young people with information and knowledge to enable them to participate actively in the public democratic processes. Zadnikar claims that it is impossible to internalize democracy through civic education. One can internalize democracy, tolerance, responsibility and other values only by experiencing them in everyday life, in society, with parents, teachers and classmates (Zadnikar, 1994).

Another source of conjecture in moral education in Slovenia is the word 'education' itself. In the Slovene language two words are used to convey the meaning (and translation) of the word 'education': 'vzgoja' and 'izobrazevanje'. The first emphasizes moral and values education, while the

113

second emphasizes the intellectual and instructional aspect of education – that is, instruction and learning of curriculum syllabuses.

From time to time, there are discussions about the balance or prevalence of either intellectual or moral instruction. Sometimes these discussions are also politically and/or ideologically coloured. The opinion is frequently expressed (especially in the media) that there is complete moral ignorance and emptiness (a 'moral vacuum'), especially among youth. It is also claimed that this 'moral vacuum' is the consequence of the prevailing intellectualism in Slovenian schools. This argument is based upon two objections – the first being that the school does not educate effectively in the moral sense, and the second that the values on which school education is founded are inappropriate.

The proposed solution to the 'moral vacuum' problem is the introduction of new 'educative' subjects and the devoting of more time (more curriculum hours) to moral education. On the other hand, other critics of the education system are not satisfied with the intellectual function of the school; here the solution suggested is more time (more curriculum hours) for 'pure' instruction without any moral and value-laden content (Zgaga, 1990: 25).

Both solutions are aimed at finding a way out of the dilemma. It seems that 'more time' is not the solution for any of the dilemmas mentioned above. It may be that the question should not be 'how many' (subjects or hours), but rather 'why teach this subject?' (the goals), 'how will it be taught?' (the methods), and 'who will teach it?' (the teacher and her/his qualification and personal values).

The goals of moral education in schools, as described by Cencic (1986: 6), were:

- developing a system of values as a guide for moral behaviour;
- developing feelings and interest for moral experiences and sensitivity for the world of values;
- developing the motivation (willingness) for congruency between behaviour and values;
- developing the whole system of the qualities of an individual (character) which assure one's moral behaviour.

The highest goal was to overcome egocentric, conformist and pure rational morality and to reach the level of moral autonomy, where the individual is capable of critical and mature judgement (evaluation) of different life situations, and able to make autonomous moral decisions. The predominant methods were reinforcement, instruction and persuasion, usage and prevention (Cencic, 1986).

Nearly a decade after Cencic outlined these goals and methods, it is stated (Ministry of Education and Sport, 1994: 22–3) that the fundamental goals of primary education in the Republic of Slovenia are:

- to enable a pupil's personal development according to his abilities and level of development;
- to convey the fundamental knowledge and skills which ensure independent, effective and creative contact with the social and natural environment, and the continuation of education.

Specific goals are:

- encouragement of mental development, independent critical thinking, intuition and imagination, and the ability to communicate;
- immersion in the Slovene cultural tradition and acquaintance with other cultures and civilizations;
- development of the ability to live in a pluralistic and democratic society; formation and encouragement of a healthy way of life and a responsible attitude towards the natural environment;
- equal opportunities together with respect for differences among children and the right of choice and of being different.

For secondary education the following principles should constitute the basis of the curriculum (ibid.: 36):

- the right to education, the principle of democracy;
- the principle of choice and responsibility;
- the principle of professionalism, autonomy and accountability;
- a holistic, complex and interdisciplinary approach.

Some educational goals of grammar schools (secondary level) are:

- to develop the ability to reflect upon the world;
- to foster an awareness of belonging to the Slovenian culture in the international context;
- to encourage theoretical study and develop the ability for independent reflection and judgement.

The above goals can also be treated as a list of values which the Slovenian educational system should try to uphold and which can serve as some kind of value orientation for the teachers. Both aspects of the word 'education' are included within these goals. The problem is therefore not the absence of values in the school system but rather may be perceived to be the critics themselves, who demonstrate dissatisfaction with pluralistic solutions.

Hill states:

the development of an independent and well informed mind is certainly an indispensable element in the modern concept of education, but there is increasing recognition that the schools also encourage the adoption of values held in high regard in civilized society . . . these two aims can and should go hand in hand.

(Hill, 1991: 9)

This statement appears to have some importance in the Slovenian context especially as it moves through a period of renewal, reconstruction and transition.

RESEARCH INTO VALUES AND VALUE ORIENTATIONS IN SLOVENIA

Janek Musek, Professor at the Department of Psychology, Faculty of Arts, University of Ljubljana, has undertaken a number of studies which focus on categories of values, personality traits and value orientations, in relation to the crisis over morality and values.

Musek's (1993a) concept of values is related to the concept of motivation. Motives are forces which push us towards biological, social and psychological goals, while values pull the person towards the behaviour by which some values can be realized; values, according to Musek, influence the individual when making choices between possible actions or when giving priority to certain ideas and judging certain events. According to him:

a growing interest in psychological research into values can be observed in the past two or three decades and several reasons might account for this. . . . One of them could be the famous gap between values and moral reasoning on one hand, and actual behaviour on the other, which disproves the traditional understanding of moral principles and values as simple regulative transition in the systems of values that have recently been observed in many societies. This can also not be understood properly without a thorough psychological reflection.

(Musek, 1992: 12)

Several studies were made by Musek in which 22, 37 or 54 values were rated by subjects on a rating scale. The numbers of subjects in the respective studies were 90, 133 and 198. Respondents of different ages, between 17 and 80, and of both sexes were represented. Several multi-variant correlational analyses were carried out within those studies.

Factor analysis (37 selected values, 133 subjects) allowed the extraction of ten factors explaining more than 76 per cent of the total variance (Musek, 1992: 13), and accounted for nine factors when sets of 54 values and 198 subjects were included in the investigation (Musek, 1994: 13–27). All those factors or value orientations can be unified into a hierarchical structure with

116

two value super-dimensions, four categories of value types and nine value orientations (Musek, 1993a: 146).

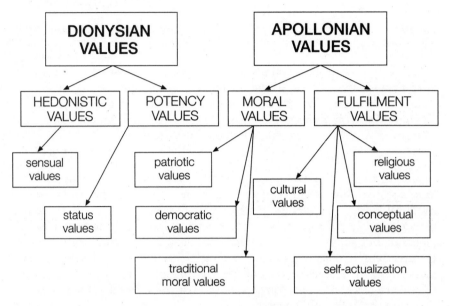

Figure 6.1 Hierarchy of value orientations
Source: Musek, 1993a: 146 (reprinted with the permission of the author)

Relationships between personality traits and the ratings of different values, value categories and value types were also examined in other studies (Musek, 1992 and 1994). The overall results demonstrated low or modest correlation between two sets of variables. A considerable number of these correlations revealed significant connections between personality traits and other personal variables (for example age, gender, education).

In another study (Musek, 1993b), value orientations through life were investigated. The author attempted to establish how persons of different ages rate the importance of cardinal values, value types and value orientations. The overall results obtained in this study show a general decrease in the importance of Dionysian values (hedonistic and potency values) and a relative increase in Apollonian values (moral and especially fulfilment values) through life. The author suggests that the problem of the conflict between generations might be explained by reference to different value orientations.

With regard to the 'crisis' of values and the moral 'crisis', the issues which are of current concern, according to Musek, are:

> that these have been encountered in past times also and maybe the
> most accurate observation could be expressed by the statement that

each human generation lives and deals with its own crisis in a specific way.

(Musek, 1993b: 124)

He also makes the following statement regarding the perceived moral and value crisis:

the analysis of the conceptions of moral and value crisis compels us to distinguish more clearly between different events concerning values, like the vacuum of values, the confusion of values and the conflict of values. In many respects the crisis of values appears prevalent in the form of confusion and conflict in the value systems.

(ibid.)

Musek (1993a) does not appear to search for a new value system (for the 'new age'); an interpretation of his theory may rather be that within each historical period a different perspective of values or even a different hierarchy of values may prevail. He advocates value tolerance and value pluralism, but not in the sense of value relativism. Values can be treated as an extrinsic reinforcement of our behaviour, connected with a developmental hierarchy: from hedonistic (exciting life, enjoyment) values through to values of potency (success, reputation, power), morality (duty) and to the values of sense (meaning) and fulfilment.

That kind of developmental hierarchy of values may help to overcome the apparent human crisis involved with valuing, and with moral and personal conduct. By following the natural development of value orientation, an individual may successfully cope with moral and other personal problems. 'The life sign-post – that's what values are for' (Musek, 1993a: 266).

Another author noted for work in the area of values in Slovenia is Zupancic (Zupancic and Justin, 1991). Her research is predominantly about values in adolescence. According to her, some differences may be observed between pre-adolescents and adolescents. Among the first group (aged 13–15) the materialistic (hedonistic) value orientation may be observed, while among the other group (aged 16–19) a more spiritual, humanistic and social value orientation may be seen as the prevailing one.

Zupancic also undertook research into the importance of particular values for a group of pre-adolescents (aged 15). The ranked list of the first ten values seen as of particular importance is: friendship, happiness, family, health, love, work and profession, school success, honesty, life success, music (Zupancic and Justin, 1991: 210). In this study some important differences were found between young people from general secondary schools as compared with the group from more professionally oriented secondary schools. The first group attached more importance to humanistic and social values, while the other group stressed materialistic and hedonistic values. Within the first group, differences between humanistic- and language-oriented students on the one hand, and the natural science-oriented students on the other, were also evident. The natural science pupils valued rationality and science, while the others stressed values connected with humanity, social relations and feelings. Those differences may not be due to the impact of school orientation only. It may be that value orientation was already one of the factors which influenced the choice of school. The impact of school and its (overt and hidden) curricula on value orientation of young generations, however, still remains an issue to be considered.

VALUES IN EDUCATION: SLOVENIAN SURVEY

The data collection process

The population surveyed

The survey was conducted with 20 practising primary school teachers and with 56 primary pre-service second-year teacher education students from the Faculty of Education, University of Ljubljana. All the surveyed teachers were female.

Practising *teachers* were from different schools throughout Slovenia. Ages ranged from 24 to 45, years of experience varied from one to eighteen and the average length of service of the respondents was ten years. All teachers were attending part-time (evening) studies for primary teachers in order to upgrade their education. They listed from one to ten in-service (INSET) seminars they had attended within the last five years.

With primary pre-service teacher education *students*, ages ranged from 20 to 21 years. Students were from the second-year course for primary (classroom) school teachers. The average length of their practical experiences within the primary school context was about two weeks.

Methods

The data collection methods applied included an open-ended questionnaire consisting of five questions. Questions 4 and 5 also consisted of four (question 4) and two (question 5) sub-questions. Altogether, the respondents answered nine open-ended questions.

Questions were prepared by the Australian team (Ling, Burman and Cooper), and translated into the Slovenian language. In order to avoid misunderstandings and to facilitate the comparison of the results, anticipated answers to the translated questions were discussed with the Australian team.

After gathering (March 1995) the anonymously written answers of all respondents, responses were analysed and a qualitative interpretative approach involving clustering the responses into conceptual groups was employed. The initial clustering was based upon similarity of responses. Subsequently an interpretative framework involving four models for values interpretation based upon those proposed by Brian Hill (1991) was applied (see detailed description on p. 13). An attempt was also made to interpret the results in the (Slovenian) framework of value orientation proposed by Musek (1993a).

In order to produce some pertinent conclusions, recommendations, and practical strategies and approaches, the data from 1994 was also used. (In 1994 an international study of values had been undertaken; see Polak and Razdevsek-Pucko, 1994).

During the administration of the questionnaire, the students in particular commented that they had not previously thought about values education. Some students stated that these problems or issues had not yet occurred to them. Students perceived that answering the questionnaire, however, helped them to become aware of these problems.

Some of the students voiced the opinion that the faculty should prepare them more effectively for the teaching of these topics. Learning how to teach values (live them and express them) and how to form (or re-form) pupils' attitudes should be an important part of teacher education, students indicated. The first condition for effective teaching of values might be the students' awareness of their own attitudes and values.

At the end of the questionnaire many students emphasized the fact that the teaching of values should be seen as an important part of a teacher's role. This survey represents an initial attempt to comply with the request made by students for a greater concentration on the teaching of values as a component of teacher education courses.

Results

Responses of student teachers and practising teachers and interpretation of data according to a common interpretive model (Hill, 1991)

In the fifth question, the respondents were asked to enumerate the values which the values education in schools (5a) and in teacher education (5b) should address.

The answers to this question may be interpreted and discussed within the framework of the model proposed by Hill (1991). Special attention is paid here to the differences between the two groups – student teachers (*students*) and practising teachers (*teachers*).

Question 5a: What are five of the most important elements which values teaching in schools should address?
Fifty-six students made 184 responses and twenty teachers made 67 responses to Question 5a.

120

Question 5b: What are five of the most important elements which values education components of teacher education courses should address?
Fifty-six students provided 135 responses and twenty teachers provided 44 responses to Question 5b.

Because of the apparent similarity of questions 5a and 5b, the same approach was used to analyse the answers, and the findings for both questions are considered together here.

After initial clustering of similar themes and concepts arising from responses, it became apparent that there was an absence of any religious values in responses from both groups and for both sub-questions. At the same time there appeared to be an absence of answers which could fit into the category of moral vacuum. The majority of respondents emphasized the values of moral universalism (traditional values such as honesty, justice, peace, universal values such as human rights and the rights of children) and consensus pluralism (respect for all people within the society, understanding and tolerance of all kinds of differences). In common with the observation reported by Zuzovsky from Israel (1995), some Slovenian respondents emphasized national values (especially the Slovenian language and culture). It was decided to add a specific category termed 'national values'.

For Question 5b a specific category was introduced for answers which mentioned the methodology of teaching values, and was entitled 'methodology of teaching values' (how to teach values, that is, methods which seem to be appropriate).

Three categories of answers to Question 5a, and four to Question 5b were formed and the percentages of responses for each of them are presented in Figure 6.2.

In order to compare the answers from the two groups, the answers for students and teachers are represented separately. In the students' answers to Question 5a, it appears that about one-half of their answers concern the values which form the category of moral universalism, while the other half of the responses belong to consensus pluralism (43 per cent) and to

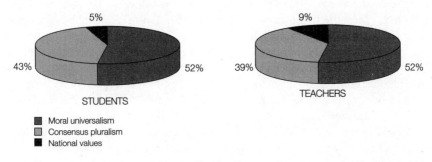

Figure 6.2 The most important values which values education should address (according to Hill's model)

121

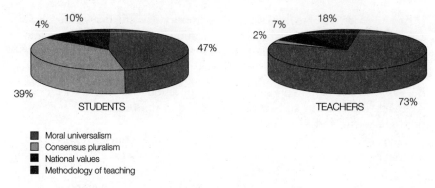

Moral universalism
Consensus pluralism
National values
Methodology of teaching

Figure 6.3 The most important values which values education within teacher education should address (according to Hill's model)

national values (5.5 per cent). The experienced teachers cited values of moral universalism in nearly the same percentage as did the student teachers, while the category of national values was slightly more evident (9 per cent) and the category of consensus pluralism was a little less emphasized by the teachers (39 per cent) than by the group of students.

After analysing the answers to Question 5b, it appears that the values within the model of moral universalism are the prevailing ones with students and particularly with teachers. Students also emphasized the values which fit into the category of consensus pluralism (understanding, respect and tolerance for all). National values are present only in a few answers. When thinking about preparing teachers for the teaching of values in education, both categories of respondents, especially experienced teachers, emphasized not only *which* values they found important, but also *how* to teach them.

Categorization of responses in the Slovenian context according to Musek's (1993a) value orientation

In the context of the theoretical background in values research in Slovenia, we have presented the model of value orientation and value hierarchy, according to research into values led by Musek (see Figure 6.1). In order to particularize the value categories for the Slovenian context, a second meta-theoretical interpretative level (Musek) has been used. An attempt has been made to categorize the answers of both groups, that is, experienced teachers and student teachers, to question 5a (*which* values) according to the model of eleven values orientations (Musek, 1993a: 144–5).

One finding was the absence of Dionysian values within both groups. None of the respondents answered with a response which could be categorized as a hedonistic value orientation (sensual, exciting life) or a potency one (status, power, reputation, success) (Dionysian values).

Among Apollonian values, the orientations which fit into a broader category of moral values prevail. The orientation towards traditional moral values is emphasized (honesty, solidarity, altruism, diligence), especially among students (50 per cent of all responses), while teachers more frequently responded in terms of democratic and social value orientation (equality, tolerance, peace, human rights and the rights of children). Both groups mentioned family happiness and health orientation with a high level of agreement.

The absence of responses which could be categorized as religious orientation (faith, God, the church) within the Apollonian dimension can be observed, as well as the absence of conceptual orientation (truth, wisdom, art). Detailed results are presented in Figure 6.4.

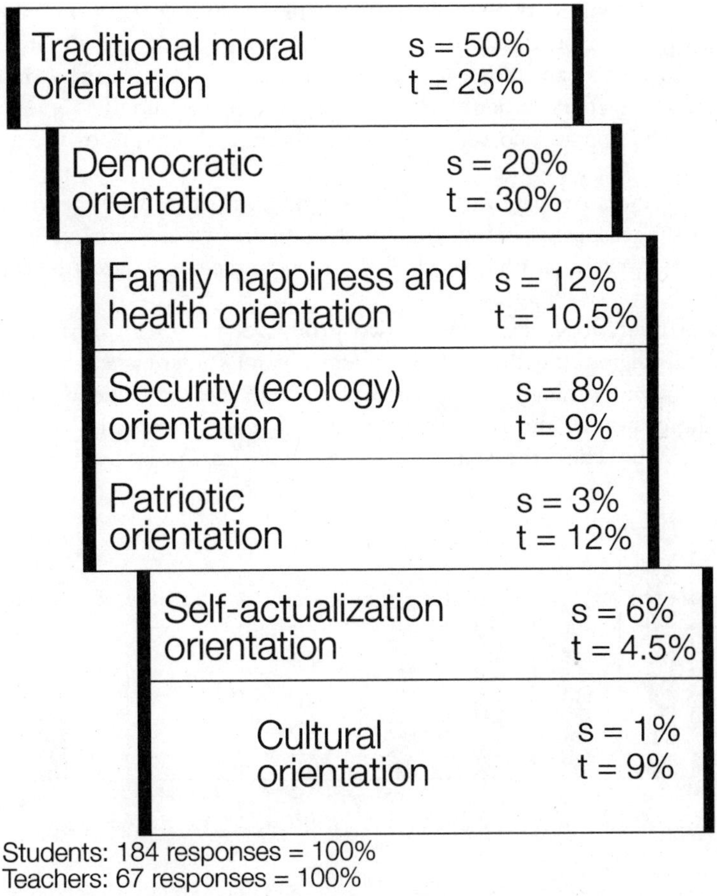

Traditional moral orientation	s = 50% t = 25%
Democratic orientation	s = 20% t = 30%
Family happiness and health orientation	s = 12% t = 10.5%
Security (ecology) orientation	s = 8% t = 9%
Patriotic orientation	s = 3% t = 12%
Self-actualization orientation	s = 6% t = 4.5%
Cultural orientation	s = 1% t = 9%

Students: 184 responses = 100%
Teachers: 67 responses = 100%

Figure 6.4 Value orientations of *student*(s) and *teachers*(t) (according to Musek's value orientation)

Religious orientation within the responses of Slovenian student teachers and practising teachers

Unlike the students and teachers in Israel or in the Irish Republic, Slovenian students and teachers who responded to the questionnaire about values in education do not have any experience with religious education within the school system (the oldest practising teacher was born after the Second World War, when religious education was no longer incorporated within the school curriculum).

At the time the questionnaire was administered (March 1995) there was a vigorous debate about the relationship between religion and school in Slovenia. It might, therefore, have been expected that there would be more responses concerning this issue. The only question to which such a response occurred was Question 3, where religion was mentioned as a cultural issue which the respondents perceived as having an influence upon the value dimension of the curriculum. The total number of students' responses was 276 (56 students) and 20 teachers gave a total of 85 answers. Among all responses 4 teachers (5 per cent of responses) and 18 students (6.5 per cent of responses) mentioned religion and/or the church as one of the cultural issues.

The numbers of respondents (not the number of responses) who mentioned other issues as being influential upon the values dimension of the curriculum were also compared. Results, in percentages, are presented in Figure 6.5.

Some differences between the two groups can be seen, not only with regard to religion and the church (where several students perceived this as one of the predominant cultural issues having a major influence upon the value dimension of the curriculum in the Slovenian context), but also to a greater extent when the state and political parties (more teachers), media

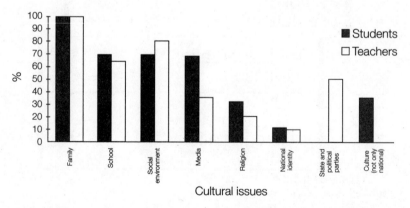

Figure 6.5 Predominant cultural issues with influence upon the values dimension of the curriculum

and culture (more students) are under discussion. Practising teachers also mentioned the social environment (urban, rural) as a significant cultural issue more frequently than did pre-service students.

The answers to Question 3 are compatible with answers to Question 4a (Whose knowledge forms the basis of the course?), in which teachers (6 out of 20, or 30 per cent) and especially students (39 out of 56, or 70 per cent) emphasized the role of the state (Ministry of Education).

After the establishment of a parliamentary democracy in Slovenia several political parties are in a battle for control of the 'school field'. Each political party is trying to 'plant' its own ideas, and, as future teachers, students are sometimes confused and worried about this situation. An experienced teacher, however, perceives that ultimately the teacher him/herself is the most important decision-maker about values in the classroom context.

No definite answer was given as to the role religion or the church played as the source of knowledge which forms the basis of the values education within the school.

Values education and approaches within the classroom (in the Slovenian context)

As was stated in the theoretical background to this chapter, education is never likely to be neutral. Without any special subject pertaining to values teaching and learning, values are nevertheless present in schools. In Slovenia, a special subject called 'ethics and society' has been part of the curriculum for grades 7 and 8 of compulsory school. Students and teachers participating in this survey had some experience of values education, in the roles both of pupils and of teachers.

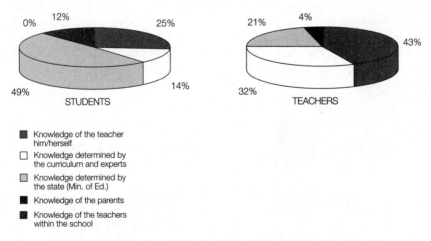

Figure 6.6 Whose knowledge forms the basis of values education?

Question 4c of the questionnaire was 'How is knowledge imparted to the learners?' (Teaching methods employed). A range of answers was given. In the first place students listed explanation, discussion, demonstration, analysing concrete examples, literary texts, group work, practical work. They also mentioned the teacher as a role model. Some answers emphasized that the method depended on the teacher him/herself. Most of the teachers (15 out of 20) mentioned discussion and careful listening to the pupils, half of them (10) experiential learning, practical work and/or interactive games.

All answers were divided into two categories, according to the criteria: 'Whose activity, who is active, who is playing the active role: teacher or pupil?' The results are given in Figure 6.7, and the trend which emerges in the responses is that in the case of the student replies the active role of the teacher is stressed. We may assume that their answers derived from their own experiences as learners. The practising teachers also gave more frequent responses which emphasized their own active role.

Similar answers to those for the previous question were given when respondents were asked to 'Outline four specific strategies which you employ in the area of values development and teaching within the classroom context.' Students and teachers acting in the role of teacher listed very similar methods, except that more emphasis was placed on an active role for pupils by the teachers. The answers to this question in the most recent questionnaire were consistent with those obtained in the survey (Polak and Razdevsek-Pucko, 1994) conducted in May 1994 (with 102 student teachers at the Faculty of Education, University of Ljubljana). In 1994, the question was: 'What approaches should teacher education courses adopt for their role in the teaching of attitudes and values in the classroom?' Student teachers listed a range of strategies and skills in their responses. The common elements of their answers can be categorized into the following groups: methods where the pupils are active participants (discussion with arguments, role play); methods where the teacher's indirect impact is predominant (his or her system of values and personal example); and the list of indispensable characteristics of approaches with tolerance in the first place.

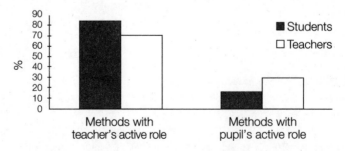

Figure 6.7 Methods of teaching values education in schools

In considering the frequency of answers to the above question, the categories were defined as follows:

- In the first group of answers (the greatest number of answers) were those where mention was made of discussion (including listening to the pupils, considering their opinions, clarifying the dilemmas). Students stressed the need for arguments to be presented during the discussion, as opposed to discussing values from the authoritative position of the teacher.
- The second group of answers demonstrated the need for developing the teacher's own value system, broadening the frame of his/her knowledge and the need for teachers to be broad-minded in terms of values.
- The third group of answers concerns characteristics of methods and approach: tolerance, critical approach, reliance and confidence.
- The next group of answers incorporated those which emphasized the need for non-enforcement of values; teachers have no right, it was perceived, to impose their values on their pupils, and thus teachers require skills of indirect communication. Student teachers especially stressed the importance of the personal example of a teacher with regard to values.
- The last (according to the number of answers) group of answers provided some specific approaches to the teaching of values (active methods) such as role play, problem solving, project method, learning through experience.

Some differences between the students, regarding the extent of their practice, were noticed: the students with less practice stressed the importance of the teacher's value system, the teacher's knowledge and the characteristics of the approach, while the students with more practice tended to think in a more practical fashion, mentioning the concrete approach more frequently, especially discussion as an approach involving the active participation of pupils.

Student teachers' opinions about values education and the approaches within the classroom

Six second-year (at the end of the second year) student teachers (female) were interviewed about their own experiences in values teaching. The interviews were undertaken individually, recorded on tape and analysed.

- All six student teachers stated that the problem of values had not been sufficiently considered during their school practice period. Sometimes they came across the values involved in language teaching (Slovene, English), when the teacher focused on values regarding the literature or lesson content. They had also experienced value discussion during their own schooling when conflicts or behavioural problems demanded that kind of approach.
- A special school subject (ethics and society) could provide an opportunity

to talk about values, but the students found this subject too theoretically oriented. They mentioned that they listened to the lessons about some (abstract) values such as patriotism, humanity, justice, but they did not deal with the concrete value-laden problems within the classroom, school and society.

- Students see the direct instruction teaching method, where pupils have no active role and where the level of their emotional involvement is very low, and all directive methods such as persuasion and the teacher referring to her/his own attitudes and values only, as inappropriate methods for values education.

- Student interviewees claimed that discussion, co-operative work, co-operation with pupils' parents and project research were appropriate methods for addressing the area of values teaching. They also suggested that values could be addressed by analysing life-experiences, practical work, relationships between pupils and the school staff, teamwork, group activities and by different kinds of school activities such as sending letters, non-verbal communication and interpreting poetry.

- Students also mentioned co-operation between teachers and parents and stressed that this co-operation is an important and influential factor which contributes to more harmonious values education in schools. They are worried about a possible discrepancy between values stressed by parents and those which are directly or indirectly taught in schools. Students emphasized that the lack of harmony in values education can be especially harmful in the case of children in primary education.

CONCLUSIONS AND RECOMMENDATIONS

In the theoretical background to this chapter it was stated that education cannot be value-neutral. Even the absence of values portrays a value and may be described in terms of a moral vacuum. Or, according to Hill (1991: 18), 'the encouragement of critical thinking in the function of preventing indoctrination is the orientation to critical rationality and is itself "value-laden"'. It means that a values stance is evident equally in the school which treats values as a special subject on the curriculum and that which does not.

Among important questions connected with values education, stress is placed here on the following: *Which values? Whose values? When* and *How* is values education organized? and *Which methods* are used within the values education process?

The survey conducted for this study outlines a traditional value orienta-tion, including values connected with the family, together with a democratic and pluralistic values orientation which accentuates human rights and the rights of children. These are the values most frequently stressed by the students and practising teachers who participated in the survey. Ecological values (for example, respect for nature) were also emphasized and became incorporated into universal values. The absence of more sophisticated and spiritual (religious) values is evident. This may be seen to be the consequence of social circumstances in a time of transition, where basic moral values and basic democratic values are seen as important. The results of this survey are consistent with those, reported by Musek (1993a), regarding the development hierarchy. Respondents, that is, students as well as practising teachers, are not of the age where (according to Musek) an increase of fulfilment values may be expected (after age 45).

The absence of potency values, which may be expected at the age of respondents in this study, may be explained by the orientation of the teaching profession, which in Slovenia is described as 'idealistic'. Religion is mentioned as an important cultural issue, having an influence on value orientation and values education in schools, not so much in the spiritual but more in the cultural and traditional sense.

According to the opinions of student teachers, discourse about values in schools is too theoretical to influence behaviour. Only active methods, such as role play and social games, project work where experience with others and with those who are different (disabled, old, sick, powerless, refugees) is included, where the pupil really becomes a subject of his/her own education, have significant influence on value development.

As an example of active methods special projects may be organized with students, where values education takes place through drama or some other kind of performance, in activity-based lessons which include simulations, conflict resolution and story-telling. An important element is also the role model of the teacher and reciprocity in communication between pupils and teachers.

To practise such methods, teachers are required to develop more effective skills of listening to others' views and expressing their own. In order to participate in group decision making, they should develop more effective communication skills, and should have more practice during their own teacher education in creating the atmosphere and using such methods as will be expected from them as teachers.

The message which has emerged from this survey is that what is needed is to be open to a range of values and to support values education with a range of approaches within the classroom as well as within teacher education programmes.

As a conclusion to the discussion of methods and approaches in values education, the thought that 'someone can internalize democracy, tolerance, responsibility and other values only by experiencing them in everyday life, in society, with parents, teachers and classmates' (Zadnikar, 1994: 76) appears to be applicable.

It is not only the methods of values teaching that need to be considered. Values education should also be adjusted to changing times. US President

Abraham Lincoln stated many years ago: 'The dogmas of the quiet past are inadequate to the stormy present. . . . As our case is new, so we must think anew and act anew.'

REFERENCES

Cencic, Mirs (1986) *Dinamika vzgojnega dela v soli* (Ljubljana, Drzavna Zalozba Slovenije).

Gaber, Slavko (1990) 'Za nevtralno javno solo!' *Verouk v sole?!*, Solsko polje 4, Ljubljana & Skofja Loka, 9–21.

Gaber, Slavko (1995) 'Spremembe v solstvu', *Republika*, 3 September, 10.

Hill, B.V. (1991) *Values Education in Australian Schools* (Melbourne, ACER).

Kanduc, Zoran (1994) 'Anomie and School Education', *Drzavljanska vzgoja, Casopis za kritiko znanosti*, st. 172–3, 107–18 (abstracts in English).

Kodelja, Zdenko (1995) *Laicna sola, Pro et Contra* (Ljubljana, Zalozba Mladinska knjiga).

Ling, L., Cooper, M., Burman, E., Killeavy, M., Zuzovsky, R., Yakir, R., Gottlieb, E. and Stephenson, J. (1995) 'Values – Valid or Vacuous? An International Perspective on Values Education', paper jointly presented at the Annual Conference of the Association for Teacher Education in Europe (ATEE) (Oslo, Norway).

Marentic-Pozarnik, Barica (1993) *Slovenia: System of Education* (Ljubljana, Board of Education and Sport).

Ministry of Education and Sport (1992) *Development of Education in the Republic of Slovenia, 1990–1992* (Ljubljana, Ministry of Education and Sport).

Ministry of Education and Sport (1994) *Development of Education 1992/1994, Slovenia*, National Report (Ljubljana, Ministry of Education and Sport).

Musek, Janek (1992) 'Dimensions of Personality and Value Orientations', in *Department of Psychology, 40 Years*, collection of scientific papers, University of Ljubljana, 11–27.

Musek, Janek (1993a) *Osebnost in vrednote* (Ljubljana, Educy).

Musek, Janek (1993b) 'Value Crisis, Values and Psychology', *Horizons of Psychology*, 3/4: 123–41 (abstracts in English).

Musek, Janek (1994) 'Personality Traits and Value Orientations', *Horizons of Psychology*, 1: 13–28 (abstracts in English).

Pecek, Mojca (1994) 'From Social and Moral Education to Instruction in Human Rights', *Drzavljanska vzgoja, Casopis za kritiko znanosti*, st. 172–3, 119–25 (abstracts in English).

Polak, Alenka and Razdevsek-Pucko, Cveta (1994) 'Values for a Changing Context: A Global Perspective, Results from Slovenia', paper presented at the Annual Conference of the Association for Teacher Education in Europe (ATEE) (Prague, the Czech Republic).

Statistical Yearbook 1995, Republic of Slovenia, Ljubljana.

Zadnikar, Darij (1994) 'Civic Education for Postsocialism?' *Drzavljanska vzgoja, Casopis za kritiko znanosti*, st. 172–3, 73–89 (abstracts in English).

Zgaga, Pavel (1990) 'Religija, etika, vednost: med vzgojo in izobrazevanjem', *Verouk v sole?!*, Solsko polje 4, Ljubljana & Skofja Loka, 25–35.

Zupancic, Maja, and Justin, Janez (1991) *Otrok, pravila, vrednote* (Radovljica, Didakta).

Zuzovsky, Ruth (1995) 'Values in Education: Valid or Vacuous, Israeli Study on Values in Education', paper presented at the annual conference of the Association of Teacher Education in Europe (ATEE) (Oslo, Norway).

7

A PERSPECTIVE FROM ENGLAND

Joan Stephenson

INTRODUCTION

In this report of a study carried out at De Montfort University in Bedford, the title is deliberately restricted to part of the United Kingdom only, since Northern Ireland and Scotland have their own educational systems and variations of training and practice. It could, therefore, be that a similar study done in either of those regions would give different results. The fourth member of the kingdom, Wales, shares the same system as England, but although there are teachers of Welsh origin included in this sample, no schools in Wales were involved.

Outline of the cultural, political, social and economic context in England

State education, with which we are concerned here, as all our respondents are teachers in state schools, is free to all children in the United Kingdom, between the ages of 5 and 18. All children must attend until they are 16. Schools are largely organized on a regional basis by county and each has a board of governors responsible to the government authorities for its running. Until recently schools were administered and funded solely by the Local Education Authority (LEA), which is an arm of local government. Over the past few years schools have been able to 'opt out' of the system and to be funded directly by central government through the Department for Education and Employment. These schools have a totally devolved budget, while LEA schools have varying increasing percentages of their budgets devolved, making most financial functions the responsibility of the head and governors of the individual school. The vast majority, however, still remain under LEA control, even those which do not continue to share similar aims and ethos. Governors are also responsible for the curriculum and academic and social welfare of pupils in their school, subject to the requirements of the Secretary of State for Education.

Each regional area is free to organize schools in age phase bands, school type and size as it wishes. This leads to some variation from region to region but most state schools cater for pupils of both sexes, of all abilities and in primary and secondary modes of roughly 5 to 11 years and then 11 to 16 or 18. There are, however, some selective grammar schools where pupils are chosen by ability and there are also some single-sex schools.

In addition to these variations there is also the right for denominational religious groups to form their own schools and receive funding from the state. The largest groups within this sector are those schools with an allegiance to either the Church of England or the Roman Catholic Church, although in certain urban areas there are Jewish schools and an increasing demand for faiths from the Commonwealth to have similar privileges granted to them.

Funding for education as a whole, although increased in numerical terms, has in fact become tighter over the last few years, reflecting the general down-turn in the economy. Resources in schools have been affected, as too have the number of teachers which a school with a devolved budget can afford. Many experienced, and therefore expensive, teachers have retired early. The general level of morale among many who remain is not high. Class sizes are now larger than for many years, particularly in the primary sector. There is not nursery school provision for all who need or desire it. Child-care is often a problem for working mothers, whether single parents or not. This, coupled with the lack of resources, poor physical condition of many school buildings and the increasing number of children from homes where neither parent is in paid work (or there is only one breadwinner, who may have no employment or a lowly paid job), has increased the pressure on schools. The breakdown of the general pattern of the male as head of household and major earner has also contributed to family strife and separation in many sections of the population and is not confined to the lower-earning or less skilled sections of British society.

All schools which receive funding from the state must follow the National Curriculum. This lays down the subjects and levels to be taught, but not the methods. Most teachers feel under considerable time pressure to fit in all the work demanded by the National Curriculum. Children at the ages of 7, 11 and 14 must complete national Standard Attainment Tests (SATS), the results of which are published as 'league tables' of individual school performance.

All schools are subject to inspection by the governmental Office for Standards of Education in Schools (OFSTED) and it is in this process of inspection that the children's spiritual and moral development must be gauged as well as their academic standards. Under the terms of the Education Reform Act (1988), Section 1, schools are required to address 'the spiritual, moral, mental, cultural and physical development of pupils'. The areas which fall within the remit of values education could be said to lie largely in this field. As part of this, although it is not a National Curriculum subject, all schools must teach and promote religious education. After recent legislation this must have a Christian focus, although only those partly funded by and with an allegiance to a religious body are permitted to promulgate sectarian beliefs or worship. In an increasingly multicultural society, with British-born ethnic minority parents of today's school body demanding their constitutional rights, this edict has left many schools with an ethical dilemma.

The National Curriculum Council (1993) gave guidance to teachers through the use of themes, dimensions and skills, pertaining to values, to be addressed in the classroom. The subsequent Dearing review of the curriculum (1993), while stressing the importance of the components of values education, has offered no guidance as to how National Curriculum subjects could be used as a vehicle for its inclusion in schools. In a sense it has taken away what clues and suggestions there were, a fact acknowledged by OFSTED in the report it published as its response to the Dearing consultation.

> Some statement of the principles underpinning the National Curriculum and of the values it seeks to foster and develop through individual subjects would appear to be timely. Such a statement could form part of an overview statement about the curriculum as a whole and, in this way, help to develop a sense of unity of purpose among the teachers of the various subjects and their pupils. The advantages of a unifying set of educational principles to which all of those involved in education can subscribe, are overwhelming. Such a set of principles should be drawn up so that the spiritual, moral, social and cultural goals which the curriculum is in law charged with serving will be made more explicit and linked more closely to the work of individual subjects.
>
> (1994)

In an increasingly secular society the reliance on religious bodies to foster a value system for succeeding generations has largely broken down, at least among the indigenous population, and schools are increasingly being seen as places in which children form or have formed their value systems, by a public who feel threatened by a lack of discipline and an increasing crime rate. To date, for the most part, values education in schools has been covered in religious education and more recently under the title of civic education or citizenship education. The difficulty of motivating pupils, particularly in secondary schools, is seen by some as a major failing of this approach (Davies, 1993: 165). This expectation of the school filling the moral vacuum is even more forcibly underlined by politicians through the popular press. There is no consensus as to what the 'moral development' of pupils in school might encompass. Some see the process as a linear one where 'right' attitudes and behaviours are accumulated by the maturing child. The term development itself is problematic in interpretation, one debate being whether the objectives are of quantity or quality, depth or complexity. While a linear notion is challenged by the school of thought that sees development as erratic and multi-directional, encompassing steps both forward and backward on a number of fronts, evaluation is not easy. The perhaps long delayed nature of cause and effect on any one individual, resulting from a programme of values education, also means that a true measure of the worth of the programme may not be possible until many years have passed.

Who is to be the arbiter of the ultimate 'value' or moral code, in its widest sense, has not yet been overtly addressed. The notion of a body of 'accepted' rules for social order, subscribed to by all, where values education is seen as instruction in moral rules followed by the individual learning to subscribe to these and adopt them as their own, is an over-simplification which could have disastrous consequences, and needs to be challenged. Individual responsibility has to be fostered and in order to do this, any programme has to go beyond the inculcation of a more dominant body's mores, into a searching for and understanding of morality underlying personal action. This cannot be achieved in the classroom alone. Values education involves both inner exploration and social discovery influenced by shared cultural and social experiences, and schools now face a range of issues in developing a climate to nurture the place of values education in their curriculum. Many argue that the demands of the National Curriculum have reduced the time available to develop an appropriate environment and atmosphere for values education. With a crowded timetable it is difficult to create the space and time needed for discussion and reflection on issues of crucial importance. There is a tension between delegating all responsibility for moral and spiritual issues to Religious Education lessons, as in some cases in the past, given not only the potential conflict of views between those who take a theistic or a humanistic stance, but also the multicultural and multi-faith composition of modern Britain, and the integration of values education in all other subjects in the curriculum.

In this climate, with no National Curriculum slot labelled 'values education', where time is largely taken up by the pressures for attainment in the National Curriculum subjects, schools and teachers must continue to educate children to the best of their ability. Some schools and teachers are aware of the problems, some are not. This study gave the opportunity to hear the views of a cross-section of practising primary school teachers.

THE DATA COLLECTION PROCESS

The project discussed in this chapter uses the data gathered from the final phase of the international study, where practising teachers in schools were targeted.

In common with the agreed research method for this international study, a qualitative approach was taken making use of triangulation (Cohen and Manion, 1994), a strategy of acquiring data on the same features of interest

from a variety of sources or perceptions; evidence was sought in three different ways. A questionnaire, common to all countries participating in this
study, posing five open-ended questions, was given without modification or
amendment to a cohort of 20 practising primary school teachers working in
state schools. Their stated age ranged from 36+ to 45+. The preponderance
of 'older teachers' reflects the current demographic picture within English
education. Only two were male. This also reflects the position in terms of
gender balance in English primary schools. All but one female member were
white and all followed what would, in England, be termed a middle- or lower
middle-class lifestyle, though some claimed to have come from working-class
backgrounds. Most of them were educated to degree level (since 1974 a
graduate qualification is required of all new teachers). Teaching careers varied from 9 years to 30 years in schools. The average length of service was
20.5 years. The teachers were self-selected, although the schools at which
they taught were chosen to give a spread of school size and geographical/
social area. All agreed to the data collected being used as long as anonymity
was guaranteed. Not all teachers gave answers to all the questions and, where
a stated number of responses was requested, the answers were sometimes
partial. The data was then analysed in clusters through the use of Hyperqual,
a data analysis software package.

Semi-structured interviews and discussion with 15 of the teachers constituted the second line of inquiry. This enabled more detailed data on
areas of ambiguity or common or unique response from the questionnaire
to be gathered. This was in accordance with the agreed international
research approach for this study; but a larger number of people than the
suggested percentage opted, when invited, to develop their input through
discussion. Since the number surveyed was a relatively small one, although
wide-ranging in coverage, a greater emphasis on interview seemed both
desirable and potentially useful. It allowed for correlation of questionnaire
responses with orally expressed views, often revised or restated in the
delivery, and the fact that one of the sessions was conducted as an open
discourse meant that expressed views were further explored and illumi-
nated through the responses and remarks of the peer group. The 12
teachers in this group were attending an award-bearing course in the university. As such a large percentage volunteered, skew or bias is less likely,
at least within the confines of this self-selecting group, and the mix of ages
and types of school continued to be reflected. The other three interviews
were with individuals.

As a final source of information observation sessions were conducted in
three classrooms in separate schools, chosen to reflect age phase, social area,
size and methodological differences. All these schools were accustomed to
having visitors and educationalists in their classrooms. The single 'observation session' took place as part of a series of visits for other purposes in
order to minimize the likelihood of non-typical behaviour on the part of

both teacher and children. These three methods of data-gathering – questionnaire, interview and observation – gave the checks and counterbalances which are the features of a triangulated approach.

ANALYSIS AND DISCUSSION OF DATA

Questionnaire

In an attempt to classify the English findings in accordance with the common interpretative model as presented in Chapter 3, it is necessary to look at findings from all three aspects of the research. Within the questionnaire not all individual questions are directly applicable to an analysis of the teachers' values model as defined by Brian Hill, Question 2 (Appendix 2) for example being concerned with teacher performance rather than belief; however, Questions 1, 3, 4a and 5 give some indication of the stance taken by this set of respondents.

The data arising from the questionnaires can be summarized as follows. In all, teachers identified sixteen principles on which they based their decisions with regard to the teaching and development of values education. Moral values, cited by just under half of the respondents, were mentioned most. Whose values form the basis of decisions for teaching values is not clear, but the categories of personal value systems, school ethos and societal parameters would suggest that the 'ruling majority' values were being taken as a 'baseline' or norm. The overall emphasis of the responses was on individual responsibility or duty to others. It is interesting to note that religious education or mores are not directly referred to as an underlying principle. The National Curriculum, which features largely in teachers' thinking in other aspects of their work, was mentioned by less than a quarter of teachers. From this set of answers religious monopolism would not appear to be a dominant feature. However, the lack of clarity as to where the 'moral values' the teachers saw as most important came from, may make such a judgement premature. More insight would be needed before a firm position could be taken. The data would seem to indicate that moral universalism in either of its forms is demonstrated here, but similar reservations apply. Consensus pluralism, in that it encompasses all codes, given that responsibility and duty to others feature so strongly, appears to be the most probable interpretation of teacher stance with regard to this question.

All the issues cited by teachers in this study in response to Question 3 (see p. 138) concerned a macro rather than the micro consideration of the subject. The central position of racism/ethnicity and gender as dominant determinants on teachers' thinking reflects the current debate in England and the United Kingdom. The gender issue not only concerns the place of women in society, but also links with ethnicity and religion in that divergent views of the values favoured by different cultural and ethnic groups are

136

Question 1 Briefly state three essential principles upon which you make decisions with regard to the teaching and development of values in the curriculum programme.

	Cited by	Age phase	Experience	Age	Gender
moral values	9	P/I*	12:18:20:21	45+:36–45	F
tolerance	7	P/I	26:29:20:30	45+:36–45	F
esteem for others	7	P/I	18:21:29:20:30	45+:36–45	F/M
school ethos	4	P/I	16:20:22	?36–45	F
societal parameters	4	P/I	12:20:22:25	45+:36/45+?	F
community values	3	P/I	12:22:30	?36–45	F/M
personal value systems	3	I	22:20:12	36–45	F
standards (NC)	3	P/I	18:20:29	45+:36–45	F
children's own ideas	3	P/I	16:26:20	45+:36–45	F
consistency	2	P/I	20:30	45+	F/M
permeation	2	P/I	20:30	45+	M
good examples	2	P/I	20:25	45+:36–45	F
self-esteem	2	I	20	45+:36–45	F
responsibility to others	1	P	12	45+:36–45	F
no principles	1	P	25	45+	F
responsibility to self	1	P	12	?	F

* P = Primary; I = infant; ? = indicates age not stated

affecting the call for change in the type and format of schooling. Shades of religious monopolism or anti-religious monopolism could be one interpretation of this. Since religion is cited high in the ranking, then the neutral position adopted by moral universalism seems, on the face of it, to make consensus pluralism, with its concern for gender issues and acceptance of religious concerns, a possible label here. However, any interpretation is beset by difficulties and the inclusion of categories of welfare/availability/ dependency and failure of social structure, together with the two respondents who saw economics and law and order as one of their five predominant

Question 3 List five of the predominant cultural issues which you perceive exert major influence upon the values dimension of curriculum in your context.

Cultural issues	Cited by	Age phase	Experience	Age	Gender
racism/ethnicity	11	P/I	12:30:18:21: 25:?	?45+:36–45	F/M
gender	10	P/I	12:18:30:21: 25:20	?45+:36–45	F
religion	6	P/I	16:12:29:26:25	?45+	F/M
social group	5	P/I	12:25:20:18	?45+	F/M
environment	4	P/I	30:26:20:12	45+:36–45	F/M
welfare/availability/ dependency	4	P	9:21:25:18	45+:36–45	F
community	4	P/I	9:26:18:20	45+	F
failure of social structure	3	P/I	9:18:21	45+:36–45	F
none given	3	P	25:20:22	45+	F/M
politics	3	P/I	21:20:18	36–45	F
beliefs	3	P	9:16:20	36–45:45+	F
heritage	2	P/I	30:16	36–45:45+	F
relationships	2	P	9:25	45+	F/M
the arts	2	P	30:26	45+	F
economic climate	1	P	45+		
law and order	1	I	30	45+	F
place of education in society	2	I	21:25	36–45:45+	F/M

cultural issues, would imply that for some of these teachers, a moral vacuum model was a distinct possibility.

Teachers' own knowledge was seen as the basis for courses and curriculum in values education by all respondents' either explicit or implicit

Question 4 Write one brief comment on these four questions as they relate to values development and teaching in your context.

a. Whose knowledge forms the basis of the course?

	Cited by	Experience
teachers	8	across all range
no comment	4	
teacher and children	2	25:12
teacher/school society/s	2	16:30
staff	2	30:25
children/politicians/teachers	1	21
head/staff/governors/parents	1	22

responses to Question 4a (above). Whether respondents question how this knowledge was acquired and how its origins affect their attitudes to the content, purpose and delivery of values education was not explored. This is an omission which should be rectified before future values education programme planning takes place, if the question of access to this knowledge is to have any hope of achieving the equality that this group of teachers was

Question 4d To which individuals or groups of learners is the knowledge pertaining to the values dimension of the curriculum available?

	Cited by
equally	17
equally in theory	2
equally in this context	1

claiming (see Question 4d). Which model is identified by these responses would depend on the values to which the individual teachers subscribed and their attitude of tolerance of or hostility to those views held by other sections which did not match their own. Hill warns that even when consensus pluralism is achieved, a holding-together of accord reached is still threatened if the differences remaining between views are sufficient to 'subvert the agreements which have been reached' (Hill, 1991: 30).

Without knowing on what basis all these teachers were claiming equality of availability of knowledge pertaining to the values dimension of the curriculum, it would be bold to conclude that this is possibly a naive response. The underlying aspects are so complicated that it seems unlikely, however, that such unanimous agreement can be a fully considered answer. This also could have a consequence on the extent to which a teacher facilitates the opportunities for individuals or groups of children to have open-ended philosophical discussions about issues they see as important.

Matthew Lipman (1991), in his adoption of philosophy for children, sees a

Question 5 What are five of the most important elements which (a) values teaching in schools, and (b) values education components of teacher education courses, should address?

Elements	Cited by	Age phase	Experience	Age	Gender
caring/compassion	11	I/P	18:20:26:29:30	36–45:45+	F
race	8	I/P	12:30:20:16: 21:12	36–45:45+	F/M
respect for all	8	I/P	18:20:16:25:30	36–45:45+	F/M
social structure	8	I/P	12:30:16:20: 25:21:22	36–45: 45+	F/M
gender	7	I/P	12:21:25:20:30	36–45:45+	F/M
class	7	I/P	30:20:16:25:18	36–45:45+	F/M
tolerance	7	I/P	18:20:26:29:22	36–45:45+	F
honesty	4	I/P	18:20:26:30	36–45:45+	F
responsibility	3	I/P	22:26:25	36–45:45+	F/M
respect for society/ property	3	I/P	18:30	45+	F
enthusiasm	2	I/P	29:26	45+	F
equality	1	I	22	36–45	F
no response	1	P	25	45+	F

model of a class as a community of inquiry. If the topics of this inquiry are to be controlled by the teacher and are at the same time restricted to their 'received view' this could be significant for children's development. Rowe (1995), writing of a recent research project using Citizenship Foundation material with practising teachers, reports that several of the teachers involved were surprised that 'the preoccupations of the children were different from what they imagined them to be'. If knowledge and therefore content and parameters are set by teachers with the same characteristics as those in this study then motivation and flexibility will be hampered. We will hope the fault lies with the question and the teacher's understanding of its deeper ramifications rather than this being an accurate picture of the situation under discussion in this section of the questionnaire.

There was overlap between the predominant cultural issues given in answer to Questions 3 and 5 the elements cited here, which may be categorized as care for others, their feelings and sense of worth. These are obviously very important factors for these teachers. Religion, as such, is, however, not mentioned. A case could be made that what is shown by the data is a range of attitudes which could be recognized as common to all moral principles and that this underlies a moral universalism position. The teachers who are opting for moral universalism appear to believe that religious disagreement is a complication in moral education and as such should be ignored while looking at the 'universal truths'. The inclusion of the current 'big' concerns of the moment, such as gender and race, would seem to indicate that the differences between the 'moral truths' of various religions or cultures are being recognized, and that these are an illustration of consensus pluralism. It is interesting to note that the structure of society and an element of respect are also raised, echoed later in the feeling of moral decline and breakdown of societal mores raised by some teachers. This accords with the moral vacuum model of the analysis. The low rating of 'equality' is perhaps further comment on the misconception or lack of comprehension of all the ramifications displayed in responses to Question 4d.

INTERVIEWS

Interviews of a semi-structured nature highlighted many of the areas raised in the questionnaire and also clarified some of the uncertainties and ambiguities caused by a lack of detail in questionnaire compilation or responses. They also reflected the average teacher's unfamiliarity with the concept of 'values education' as a discrete area of the curriculum. The teachers largely equated values education with personal and social education in this study, with a concentration on the behavioural aspects of a child's conduct, either in the realm of discipline, or in attitudes towards work in school. The interviews took place in a discussion group of twelve teachers on a post-graduate in-service course and individually with three teachers of different ages.

An analysis of responses revealed three main clusters. These were:

- areas covering aspects of principles as in Question 1, cultural issues as in Question 3 and, of course, elements as in Question 5;
- methods, where Questions 2 and 4b/c were paralleled;
- knowledge-base largely expanding on 4a and so an appropriate issue here.

Interview responses confirmed stances taken in the questionnaire. For example, in Question 1, which covered the five most often-cited principles (moral values, esteem and tolerance of others, collated with societal community and personal value systems), and the elements of Question 5 with which it was closely related (care, compassion, respect and social structure emphasis), gave rise to the question: 'Couldn't values education be something bigger though than whatever it is we're teaching, sort of a set of, sort of an ethos really?' This question brings up the issue of ethos being expanded into the notion of a 'received' set of values from a distinct source, as in:

> 'but then we wouldn't be teaching that would we? It's what we should expect from our children . . . and what can we teach in the areas like how should we behave in society, that we could teach them [pause] you wouldn't be specifically teaching.'

> 'I suppose that is a sort of behaviour isn't it? It's the sort of behaviour that we want in society but surely that's a value issue?'

This teacher introduces personal respect and implies that it goes beyond inculcation: 'But I think when it's things like personal respect for other people – er – within your society, your society and things like that, then I . . .' Here the teacher acknowledges the difficulties and the complex nature of values, even within a setting where from the appearance at least it might be reasonable to expect similar values to be shared:

> 'In mixed classes where everyone's tolerant and looking after someone else then it's there ready for you, but if you're in middle class even where there are no differences you may be walking into a nest of prejudices, etc.'

The consensus pluralist approach is echoed by a teacher who acknowledges a plurality of sets of values: 'There isn't a right answer could be a principle.' A similar stance might be echoed in this comment: 'I see the ideas of value being what we are.' This comment might suggest not tolerance, but a monopolistic belief in one truth, but on what the truth is founded is unclear.

The idea of understanding and explanation is introduced here, again by a teacher who recognizes other acceptable value systems than her own and brings the child and its contribution to the formation of a value system into the frame:

> 'if the child does something that's not acceptable, not acceptable not just within the school context but not acceptable within society at large,

then you've got to first of all make it clear to that child that first of all it's not acceptable and why! Which is not the same thing as leading by example . . . no . . . but to me brings other values in.'

The sentiments expressed in the previous comment are developed further by the teacher who said: 'and even eventually children have got to decide their own values'. This respondent underlines both universalist and consensus views: 'and we must accept that we have different sets of "acceptable values"'.

The question of what or how to teach values, is however, purely academic for some:

'But you can't teach it. You can't teach "this is right and this is wrong" and you just say what it is you believe and you encourage the child to form a belief, or an attitude on a particular issue.'

Values are 'caught not taught' was the view of a sizeable minority.

It is in the last of the cluster categories, that of knowledge, that there is the widest discrepancy between questionnaire responses and spoken opinions. The responses in the questionnaire were overwhelmingly of the opinion that teachers dominated and set the knowledge pool for values, that they were the arbiters of what was and was not of value in current society.

It is recognized by some that sub-groups exist within one larger society:

'where they have different expectations of the children and ways of dealing with them. I mean the children need to learn a variety of different values though perhaps within one framework, one impression of what is right and what is wrong. They need to learn what is acceptable to their parents is not acceptable to their friends' parents, I mean there are degrees even within society . . .'

What was not elaborated on in the interviews, in spite of the opportunity being given, was the accessibility issue raised in 4d of the questionnaire. This is an area of concern for any initial or in-service educator, and an issue which requires investigating more closely, both in a national and in a comparative international context. One somewhat more cheering exception was the view that:

'I would have thought that all the groups, you could give similar access to what you will try to teach at school but the uptake of it and whether they could go along, would they be able within their own social or ethnic group to be able to develop their own set of values as opposed to those perhaps instilled on them by other groups of people or other religions, especially if they conflict. I mean that is the bit where it's going to differ, isn't it? I mean you could present it to them as equally as you like at school but the uptake of what you have presented is obviously going to be environment affected, isn't it?'

The need for positive intervention in the cause of consensus and pluralism was raised in the following comment:

'I mean that's why you have policies on things like race, culture, equal opportunities and suchlike with the school. The things that affect our moral development and our own sense of value, so that everyone does pull in the same direction within a school, so that a school can – em – present a given set of values.'

If the last phrase does rather spoil the impression of the liberal, flexible approach that the statement appeared to be advocating, it does at the same time reinforce how difficult the average teacher finds the whole area of values education, their own moral values system and their part within society.

The last words should perhaps be given to three statements, all of which are thought-provoking in their way, and could each serve as the basis for further research within the English teaching profession:

'I think it's got to be largely your own, you can't teach somebody else's values.'

'In a way we are teaching our values, as a reflection from society, I mean they are not own values, they are not my personal values, they are what society expects from you.'

'I don't think it's an imposition but there is a degree of indoctrination.'

OBSERVATIONS PRINCIPLES

Three observation sessions in classrooms with Yr 2/3, Yr 5 and Yr 6 children (6/7, 9, 10/11 years old) and their teachers would seem to give support to the questionnaire data from Questions 1, 3, 4 and 5 on the matter of underlying principles, but only in a limited number of areas. In these areas teachers practised what they preached on the whole, though there was one notable exception.

The often-cited element of gender was evident in both positive and negative ways. As far as the researcher could observe this was considered positively by two of the teachers. A tally of teacher–child interactions showed equal attention given to boys and girls. The third teacher (a male) had more interactions with boys than girls. Children were seated in mixed groups in all rooms. There appeared to be no restriction of activities according to sex. Both girls and boys were chosen as leaders, but in two of the rooms they still 'lined up' by sex. Analogies about sport were more prevalent with the older children, and may have reflected a discipline-strategy on the part of the teacher to control a disruptive element among the boys.

Tolerance of difference, another of the cited principles/elements, was very marked in the classroom ethos of one school (Year 5) where there was a mix of ethnicity and special-needs children present. A feature of this teacher's interchange with the children was her readiness to explain the why, how and what for, before, during and in summary, of the multi-topic group work her class was doing. She also used children as resources, encouraged peers to evaluate each other's work in an attempt to raise self-esteem and respect for all. From the evidence provided, this had worked in a school drawing children from an estate of local authority housing with multiple social and economic difficulties. She spoke positively about her students, the school organization and management and stressed the importance of the social structure within the school. The school had written policies for Equal Opportunities, a discipline code and frequent staff meetings. Children were involved in writing the school rules.

In another school, with children of similar social/economic background, there was also a written Equal Opportunities policy, but no evidence of the policy being more than rhetoric in the classroom observed. Comments on pupils were negative, for example, 'That one's been excluded from three schools . . . '; 'They're not interested in learning . . . '; 'This is the worst year I've ever had.' Although the 'espoused theories' adopted by the school are politically correct the 'actually used perspectives' used by the teachers were quite different. The reality-and-rhetoric dichotomy in action was evidenced by practitioners who appeared to believe genuinely that their conduct was in accord with their expressed public policy.

The overriding impression is that it was largely the teachers' conception of value that set the tone. This, however, showed degrees of variation. It was the teacher's own belief system, rigidly adhered to, in one classroom; the class teacher's concepts had been influenced by staff and children in another; while in the third the system showed definite signs of cultural awareness. There was direct reference to political concerns only in the classroom where the teacher felt society at large had totally failed. To set these observed behaviours within the common interpretative model, given that a limited range of principles was on view, is difficult. All teachers exhibited care and concern for their children and all to a greater or lesser extent tried to present and encourage a plurality of values at least in the treatment of others in the classroom. Societal, or at least school, versions of a preferred set of values were, however, stressed. This may be a function of the make-up of the classrooms in two cases or the age of the children in the other. Parental expectations certainly played a part in the smallest of the schools and the expressed values of these teachers would indicate that all see themselves as at least open to consensus if not implementing it in practice. All that can be stated is that no aspect of religious monopoly was manifest in the course of the observations which were undertaken for this study.

APPROACHES WITHIN THE CLASSROOM

In an attempt to discover how the respondents went about introducing, teaching or making accessible to the students in their class the issues covered by the term 'values education', a questionnaire item related to the use of formal and informal strategies in the classroom. In some cases teachers did not see a clear divide between formal and informal teaching strategies. This is not surprising given the philosophy of primary education current in English schools, where work is child-centred, often individual or group based, and includes a proportion of cross-curricular topic or project work. The emphasis is on sharing and caring and as much attention is given to learning through the 'hidden curriculum' (that is, ethos forming) as in the formal planned curriculum of the school.

An attempt was also made to look at the curricular provision for the area of values in these particular classrooms and across the whole school in sub-parts of Question 4. Question 2 provided the most responses:

Question 2 Outline four specific classroom strategies (two informal and two formal) which you employ in the area of values development and teaching within your classroom context.

Informal strategy	Cited by	Age phase	Experience	Age	Gender
praising	8	P/I	18:22:20:26: 29:30	45+:36–45	F
using good examples	7	P/I	18:20:29:30	45+:36–45	F
talking about attitudes	5	P/I	18:21:20:25:12	?45+:36–45	F
expectations of standards	5	P/I	12:20:9:22	45+:36–45	F
classroom organization	5	P/I	21:20:25	45+36–45	F
seating	2	P/I	20	36–45	F
criticizing	2	P/I	22:25	45+:36–45	F
positive work/ behaviour attitudes	2	P/I	20:22	36–45	F
inclusion in lessons	2	P/I	12:29	45+:36–45	F
group working	2	P/I	12:26	45+:36–45	F
rewards (e.g. stars)	1	I	18	45+	F
teacher example	1	I	30	45+	F
national curriculum	I	I	25	36–45	F
role play	1	P	20	45+	M

Formal strategy	Cited by	Age phase	Experience	Age	Gender
discussion	9	P/I	18:26:20+:29:30	45+:36–45	F
planning	6	P/I	18:21:26:20:30	45+:36–45	F
through stories	2	P/I	18:25	45+	F
RE	2	P	9	45+	F
curriculum permutation	2	P/I	25:21	45+	F/M
school policies, e.g. EO	2	P/I	25	45+	F/M
assemblies	2	P/I	12:20	36–45	F
drama	2	P/I	12:25	?45+	F
PSE (personal and social)	1	P	9	45+	F
selective questioning	1	P	29	45+	F
organization	1	I	18	36–45	F
history	1	P/I	12	45+	F
topic choice	1	I		45+	F
role play	1	P	20	45+	F

The most striking point of both the informal and formal strategies responses is the indication given of the importance of talk within a primary classroom. Both in the informal methods, where talk seems to lie predominantly with the teacher, and in the formal methods, where in discussion teachers can encourage the pupils to make their contribution (see here 'children's own ideas' in the 'principles' responses), the overwhelming popularity of verbal communication as a learning vehicle is evident. The opportunity for voicing their views is important for all children. The teachers' belief that they themselves control and dominate the ethos of their classroom, at least in theory, is also illustrated by the high priority given to the control mechanisms implicit in expectations of behaviour and classroom organization, while planning and the use of good examples again emphasize the perception of central responsibility of the teacher. Given the pre-eminence accorded to National

Curriculum matters over the past five years, it is perhaps surprising that most strategies employed are of the type that could be applied in any context and do not specify the curriculum in any detail.

Question 4 Write one brief comment on these four questions as they relate to values development and teaching in your context.

4b How is the knowledge organized for the learners?

	Cited by
integrated	8
integrated and discrete	7
discrete	3
no comment	3

Discrete treatment of values education appears to be the least favoured teaching method for values education by these teachers. This could be because there was an uncertainty about what values education consists of, or because like other aspects of the primary curriculum it is seen as containing elements that are all-pervasive, which cannot be treated in isolation and must be addressed whenever the opportunity arises during the day-to-day activities in the classroom or school. The emphasis on behavioural control when forming values could be seen as evidence supporting this notion of pervasiveness. On the other hand, given the packed nature of the National Curriculum, it could be that there simply is not time to teach values as a discrete subject.

The responses to Question 4c again underline the predominance of the spoken word within primary teaching methods and the importance attached to the general ethos of the classroom and the strategies applied by the teacher to achieve this ethos.

Interviews

Quotations, observations and questionnaire findings suggest that 'values' are mostly integrated within other subjects and topics or arise in an 'opportunistic' way:

'The idea is that within a story there could be ideas that are values, I mean, you could choose to do a topic that would involve values.'

Question 4c How is the knowledge imparted to the learners?

	Cited by
teacher/pupil example	9
discussions	8
small-group work	5
projects	3
praise/approval	3
drama	3
story	3
expectations/standard of behaviour	3
individuals	2
class lessons	2
assembly	2
movement	1
reading	1
circle time	1
RE	1
listening	1
writing	1
incidental learning	1
visiting speakers	1
role play	1
through classroom organization	1

'Yes, I mean secondary school's going to be more . . . but it's not, not taught as such, in the formal sense, I think it's more a sharing of information and that sort of thing. They're given a certain amount of information, but it's attitude forming.'

149

From an analysis of interviews, values education is taught in schools through:

- assembly (the obligatory coming together of the whole school in a collective act of worship and sharing; it should reflect predominantly Christian principles but in an increasingly multicultural and secularized society has, in many cases, lost this emphasis; the Education Reform Act (1988) again stressed its statutory and Christian emphasis)
- a role model of behaviour:

    'That's what we'd question, you know, do we expect this kind of behaviour for yourself? If the answer is no, then you shouldn't have done it but there's something wrong.'

    'You pick up a lot of values for life from the people you want to emulate.'

- reinforcement of 'good' ideas:

    'Yes, but you can encourage that by how you act in your own classroom, if you're always there early and ready, with lots of exciting things to do, well that's going to be helpful surely, in well, getting that sort of message over, I think.'

- 'enabling' – children to discuss own values, etc.

    'Your values are going to alter according to the children.'

- PSE (Personal and Social Education)
- RE (Religious Education)
- within classroom – management
                        – ethos
                        – organization

    'You're talking there really about policies set by schools for the staff to follow in their general behaviour and their teaching methods but there's a separate issue as well, I think. You must accept there's another issue, surely, what the children actually . . ., to take an example you gave, "you can write down you're not going to hit the person next to you" but surely there's a why and that's what must come into it from the first place.'

- parameters
- 'live it'
- teachers' example – through explanation
                        – communication
                             verbal
                             non-verbal
                        – by active involvement
                        – by saying 'this is right'

150

'I think to expect everybody to become indoctrinated? I mean that way [pause] we just give them an example, you know detail, teacher can be given as an example, but you know you don't expect that everybody will behave in a better way.'

'Think how is it going to work in real life before teaching anything – which value is going to . . .'

Values education topics were identified as being wide-ranging but largely behavioural. The topics do at least link in with the questionnaire principles and elements given in Questions 1 and 5. What the teachers chose as topics here bears out the stated beliefs and models of values education. Whether this carries through into the classroom could only be borne out by observation, a study of the experience of the children involved or research with the children themselves. Areas of importance in values education from interview data include:

- self-awareness of good and bad deeds, etc.
- praising
- giving recognition
- rejection of stereotypes
- taking of responsibility
- caring
- empathy
- tolerance
- responsibility
- dealing with conflict
- helping one another
- consistency
- compromise
- protecting own standards against others' bad influence
- appreciation of others
- valuing diversity
- acceptance of others, e.g. cultures
- nurturing
- kindness
- respect
- consideration
- environment
- sharing
- scepticism, i.e. questions
- words/not blows – discussion
- discipline

The practice of teachers' using themselves and their behaviour as examples came over more strongly in interviews than it had done in the questionnaires.

OBSERVATIONS PRACTICE

The teachers' reliance on the human voice in terms of affecting values and attitudes was borne out in the observation sessions, as was the reliance on praise, opportunism and the use of many areas of the subject curriculum as vehicles for the introduction of values teaching. In the matter of demonstration, all three teachers demonstrated the use of examples by adults, for example, saying 'Would you please . . . ' 'I'm happy to see everything is cleared away . . . ', thanking children for doing things and showing in non-verbal ways they approved, recognized, esteemed and appreciated pupils' work, attitudes and behaviour.

The reverse was also true. The teachers of the youngest children and the oldest children in particular used both verbal and non-verbal means of showing disapproval of actions and attitudes, both towards work and towards other people – 'teacher looks at child, does not smile, shakes head, mouths child's name' (extract from notebook). 'Teacher crosses room, lifts up child and separates him from the group, speaks to him quietly (couldn't hear what was said), child remains isolated as a reminder of his anti-social behaviour' (extract from notebook). Use was also made of good examples by children, for example, 'That is kind of you, X . . . ' 'Look what good work X has done . . . ' 'Thank you for sharing with Y, X . . .' 'Stop, everybody, let's watch what exciting shapes X is making . . .'

All teachers stressed responsibility for others – through safety in PE (physical education); that everyone had apparatus in Mathematics; that everybody's share of project work should be finished by lunchtime so as not to let others down, etc.

When looking at teaching methods for developing values, the integrated approach through the curriculum and through the 'hidden curriculum' seems to be more prevalent in practice. Despite a request to attend a discrete teaching session on values education no invitation was received by the observer in any school, except to attend an assembly. This assembly illustrated the widespread claim to the use of stories, drama, example and praise which have been cited as vehicles for values education. Children were involved in the assembly, presumably raising their self-esteem, and the sharing, caring celebration of difference was illustrated in the playlets and performances seen (stories of Sita, involving all religious groups). Morals were drawn out in the form of a homily. This was the only instance seen of the use of a story or narrative in pursuit of values education in practice, although teachers referred to their use of this strategy in both the questionnaire and interview replies.

'Story-telling', through which abstract concepts can be introduced to children via their own actual experiences, provides, as Lipman *et al.* (1980) advocate, a philosophical context for children's moral development. Both pre- and in-service courses and materials need to be developed to enhance story-telling, which can include most areas of the curriculum and which is, in the primary classroom at least, one of the favourite activities and vehicles for imparting knowledge by both teacher and pupil, and provides another area which is ripe for development and inclusion in teachers' current strategies.

In the classrooms, examples of 'values' being fostered in small-group work (for example, co-operative work) and through discussion, both formal (teacher-initiated discussion on a story chosen to illustrate bullying) and informal (teacher using an example of a child needing comfort) were present. Formal use was also made of 'show time' (youngest groups) where children were encouraged to share each other's success, joys or sorrows, the children choosing to speak of or show their own preoccupation of the moment (for example, picture of new baby, letter from grandma, new toy, news about death of a pet, etc.). No clear examples were seen of a teacher working with concepts beyond a child's developmental level, essential for growth according to Kohlberg and Blatt (1975), other than in the instance of a child being asked to think how he would have felt if treated in a similar manner and the general call for empathy over the death of a pet. The question 'why' was asked, but by the teacher rather than as part of a questioning of moral attitudes on the part of the children themselves.

Praise was very evident. In two of the rooms and in the assembly, children were encouraged to praise one another. 'Claps' were given, merit stars and privileges of special jobs, being allowed to choose what to do in 'free time', work on wall, taking work to Head, etc. 'On report' was used as a sanction, as were reminders of skills when noise levels rose, parental expectations and the withholding of 'agreeable' pastimes such as games, painting, etc.

Curriculum areas used as vehicles for values issues included Physical Education, Mathematics, Humanities, English, Art and Science. Organization/planning were utilized in coming in, clearing away, leaving, changing occupation, giving out and collecting in resources, moving around the classroom, moving around the school, greeting visitors, addressing one another.

CONCLUSIONS AND RECOMMENDATIONS

What is overwhelmingly clear from an initial analysis is that English teachers do care about the standards of behaviour of children in their charge, and accept this as partly their responsibility. They equate education with raising these standards and the place afforded to schooling for life, but have no access to clear philosophical concepts or debate as to what or where these values come from and who should set or 'police' them in a formalized way. In this they reflect middle-class society in England in 1995. Wilson (1990), in suggesting that significant psychological reasons are at the root of many teachers' unwillingness to tackle values education, underlines a long history of uncertainty in dealing with social and moral values in schools. He suggests that it is because the subject has more basis in reason than authority. The teachers' dominance in the classroom as shown in this study may serve to confirm this, if not to supply strategies to overcome it.

Looking at the four categories used in the analysis of models within the international study, the attitudes and practices of this group of teachers in England appear to illustrate a particular trend. If we consider Hill's models of religious monopolism, moral universalism, consensus pluralism and the additional model of the 'moral vacuum' model as a theoretical framework, a pattern appears to emerge.

Examination of the data from all parts of the tripartite approach used in the collection of teachers' views, beliefs and practices shows that the subject of religion does not feature to any great extent. It may be extrapolated from this that the idea of 'tolerance' cited in response to Questions 1 and 5 in the questionnaire may suggest the need for religious openness and tolerance as was suggested in some of the responses during the discussion. Characteristics of moral universalism can be found within the common shared values found in the elements and principles upon which values education is founded, such as respect, honesty, courtesy, and it would seem that an element of moral universalism underpins the thinking of teachers in the area of values in England.

The overwhelming impression is that consensus pluralism forms the main philosophical base for the group of teachers studied, at least as a considered reaction to questions and this is to some extent backed up by the observations of practice in the classroom. There was a strong emphasis on the recognition and acceptance of difference. This emphasis on the importance of 'empathy' indicates, in theory at least, that one of the major factors identified by Gibbs *et al.* (1992) as influential in pro-social behaviour is present in these teachers' concerns and practices. Given teachers' concern with aspects of values education and Seery's (1994) study, among others, showing positive correlation between empathy and behaviour, this 'halo' effect could be one means of motivating teachers into reconsidering the place of values education within their curriculum, both taught and hidden.

To consider such things as race and gender, to take into account the effects of economic background and class, and to set values within a political reality was seen as very important by the respondents. These elements were sometimes at variance with responses to other questions, most noticeably that of the knowledge base for 'values' and the consideration of access to this knowledge by members of their class. This would seem to suggest that the fourth model, that of the 'moral vacuum', may be contributing more than overtones to the emerging attitudes and practices of teachers at work in the primary sector today.

Teachers' lack of certainty about moral values and the diminution of the influence of traditional arbitrators of 'good' and 'evil', such as religious bodies, elders and the judiciary, may be contributing to the stance teachers are taking in schools and thus may be reflected in the anomalies found within their responses. The status of 'values' as a control medium, and the way that the teacher has dominance over life in the classroom, is most striking in this investigation. It seems to cover a reasonably wide range of teacher age and experience, as well as all situations. This aspect is an important point of comparison with other countries. The dominance of the teachers' knowledge as a basis for their values work and classroom curriculum in the area of values may also be a factor in this uncertainty. We need to ask the question, 'Do the majority of teachers question where their values come from?' A realization of whose values they are and what purpose they are to be used for must be a starting point in any discussion of values teaching in schools.

Although religion was dismissed as an influential aspect in the formation of a model that teachers were following, it would be useful to investigate how strongly the values knowledge that teachers appear to rely upon was influenced by religious teachings. The place of the 'religious monopolism' model might then appear more dominant.

Mention has already been made of wider pluralist issues which are seen in the responses. Gender in particular, however, should not be seen as simply underlining the 'consensus pluralism' approach, that is, an open reaction, but also in the context of the present dilemmas facing values education, that of the 'right views' of one community forming the curriculum for values education. This is manifested in the position of church schools and the growing movement for non-Judaeo-Christian cultures to have similar rights. This movement could have an effect on gender issues with the impetus for a move to single-sex schools. This impetus in itself could be seen as an aspect of the moral vacuum in that these sections of the population feel their traditional cultural values so threatened they are impelled to do something about the situation themselves.

The findings seem to indicate that most teachers need the opportunity to explore and develop the whole concept of 'values' in its widest definition. This includes the knowledge and understanding to reflect and act on their own views and beliefs. They also need to be clear as to whether, for them, values can be viewed as objects of evaluation, whether it is extrinsic or intrinsic values they are addressing, and where the theories of philosophers of the past and present sit within their personal view (Carr, 1991). They need to be challenged to confront the issues of tolerance and difference, to address all those areas encompassed by the four models suggested in this book, and to develop their own moral cognition level in the process. The 'stages' of Kohlberg and Blatt (1975) may be considered erroneous, simplistic and out of favour, but they or something like them may serve as a starting point for discussion. If we believe that there is a maturational progression in the socio-moral awareness of children, then when their teachers are unable or unwilling to engage in dialogue on abstract principles it is unlikely that development in the classroom will take place.

We all need more knowledge of values, and the thinking underpinning them, from sections of the community outside those in which we feel most comfortable. We need the strength and humility to face and overcome our prejudices and give ground on embedded customs and beliefs, if as teachers we are to accept the role of . . . ? What role? Herein lies the greatest problem.

It might be possible to provide in-service and pre-service courses for teachers to increase knowledge – to introduce and develop, in a systematic way, the education of the teachers themselves, in, for example, moral development. It would be useful to set up diverse groups where through dialogue and meetings it would be possible to gain greater awareness, if not understanding, of how an issue appears from a different standpoint. Legislation to include values education in the school curriculum may ensure that at least every teacher tackles and every child has some exposure to at least some of the issues. Curriculum materials are being produced, by teachers and bodies such as the Citizenship Foundation and various religious and secular bodies, to gain children's interest in practical non-partisan ways. More of these could be useful, as could added resources and positive discrimination for areas of greatest need. If, along with the Scottish Consultative Council on the Curriculum and their long-term project 'Values in Education', we believe 'it's about every teacher and every aspect of school life' (Barr and McGhie, 1995: 104) then action must be taken. However, until teachers have a clear message of what it is society is expecting of them in the area of values teaching, a greater understanding of themselves and what measures the other players in the game, such as parents, religious bodies, government agencies and the media, are also bringing to the effort, the same uncertainties, dismissals, misplaced honest endeavour and frustration as voiced by the teacher who said 'Values education? – I don't hold with that. It's a waste of time!', may prevail.

REFERENCES

Barr, I. and McGhie, M. (1995) 'Values in Education: The Importance of the Preposition', *Curriculum*, 16 (2): 103–8.

Carr, D. (1991) 'Education and Values', *British Journal of Educational Studies*, XXXIX (3): 245–59.

Cohen, L. and Manion, L. (1994, 4th edition) *Research Methods in Education* (London, Routledge).

Davies, I. (1993) 'Teaching Political Understanding in Secondary Schools', *Curriculum*, 14 (3): 165.

Gibbs, J., Basinger, K. and Fuller, D. (1992) *Moral Maturity: Measuring the Development of Socio-moral Reflection* (New Jersey, Erlbaum).

Hill, B.V. (1991) *Values Education in Australian Schools* (Melbourne, ACER).

Kohlberg, L. and Blatt, M. (1975) 'The Effects of Moral Discussion upon Children's Level of Moral Judgement', *Journal of Moral Education*, 4: 129–63.

Lipman, M. (1991) *Thinking in Education* (Cambridge, Cambridge University Press).

Lipman, M., Sharp, A.M. and O'Scanyan, F.S. (1980) *Philosophy in the Classroom* (Philadelphia, Temple University Press).

National Curriculum Council (1993) *Spiritual and Moral Development: A Discussion Paper* (York, NCC).

Office for Standards in Education (1993, revised May 1994) *Handbook for the Inspection of Schools* (London, Her Majesty's Stationery Office).

Office for Standards in Education (1994) *Spiritual, Moral, Social and Cultural Development: An OFSTED Discussion Paper* (London, OFSTED).

Rowe, D. (1995) 'Developing Spiritual, Moral and Social Values through a Citizenship Programme for Primary Schools', in R. Best (ed.) *Education, Spirituality and the Whole Child* (London, Cassell).

Seery, G. (1994) 'Can Virtue Be Taught?' Unpublished doctoral thesis: Oxford Brookes University.

Wilson, J. (1990) *A New Introduction to Moral Education* (London, Cassell).

Part III
OUTCOMES

8

PRACTICAL STRATEGIES IN VALUES EDUCATION

Maxine Cooper and Eva Burman; Lorraine Ling,
Cveta Razdevsek-Pucko and Joan Stephenson

INTRODUCTION

Throughout the theoretical sections of this book and also within the reports of each of the countries represented in the research study, a common thread which has emerged has been the need for educators to acknowledge continuously and reflect upon the dialectical relationship which exists between theory and practice. The perceived gap which is imagined by some educators between the intended curriculum of schools and the lived curriculum of schools is frequently mentioned. This may be referred to as a rhetoric/reality gap. It is contended in this book that such a perception is false and that it reflects a linear and polarized mode of thought which is simplistic and artificial. Rather, it is seen in this study that there is an inextricable interdependence between the zones of practice and theory such that these two zones continuously influence, make and remake each other. One should not try to define theory without reference to practice and vice versa.

Based upon this interdependent and dialectic conception of the zones of theory and practice, this chapter constitutes an outline of some typical practical activities which derive inevitably and naturally from the theoretical perspectives which underpin the area of values education in the curriculum. These activities should not be seen as standing alone, nor should they be regarded as an inclusive array of possibilities. Rather they are included here to provide an illustration of the way educators at all levels of the education system may extrapolate theory into practice and thus ensure the links are made between the two interacting zones of meaning.

It is stressed here that in values education, as in any other area of the curriculum, teachers should not search for ready-made tricks, prescriptions or recipes for application in teaching and learning contexts. Teaching and learning and the interrelationships between the two activities are complex and idiosyncratic. To attempt to reduce teaching and learning to a set of prescribed principles, or indeed even to articulate fixed, predetermined outcomes, is seen here as simplistic and reductionist. The activities provided here, then, should be regarded as examples only and not as plans to be rigidly or uncritically implemented. The most effective classroom activities are those which are specifically designed for the context of use, taking into account the local as well as global needs of all the actors, and thus the responsibility for such design rests with individual teachers.

In this chapter an outline is provided of various ways by which teachers may introduce and develop values education in a classroom or school setting. In many cases these activities can be adapted for tertiary settings. These ideas are based on the data analyses and interpretation arising out of the research outlined in the earlier chapters.

In this section a number of principles and implementation approaches arising from these findings for the area of values education are discussed. They are intended as guidelines only and as such are open to adaptation for individual educational contexts. This customization will depend on factors such as the developmental stage or age of the students, the school philosophy and current objectives, classroom planning approaches and the availability of resources. Other factors which may be considered include current curriculum policies and the particular concerns of students and teachers in the area of values such as the conflicting approaches and ideologies within local communities. These strategies, activities and approaches will provide teachers with a reference point from which to develop classroom and school practices as well as school development policy.

Activities described in this chapter which are based on a framework of approaches which includes the purpose, resources, procedures and evaluation of the activity. There are, however, a number of examples provided which illustrate how they may be adapted for different situations. For example, Activities 4 and 5 provide illustrations of a more detailed plan for a values activity while others in the chapter are presented in an outline version. Extension activities have been suggested for each activity and may be adapted to suit a range of cultural contexts and school settings.

Throughout this chapter, teachers in schools and teacher educators in tertiary institutions will be referred to as teachers. A number of activities, for example numbers 9 and 11, have been devised for students both at school and in teacher education institutions.

The role of values education in an educational setting

Values education, both formal and informal, may encourage students to:
- develop their own personal moral codes and have concern for others;
- reflect on experiences and search for meaning and patterns in those experiences;

162

- have self-respect and respect for commonly held values such as honesty, truthfulness and justice;
- make socially responsible judgements and be able to provide justification for decisions and actions.

THE SCHOOL SETTING AND A WHOLE SCHOOL APPROACH

Teachers and administrators within a school will ideally develop a 'whole school approach' to values education. The effective implementation of this approach presupposes that teachers within a school, with support from the administration, recognize and debate issues and concepts relating to values education within their own school settings. The importance and relevance of these issues and concepts to a particular school setting are then negotiated and linked to current curriculum documents so that aspects of values education may be integrated into curriculum areas as well as being taught as a discrete area of curriculum. Processes and approaches to values teaching, at both a school and a classroom level, are ideally discussed by the whole staff so that a consistent and coherent approach to values education may be implemented. At each of these stages parent and student participation is encouraged so that the curriculum and school procedures and processes reflect the diversity of values in the school community. Where a school council exists, on which staff, both teaching and non-teaching, management, students and parents are represented, this makes a good forum for on-going debate.

In order to facilitate these processes in relation to values education, teaching staff discussions may be conducted during weekly and monthly staff meetings, professional development sessions, policy development committees and at school council meetings. Students may be encouraged to participate in class discussions, school council meetings and peer support programmes. Parent and community involvement in school decision-making processes may include participation in policy development committees, school council meetings and other committees such as those organized to support a range of language and cultural groups. School community discussions and decision making may be facilitated by the administration of surveys by mail and telephone. These surveys could include methods such as interviews with community members and/or questionnaires to discern community responses to values education.

A 'whole school approach' to values education potentially provides consistency in the development and implementation of curriculum, provides peer support for teachers, and encourages student and parent participation. It also serves to minimize the difficulties which can arise when a values system promulgated by the school, or even just the management of the school, is at variance with that of its community and/or clientele.

Values education policy

A school's values education statement may include discussion of:

- the need for students, teachers and administrators to be taught and encouraged to reflect critically as a means of developing personal decision-making skills for their own growth and community involvement;
- the need to develop students who will become responsible citizens within their own community and the global society;
- the need for school administrators to provide resources to support the implementation of comprehensive values education programmes;
- strategies to be employed to address the espoused objectives of values education.

Within the 'whole school approach' individual teachers and classes are still required to define their own particular programmes to serve their unique situations and needs. This will be done in the light of the values education policy guidelines.

In some school settings, a 'whole school approach' to values education may be considered inappropriate or may be a catch-phrase only. This may occur where there is lip service given to the concept of a 'whole school approach', but where one group, for example staff or a strong parent lobby or interest group, is the formal decision maker and where involvement of other interested groups is not facilitated. The motivation for using accepted participatory terms, such as 'collaboration', 'co-operation', 'whole school', may in fact reflect a disingenuous agenda on the part of an existing or aspiring power group. If a 'whole school approach' is to be developed and implemented effectively it needs to be done with rigour, integrity and commitment. Teachers will ultimately be required to consider the role of values education at their grade level and to develop curriculum and classroom processes to address the values education area of curriculum as a discrete and explicit programme.

Some basic principles in values education

Principles which may form the basis for the development and implementation of practical strategies and approaches in the classroom include appropriateness, authenticity, practicality and transformative capacity.

In developing and implementing practical strategies some consideration of the following issues is required:

- the curriculum content in relation to values education needs to be appropriate to the students' experiences, stages and styles of learning and cultural setting;

- values education should motivate the students and arouse their interest and curiosity and take account of personal experience.

It is important to use contemporary and up-to-date examples when examining issues relating to values education so that students can relate the wider philosophical and ideological issues to real-life situations and to practical events in their lives.

In providing a values education curriculum a teacher provides opportunities for students to:

- understand and compare values and beliefs they hold and others hold, look at evidence, form opinions and conclusions;
- discuss differences and manage conflicts in non-violent ways;
- discuss and consider different solutions to personal, social and moral dilemmas;
- recognize the complexities of defining right and wrong and discussing elements of power and the role of decision makers in the community;
- communicate their values and understandings in discussion and through their behaviour;
- reflect on how their actions may affect others;
- demonstrate responsibility and initiative.

Processes involved in values education

In implementing values education in a range of educational settings, teachers adopt processes and strategies which will depend on personal, cultural and social settings. These processes include the use of co-operative learning in small groups, inquiry approaches based on individual and small-group research, problem-solving activities and collaborative decision-making activities involving group decision making.

The research data collected in this international study indicated that the collaborative decision-making process was an approach favoured by many of the respondents in implementing values education. Collaborative decision making refers to the group decision-making process which involves all participants more or less equally. A classroom where the teacher and students share power equally is recommended as the ideal to which educators are striving. Collaborative decision making involves the teachers and students in:

- the promotion of independent thought regarding social and moral issues;
- respect for laws and the legitimate rights of others;
- respect for different beliefs, ideas and practices;
- using non-violent ways of managing conflict;
- active involvement in the life of the school and the community;

- critically examining the role of democratic principles and practices in the decision-making process;
- building positive relationships within the classroom, and potentially in the community and the wider society.

The teacher as a model

Almost all the teachers who participated in the research study saw themselves as influencing the atmosphere and ethos of their classrooms by their own behaviour.

> 'Teachers need to be aware of their own values because values are often caught not taught' (Questionnaire respondent, Melbourne, 1994).
> 'A teacher should be modelling an enthusiastic approach to education' (Questionnaire respondent, Melbourne, 1994).
> 'I have to be seen to do the things I am expecting them to do and I have to respect their views if I want them to respect mine' (Interviewee, Bedford, 1994).
> '. . . teacher's values and attitudes will show through – teaching does not take place in a value-free vacuum' (Questionnaire respondent, Bedford, 1994).

The findings of this study indicate that teachers acting as role models influence values and transmit values. This role modelling occurs in both explicit and implicit ways and has the potential to be either a positive or a negative influence upon the value development processes of the students. Thus teachers are required to examine critically their own values and to reflect upon the values they portray through their teaching methods, relationships with students and colleagues, methods of assessment and evaluation and, selection of content. The learning environment they construct, the classroom climate they create and the philosophies they hold about education as a social process also need consideration. Only when such a critical examination and reflection process has occurred at a personal level is a teacher likely to be effective in actively constructing a critical approach to values education within the classroom. This underlines the importance of both initial and in-service education in the area of values education.

The respondents in this study also recognized that their behaviour affected the way the children treated each other. Teachers therefore need to be aware of students' reactions to what teachers model, say and do about values education and the effect this has on students. Barr and McGhie define teaching as 'a role, not an act, a series of "conversations" in which the language, whatever the subject matter, is inevitably moral'. In stressing the complexity of classroom life they provide a variety of issues which teachers need to take into consideration.

Values *in* education is therefore about very many things; it's about the relationships teachers have with pupils, and with each other for that matter. It's about methodology. It's about the way we behave towards each other. It's about the kind of language we use with each other. It's about the kind of climate in which we operate. It's about sharing responsibility and, most importantly, *it's about every teacher and every aspect of school life.*

(1995: 104)

Initially teachers may pose questions which encourage both teachers and students to consider the complexity of values in their own lives and the place of values education in classrooms. The posing of questions related to values education should continue to be part of an on-going process of critical reflection.

Practical activities for values education

The section which follows provides a selection of examples of possible activities in the area of values education. They reflect elements of the theories of the various philosophers cited in this book. They are drawn from a variety of contributors across the countries. In each example a similar structure for the description of an activity is followed. The purpose of the activity is outlined in order to provide a rationale and clear direction for its implementation. The theoretical context is then set. While this context of theory is not covered in detail in each activity, the basis and elaboration for this has been discussed in Chapter 1. It is considered necessary to anchor each activity in a clear theoretical context as a means to provide comprehensiveness and consistency in values education. The procedure for each activity is outlined briefly, and resources are included as a support for teachers. Where appropriate, teacher and student roles are set out. Suggestions about evaluating the outcomes of the sessions are made and comments then follow which link the activity with findings from the project. The activities are given in broad outline only, to allow educators, in a variety of contexts, to adapt and modify them as they think appropriate. Some initial questions are provided in the following sub-section in order to facilitate the critical, reflective process for teachers.

ACTIVITIES FOR TEACHERS TO REFLECT ON VALUES EDUCATION

Activity 1   Teacher reflection on values

Purpose   To reflect on personal values as a basis for classroom teaching.

Theoretical context   This activity reflects elements of the theories of Socrates and Raths in relation to values clarification approaches and of Dewey in relation to integrated approaches to learning.

167

Procedure Teacher allocates time to reflect on personal values on a regular basis. It is suggested that teachers document their reflections in a diary or journal.

Questions for reflection

What is my philosophy about the purpose of education as a social process?

What does this philosophy mean for the kinds of teaching and learning approaches I adopt in my classroom?

What model do I provide for the learners in the area of values?

What are my aims, in terms of values education, for this class?

Have I priorities in relation to values education?

What are my preferred teaching approaches?

How are these children motivated?

How do students best gain an understanding of the diversity of values and a sensitivity to other people's values and attitudes?

Should values education be integrated into the curriculum?

If appropriate, how best can values education be integrated into the curriculum content?

Are there elements of values education that need to be considered separately from other subject areas or in different ways?

If there are elements that need to have a separate focus how do I approach those through my curriculum planning and classroom organization?

How do I address the need to prepare myself and my students for life as members of both a local and a global community?

Conclusion Teachers may record their reflections in a diary, journal or on audio/videotape or on a computer disk and refer to emergent themes and trends as a basis for future action. Teachers may also share their reflections with their colleagues in small-group situations and ask colleagues to act as critical friends.

Comments

Initially teachers committed to values education will need to reflect critically on their own understandings about their values and about values education. This research study indicated that, in many cases, the respondents were unable to reflect critically on and to articulate their attitudes to values and values education. In some cases it appeared that they had avoided, consciously or unconsciously, the sources of many of their basic assumptions regarding values or were unable to understand the meaning of the questions asked in surveys or interviews.

If teachers are to undertake a form of personal critical reflection, in order to implement values education in the classroom, support and encouragement through a 'whole school approach' to values education is necessary.

Activities designed to encourage teachers to analyse their own classroom practice are recommended as a means to allow teachers to reflect on the relationship between their classroom practice and the values which they hold. Such an activity follows here.

Activity 2 Teacher reflections on personal values in relation to teaching style and classroom practice

Purpose   To encourage teachers to reflect on their personal values in relation to values education, teaching style and classroom practice.

Theoretical context   This activity exemplifies elements of the theories of Socrates and Raths in relation to values clarification approaches.

Procedure   The teacher allocates three ten-minute periods in the day to observe and record his/her own behaviour with regard to values demonstrated through teaching style and classroom practices. In recording observations it may be valuable for teachers to select two or three aspects of their teaching on which to concentrate for each day, week or other designated period. This allows for a clear focus to be identified rather than a general observation which may be potentially unfocused. In order to assist teachers to identify some issues for concentration the following questions are provided as examples.

Questions for reflection

What are the trends or patterns that emerge when I reflect on my positive and negative comments to students?

What do I perceive the tone and pitch of my voice convey to students?

Does it appear that my voice conveys the same messages as the words I am using or is the message contradictory?

Am I shouting or raising my voice?

How often do I interrupt the students?

When and for what reasons do students interrupt each other or me?

Do I cater for a range of learning styles and approaches?

Do I include all the students in my class, taking account of gender, ethnicity, socio-economic class and disability?

Do I handle conflict in the classroom in a positive way?

As a means to support or refute teachers' own perceptions of these aspects of their classroom teaching, teachers can check through various means with the learners to see what their perceptions are and whether they are consonant with the perceptions of the teacher.

Conclusion Teachers may record their reflections in a diary journal, or on audio/videotape or on a computer disk, and refer to emergent themes and trends as a basis for future action. Teachers may also share their reflections with their colleagues in small-group situations and ask colleagues to act as critical friends. Teachers may undertake this activity as an activity research project which involves co-operative research with a colleague.

Comments

Responses to the above questions may help teachers to analyse and understand the link between teachers' own values and their teaching style and classroom approaches. After critical reflection teachers may find it necessary to consider changes to elements of classroom practice.

An analysis of teaching practice based on the reflective process may indicate to teachers that their instructions are not clear and that it is necessary to clarify directions, instructions and tasks. Contradictory messages about behavioural expectations and disciplinary approaches in relation to differentiating between boys' and girls' behaviour may also become apparent. Similarly teachers may 'reward' students who are fidgety or noisy by giving them attention or may discriminate against some students by the choice of material or topic chosen. The seating arrangements, whether self-chosen or decided by the teachers, may have separated those who work best together or resulted in disruptive tactics being used within the group. Teachers may discover that they speak disrespectfully to the students or use aggressive body language, for example when reacting to bullying. Teachers need to consider whether all students are confident enough to tell the teacher about disruptive incidents. Teachers also need to consider their own attitudes and approaches to managing conflicts which occur in school and classroom situations.

Self-observation and self-evaluation have the potential to help teachers tune into any anomalies in their own behaviour and help them to develop personal strategies to refine further their classroom practice. It may be beneficial if teachers consider using video and audio recording as well as personal reflective journals and action research as a means of recording the observation data and the reflective process. Teachers could be involved in peer support programmes at a whole school level so they are able to work through this process of self-evaluation and personal observation collaboratively.

The research findings in this study indicated that teachers did not see the facilitating of values formation as a separate part of their life in the classroom. If teachers place such importance on themselves as role models as this study revealed, then it is essential that they undertake a process of reflection, analysis, discussion and collaboration in order to link role modelling and the values dimension of teaching more effectively.

As the findings of the project appear to indicate, teachers need to be provided with the opportunity to explore and develop the whole concept of values in its widest definition. Just as teachers need to have the opportunity to address and challenge their own and others' attitudes and values, so do the students in their classrooms. When teachers are considering these questions they will need to decide whether they involve students in making decisions relating to values education. They will also need to decide the level of student involvement and how processes to encourage this input into the curriculum may be implemented in the classroom. The ease with which these negotiation processes may be developed and implemented will depend on a number of factors such as the age or stage of development of students and the previous experience of the teacher and the students in collaborative decision making. Experiences such as previous involvement in decision making potentially empower students as they perceive their ability to play a valuable role in discussing, critically analysing and negotiating the diversity of attitudes, moral codes and social development within school settings.

ACTIVITIES FOR STUDENTS IN SCHOOLS AND TERTIARY SETTINGS

Based on responses to questions from the research study, the following section outlines a number of practical activities that student teachers, teachers and teacher educators may implement within a values education curriculum. Concepts that the respondents stressed were necessary components in values education included the need for equality, tolerance, self-esteem and respect for others, responsibility, fairness, honesty and empathy. The development of these values has formed the basis for the teaching activities outlined in the following parts of this chapter. Most of the activities can be adapted to suit a range of age groups and educational settings.

Below are two detailed examples of activities, one which focuses on the idea of citizenship and community life at a local and global level and the other which is on values clarification for young students.

Activity 3 'I'm from Calathumpia', a poem by Lorraine Ling (1996) Age group: 8 to 14

Purpose To develop students' understandings of culture and diversity at a local and global level and to emphasize the dialectical relationship which exists between the local and the global contexts.

To encourage students to consider their simultaneous role as the members of the local and the global community.

Through analysis and discussion students will be encouraged to reflect on values in relation to social, political and economic issues at the local and global level.

171

Theoretical context   This activity reflects elements of the theories of Socrates and Raths in relation to values clarification approaches, Nietzsche in relation to discussions about power and authority, Durkheim in relation to group interaction and group decision making and Dewey in relation to integrated approaches to learning.

Teacher's role   Facilitator, observer, knowledge provider, challenger of students' ideas, decision maker.

Procedure   This poem may be used as a basis for a single lesson but it may be more appropriate for teachers to develop a series of integrated lessons and activities which would allow students to explore local and global issues and interrelationships. Literature in any form may be used as a stimulus for this activity.

The teacher may introduce this poem in a number of different ways; for example: discussing photos of children from different countries, looking at a globe of the world, showing flags of different countries, discussing cultural traditions with students, examining sporting events at a global level, such as the Olympic Games, viewing a video of a current political event at an international level or using the Internet to focus on a particular global economic issue. Students may then be encouraged to compose poems or songs, or to express their ideas in other ways about diversity and difference and the concept of global community.

(Teacher reads the poem)

'I'm from Calathumpia'

I'm from Calathumpia
So I'm a Calathumpian
We have our own ideas
And we have our own tradition
We live in a community
We share some common ways
We have some special notions
About how to spend our days
This gives us an identity
Helps to make us what we are
And make us very proud
Whether travelling near or far
But as well as Calathumpians
We are citizens of the world
Regardless of the flag
Our country has unfurled
We communicate in an instant
With people far away

172

With different groups and cultures
We mix everyday
We all have different backgrounds
Different ways and different needs
But we share a common bond
Regardless of our creeds
We're local and we're global
So let us get together
Regardless of the weather
And decide what we can do
To make the twenty-first century
The time for me and you
The challenge is exciting
And we will see it through.

Action for teachers　　Teacher leads discussion of the concepts and ideas arising out of the poem, highlighting such aspects as:

What is it about Calathumpia that is similar to or different from our country?

What does the idea 'citizens of the world' mean?

What are some of the common bonds that bind groups of people together at a local and at a global level?

What do you think we need to do at a local and global level to prepare ourselves for the twenty-first century?

What do you think is meant by the idea that the twenty-first century is 'a time for me and you'?

Students are asked to imagine a community like Calathumpia and consider what life would be like in such a community. The teacher then organizes students into small groups with each group focusing on different elements of life in Calathumpia. These groups may focus on such areas as: designing a flag which includes local and global elements; drawing a plan of the Calathumpian community, highlighting geographical and environmental concerns; outlining roles and responsibilities of community members in home and work environments; writing rules for the community with consideration of who has power and authority and why.

Conclusion　　Groups to report back to the whole class through discussion, role-plays, creating a collage of life in Calathumpia or through drama. The whole classroom may be transformed into a mythical country called Calathumpia for a few weeks in which time the various elements of life are explored by all groups.

Resources Poem, sets of photographs, world globe, flags of various countries, videos. Questions/instructions for activities.

Evaluation of learning Students' involvement in class discussion, observation of students' behaviour and consideration and examination of students' work.

Development and extensions Students may develop and extend key ideas and concepts which have emerged from the activities. Issues and concepts for further development and discussion may include: the use of language for communication and ways of communicating with different cultural and ethnic groups; an exploration of local and global environmental, economic and political issues; traditional rites and ceremonies; and the development of responsible citizens of the world. These aspects may be integrated into a range of curriculum areas. Technology, such as the Internet, may also be used to encourage students to communicate with other students at a global level, regarding issues which have arisen from the activities. Students could attempt to compose their own poems about a mythical community or country.

Core processes and skills Making predictions, hypothesizing, observing, collating and analysing information, generalizing and synthesizing information.

Activity 4 Being friends
Age group: 5 to 10

Purpose To promote respect for others and share differing attitudes and values. To enhance awareness of difference and facilitate acceptance of diversity.

Theoretical context This activity reflects elements of the theories of Socrates and Raths in relation to values clarification approaches, Durkheim in relation to group interaction and group decision making and Dewey in relation to integrated approaches to learning.

Teacher's role Referee, challenger, persuader, observer, knowledge provider, decision maker, allocator of roles.

Procedure The teacher collects and presents a series of pictures, reads a story or a poem or shows a video relating to different forms of friendship including people of different gender, age group, class and cultures. The class discusses the ideas which arise from this introductory activity.

Questions for discussion

Why do we have friends?
How do we make and keep friends?

Who would you choose as a friend?
Why do people choose you as a friend?
Would you tell your friend's secrets to other people?
Do you always do what your friends want you to do?
Do you share things with your friend?
What activities do you like doing with your friends?

Students are provided with sheets of paper and draw themselves in the centre. They then talk to their friends and decide on something they like doing together as friends, and make a collage of the friendship and activity patterns in the classroom by gluing the pictures of themselves and their friends on a large sheet of paper. They then draw in any other components needed to describe their friendship activity. At this stage other materials such as magazine pictures, wool, raffia and textiles may be added to the collage. These large sheets of paper are compiled into a class collage which is displayed in the classroom. Teachers will need to be sensitive in ensuring that all students are positively involved in this activity.

The teacher is required to think about teacher responses to possible answers and the form of teacher intervention. Student reflections about friendship should be encouraged through open questioning that assists students to clarify their friendship patterns. If prejudicial statements are made a teacher should not ignore them but rather should give students time to react and to observe how they cope with uncomfortable situations before challenging, inviting or suggesting alternative views.

Action for teachers

1 Explain to students that they will be making a collage which illustrates their friendships and that they will need to make some choices.
2 Encourage students to discuss the questions above.
3 Encourage and support students in creating their drawings, making friendship groups and making the class collage.
4 Discussion of choices and justification for these should then follow.

Resources Sets of photographs, poem, story-book or video collection. Materials for the collage such as old magazines, textiles, glue, scissors and large sheets of paper.

Evaluation of learning Students' involvement in class discussion, observation of students' behaviour and presentation of collage.

Development and extensions Links to other curriculum areas such as literature, songs, art and role-plays about friendships and activities with friends.

Core processes and skills Analysis, testing judgements and synthesis of information.

GENERAL ACTIVITIES FOR ADDRESSING VALUES EDUCATION

Outlined below are a range of activities which are organized around some of the categories which emerged from the research data. These activities may be developed in more detail for various settings.

Discussion

Many teachers in the study favoured the use of discussion as an approach to values education. Discussion may take many forms. These include teacher-led or student-led discussions, question-and-answer sessions, debates, justification of a personal point of view or a combination of written and oral language work. As open discussion is a priority teachers need to establish a classroom environment where trust and openness are encouraged and supported by teachers and students in a creative and imaginative way. Verbal discussion and communication, active listening, critical analysis and focused arguments are skills that need to be developed in the classroom setting.

In using dialogue to explore a values education concept or attitude a teacher may encourage discussion by:

- being open to ideas and the diversity of student approaches;
- setting ground rules for fairness, active listening and respectful dialogue;
- using open-ended questions to encourage a range of thinking approaches such as De Bono's thinking hats activities (De Bono, 1992);
- asking students to justify ideas, opinions and actions, for example, 'Why do you believe this?' or 'Why did you do that?'
- comparing actions and beliefs provided by the students and asking students in small groups to justify or explain their beliefs and actions to each other;
- listening to and reinterpreting students' responses;
- encouraging students to contribute in a fair and equitable manner;
- guarding against domination by a particular individual or group.

The following activities provide examples of ways teachers may attempt to achieve the kinds of learning context where the desirable attributes listed above are present.

Activity 5 Futures: probable, possible and preferable
Age: 12 to tertiary

Purpose To encourage students to reflect on probable, possible and preferable scenarios for the future.

Theoretical context This activity reflects elements of the theories of Socrates and Raths in relation to values clarification approaches, Nietzsche in relation to discussions about power and authority, Kant in relation to global issues, Durkheim in relation to group interaction and group decision making and Dewey in relation to integrated approaches to learning.

Resources Flash cards with statements about the future written on them.

Procedure Prior to the activity the teacher should provide the students with a series of statements relating to the future. The teacher should define what is meant by the term 'the future' and provide a definite year on which students should focus for this activity. For example, the teacher may focus on the year 2025. The statements provided by the teacher might include:

All men and women will receive the same wage for the same amount of
    work.
Children will receive all their schooling while working with a computer at
    home.
People will not need to eat food to stay alive but will only need to take three
    nutrition tablets a day.
Robots will do all the housework.
There will be no newspapers or magazines.
Money will be obsolete.
The average life expectancy will be 120 years.
All private vehicles will be banned and everyone will use public transport.
Personal use of guns will be banned in all countries.
The working week will be universally limited to twenty hours per week.

In pairs, students consider the statements and write whether they think they are possible or probable.

As a second activity students choose the five statements which they think would be most preferable for themselves, and another five which they think would be most preferable for society. In small groups students would discuss which factors would support and which would constrain these developments.

Conclusion In pairs, students develop five statements which relate to how they would ideally envisage their world for the year 2025. A whole-class discussion of the compiled list of statements is conducted by the teacher.

Evaluation of learning Students' involvement in class discussion, observation of students' behaviour and consideration and examination of students' preferences about the future.

Development and extensions Students could be encouraged to develop and extend key ideas and concepts which have emerged from the activities by focusing on a particular year in the future such as the year 2050. These activities might include designing appliances, developing ideas for means

177

of transport, housing and clothing, and planning an ideal city complex. Students could also conduct a research project where they interview people from different generations about their views of the future. Technology, such as the Internet, might be used to encourage students to communicate with others.

Activity 6 Discipline in schools: a value position
Age: 12 to tertiary level

Purpose To allow students to justify their position in relation to discipline in schools. To encourage students to reflect on their level of support for a range of disciplinary approaches.

Theoretical context This activity reflects elements of the theories of Socrates and Raths in relation to values clarification, Nietzsche in relation to discussions about power and authority, Mill in relation to the study of democratic principles and Durkheim in relation to group interaction and group decision making.

Resources Teachers develop a series of statements and questions relating to issues of discipline in schools. Statements are presented on worksheet 1 and questions are presented on worksheet 2. Examples of statements include:

Teachers should reward students for acceptable behaviour and punish students for unacceptable behaviour.
Teachers should make up all the rules for the classroom because they know what is best for the students.
Teachers should remain calm when informing students that their behaviour is unacceptable.
Male and female students should both be disciplined in the same way by the teacher.
Students who act unacceptably should not be intentionally embarrassed.
Corporal punishment is an acceptable consequence of misbehaviour.

Examples of questions on worksheet 2 include:

Does one human being have a right to punish another human being?
When, if ever, is it legitimate for one human to punish another human being?
Who should decide what is acceptable behaviour?
What criteria should be considered when deciding what is acceptable behaviour?
Are rules necessary – why or why not?
What rights and responsibilities do teachers have?
What rights and responsibilities do students have?
What rights and responsibilities do parents have?

Procedure   Students work as a whole group and consider the statements separately. The teacher designates one end of the room as an 'agree' area and the other end as a 'disagree' area. They should, however, note that a values continuum should not be regarded as a polarization of concepts or elements but an interactive relationship between zones of meaning. Students consider each statement and move to a position on the continuum ranging from strongly agree to strongly disagree. The teacher asks some of the students to justify why they have taken up their particular positions. Teachers should now discuss with students the complexity of relationships which have resulted in their decision to take a particular stance in relation to the statements provided. After listening to the justifications provided by others, students are invited to readjust their position on the continuum in light of the arguments heard. Students may be asked, if willing, to explain the change in their position based upon the arguments provided. This shows how our values are influenced by arguments and justifications which are provided and shows the dynamic and continually evolutionary nature of personal and social values.

Students are divided into small groups and discuss one or more of the questions on the second worksheet and consider the various alternative possible responses.

Conclusion   The final stage of the session may be in the form of small-group feedback to the whole class where small-group responses are reported and discussed. Each group writes a final response to the question on the board which summarizes their negotiated position.

Evaluation of learning   Students' involvement in class discussion, observation of changes in students' behaviour and consideration and examination of students' work.

Development and extensions   Issues and concepts for further development and discussion might include: role-playing classroom incidents with students from other classes and different age groups, viewing videos about school life followed by a focused discussion of the disciplinary elements in the video, and reading related novels.

APPROACHES THROUGH LITERATURE

Literature has the potential to allow students to examine a wide range of experiences and values and to develop insights and sensitivity to complex and challenging situations. Dibella and Hamston (1989) suggest that:

> Literature enables children to identify and clarify their values; reflect upon their own experiences; compare situations in stories with their own experiences; become involved in new experiences via the literary

179

medium; come to terms with sensitive issues by identifying with and relating to the characters in a story.

(Dibella and Hamston, 1989: 2)

The following activities are literature-based and are designed to address the objectives listed above.

Activity 7 A 'Who am I?' poem
Age: 7 to tertiary

Purpose To develop students' self concept and to allow them to examine personal values. To examine aspects of themselves that they value.

Theoretical context This activity reflects elements of the theories of Socrates and Raths in relation to values clarification.

Resources Teacher provides an example of a poem which he or she has written of a 'Who am I?' type. The poem is written according to the acronym of a person's given name.

Procedure Discussion relating to qualities we value in other people and in ourselves. Teacher provides a personal example of a 'Who am I?' poem on the board, stressing the need to include the personal qualities students value about themselves in the poem.

The poem could be written in the following way.

MARK

M – mindful of others
A – able and articulate
R – ready and reliable
K – kind and courteous to his sisters and brothers

Other literary forms, such as free prose, could be an optional and less structured and prescriptive way of writing about yourself and others, for example, 'I am an Israeli, I am a female, I am a wife, I am a mother, I am a teacher, I am a sister, I am an aunt, I am a good cook, I am a student and I am a friend.' This kind of approach would highlight the variety of concurrent and interrelated roles which people adopt in their lives and in their relationships with other people and the environment.

Conclusion A number of students read out their poems to the class and all students' work, with their permission, is included in a classroom display.

Evaluation of learning Will be based on students' involvement in class discussion, observation of students' behaviour, and consideration and examination of students' work.

Extension activities Some extension activities may include compiling a class book of poems, reading other poems and stories, interviewing students and writing up interviews in a class paper, and art and craft activities. Music may also be another aesthetic form employed as a stimulus in this activity.

Activity 8 Quotable quotes
Age: 8 to tertiary

Purpose To develop in students an understanding of common quotations and their relation to personal and social values. These quotations will be culture-specific and thus will be selected to suit the cultural context in which they are used.

Theoretical context This activity reflects elements of the theories of Socrates and Raths in relation to values clarification and Raths and Durkheim in relation to negotiation of meaning.

Resources The teacher provides a list of appropriate quotes taken from a range of cultural contexts, for example, 'Honesty is the best policy.' 'Do unto others as you would have them do unto you.'

Procedure Prior to the lesson the teacher asks each student to speak to family members and asks them for a quotation that is based on a values position from a particular cultural context. Students write their quotation on individual sheets of paper and hand these to the teacher. The teacher divides the board into sections and selects a number of quotations for small-group discussion and analysis. S/he organizes students into small discussion groups and provides them with quotations to be discussed. Students discuss the quotation and select specific values included in the quotations. As a group they list these values on a sheet of paper which is collected by the teacher. The teacher lists all the values on the board.

Conclusion A whole-class discussion is conducted where such issues as universal values and changing values are discussed. Particular emphasis could be placed on discussion of values pertinent to society today both locally and globally.

Evaluation of learning Will be based upon students' collections of quotable quotes, involvement in class discussion, observation of students' behaviour, and consideration and examination of work samples.

Development and extensions In a multicultural classroom students would provide sayings, proverbs, metaphors or colloquialisms from their own cultures in their own languages to share with other students. Students could contact students in other states or countries by either writing to them or using the Internet to collect quotations from different cultural groups. Students write quotations one to a large page, illustrate with a comment on the interpretation of the meaning and bind it as a large class book. Students may use puppets to act out the interpretations and meanings of the quotations.

This lesson could be developed to use a range of genres and literary devices, such as proverbs, homilies, sayings, colloquialisms, metaphors or similes. This activity could integrate with language and a study of these various styles and forms of expressions. Their place in a cultural context and their specificity in terms of their cultural connotations and meaning could also be an important discussion point.

SIMULATION GAMES

'Simulation games are powerful tools for transferring values, attitudes and beliefs' (Thiagarajan, 1993: 65). As simulation imitates reality, students are given a chance to anticipate their value positions and to consider alternative approaches to constructed situations. Students should be encouraged to feel that they are able to exercise some control over the decisions they are making and to consider the effect their decisions could have on the situation and on other people.

'In simulation, reality is reduced to manageable proportions' (Baker and Marshall, 1986: 5). Students are more likely to be able to consider a range of alternative positions and solutions while working through a simulation activity. There are many approaches to simulation that may be introduced into a classroom setting. These include simulating situations through culturally appropriate board games and computer simulations. One form of computer simulation game encourages the students to become more aware of their own strengths and weaknesses in relation to personal relationships. An example is where adolescents are presented with a range of situations such as meeting the parents of their boyfriend or girlfriend for the first time and are asked to respond in various ways. Other examples could simulate group dynamics in relation to conflict and co-operation. Teachers would need to consider computer simulation games within their own cultural and educational settings.

When students participate in simulation board games they are involved in assessing and discussing real-life situations through a game format. Rules which apply to games, such as number of players and a framework for playing the game, also apply to real-life situations.

Simulation board games allow players to reflect on their own positions as well as consider a range of views and feelings that others may have about a particular situation. Players may analyse the key elements of a simulated situation and may also assess possible consequences for decisions and actions taken. Board games encourage players to pre-plan strategies for action and to assess the likelihood of pre-planned action achieving a desirable goal. This skill is one which students may then transfer into real-life settings.

Activity 9 Creating a simulation game
Age: 12 to tertiary

Purpose   To develop in students the ability to construct, create and play a simulation game that highlights social values.

Theoretical context   This activity reflects elements of the theories of Socrates and Raths in relation to values clarification, Ayer and Stevenson in relation to expounding a position or opinion, Kant in relation to human rights and environmental issues and Durkheim in relation to group decision making.

Resources   The teacher provides materials for construction of the game, such as paper, wood glue, tools, or, if students are constructing the game on the computer, a disk as well as reference material.

Procedure   Students are asked to consider what is meant by the term values and reflect on notions of personal and universal values. Teachers then discuss what is meant by a simulation board game or computer simulation game and discuss elements that need to be considered when developing or constructing one. In small groups, students are required to develop a simulation game focusing on particular social or environmental issues to be played by two or more players. The game should include details such as purpose of the game, age group for which the game is intended, number of players and the rules for the game. The teacher should discuss the need for clarity of presentation and appropriateness for a particular age group. Students are encouraged to develop a game that is both creative and challenging. Students work in small groups for a specified time to develop and try out their games. Time is set aside for groups to present their games to the whole class and for each group to play each of the games.

Conclusion   The final session allows groups to fill in an evaluation form under headings such as purpose of the game, appropriateness for age and size of the group, clarity of the rules, level of enjoyment and satisfaction of the players in relation to the purpose of the game.

The final session of the activity allows for this feedback to be provided to each of the small groups involved in creating the simulation games. Each of the groups considers the feedback provided and then decides whether any modification needs to be made to their game.

The games should be stored or displayed in a particular place in the school, such as the library or computer room, so that they can be used permanently as a form of extension activity by teachers and other students.

Evaluation of learning Systematic observation of students' involvement in simulation activity and group work.

Development and extensions Students may develop and extend key ideas and concepts which have emerged from the activities. Issues and concepts for further development and discussion may include: video-recording the simulation activity and showing it to students in other classes; developing a class or school newspaper which examines a range of issues using simulation activity focus as the basis for the first edition; and conducting a debate about the issue on which the simulation activity was based.

Teacher education activity

This activity may be used at a tertiary level where student teachers develop games linked to a particular curriculum area such as social science or environmental studies. The teacher education students would work through the processes described above with a number of additions. When developing the game, they would need to link the purpose of the game to current curriculum policy documents and clearly state how their game focuses on a particular element or elements outlined in these documents. The student teachers would also need to indicate the teaching and learning processes involved in playing the game in a classroom and how they would assess and evaluate the effectiveness of the game in the classroom setting. They would also need to show clear links between the purpose of the game and to emphasize how the game relates to values at a local and global level.

ROLE-PLAYS AND DRAMAS

By role-play we mean involving students in acting out situations which are not scripted. Students are provided with simple guidelines and a framework of a situation which they need to interpret using both verbal and non-verbal communication. Students individually are able to interpret a particular role within the given parameters and are therefore able to act out personal feelings and emotions. Role-plays also allow students to place themselves in the position of others and if the role-play is handled sensitively this can increase students' empathy and tolerance. Situations and issues may then be viewed and interpreted through another person's perspective.

In organizing a role-play a teacher will address a number of stages. Dibella and Hamston (1989) suggest that there are eight stages in this process of role-play organization, which are adapted below.

1 Warming up – teacher discusses the scenario and roles with the students and allows consideration of the context and characteristics of the roles.
2 Selecting participants – teachers should sensitively allocate students to particular roles and encourage their full participation in the activity.
3 Preparing the audience – prior to the role-play the teacher should discuss with the students the context of the role-play and provide a structure for observation and follow-up discussion.
4 Enactment – teachers should ensure that the role-play is brief and succinct. Students act out the role-play in front of the audience.
5 Discussion – the students in the audience discuss aspects of the role-play and express their ideas and reactions to the situation.
6 Re-enactment – the same or other students re-enact the scenario, after which discussions of alternative strategies may be explored.
7 Further discussion – all elements of the role-play are discussed by role-play participants and the audience. Value positions and alternative approaches, behaviours and outcomes are examined and clarified.
8 Debriefing – students are debriefed and the teacher makes it clear that the particular roles are no longer associated with individual students.

Activity 10 Role-playing a meeting about pollution in the local community
Age: 8 to tertiary

Purpose Describe a situation which presents different viewpoints on an issue and have the students assume the roles of the individuals involved.

Theoretical context This activity reflects elements of the theories of Socrates and Raths in relation to values clarification, Nietzsche in relation to power and authority, Ayer and Stevenson in relation to expounding a position or opinion, Kant in relation to environmental issues and Durkheim in relation to group decision making.

Resources The teacher provides a map of the local area.

Procedure The class looks at a map of the local area and decides on a current or potential problem relating to pollution such as air, noise or water pollution. The class then discusses which groups or individuals may be involved in causing the pollution or in solving the pollution problem. Students are then divided into groups each representing key players in the pollution role-play. Students are asked to elect a representative who will, in the next lesson, be attending a mock community meeting where they will be asked to state their case. Each group will need to consider and document its position. Time is allowed for each group to work on its arguments and values positions during the first lesson. In the second session a student is selected to act as a chairperson and the representatives of each group state their case to the whole community meeting. The chairperson summarizes possible action to be taken in relation to the pollution problem with the rest of the class taking a majority vote on suggestions for future action.

Conclusion Students individually write a report which outlines the pollution problem which formed the basis of the role-play, the process of decision making which occurred during the meeting, their personal level of support for the decision made at the meeting and whether this has changed from their initial position as outlined in the beginning of the role-play.

Evaluation of learning Students' involvement in class role-play and follow-up discussion, observation of students' interaction during simulation and consideration of knowledge of decision-making process.

Development and extensions Extension activities include: class excursion to local council meeting, examination of historical council policy documents and interviewing local members of government. Other topics that might be discussed at a mock council meeting might include recycling of house and factory refuse, local traffic issues and transport alternatives and issues related to noise, air and water pollution.

Activity 11 Advertising in the media: a role-play
Age: 10 to tertiary level

Purpose To develop skills in writing a scenario or critical incident with an emphasis on the skills which result in the creation of a newly conceived advertisement. To develop negotiation skills in students. To analyse aspects of the media with a focus on power and authority and the role of pressure groups.

Theoretical context This activity reflects elements of the theories of Aristotle in relation to role-plays of situations with opposing views, Socrates and Raths in relation to values clarification, Nietzsche in relation to power and authority, Ayer and Stevenson in relation to expounding a position or opinion, Kant in relation to civil rights issues and Durkheim in relation to group decision making.

Resources The teacher chooses an advertisement for a particular product that is advertised in a provocative way. The teacher also provides a space in the classroom for dramatic activities.

Procedure The teacher shows the students the advertisement, which focuses on a particular issue such as smoking, drinking of alcohol or the way women's and men's bodies are portrayed to advertise products provocatively. Students in small groups then develop a scenario or critical incident, in which an advertising executive from the company that developed the advertisement is approached by a small group of student activists who disagree with the approach taken by the advertising company to one of these issues. One student takes on the role of the advertising executive and the other members of the group take on a variety of roles. The students then act out the roles in front of the class and discuss each of the incidents in relation to various values positions.

During the follow-up lesson each group, which includes the members of the advertising agency and the activists, creates an advertisement for their particular product which takes into account the negotiated position of both groups. The completed advertisements are then displayed in the classroom.

Conclusion A whole-class discussion is conducted about the range of value positions held by various group members and the process of negotiation leading up to the final advertisement.

Evaluation of learning Students' involvement in role-play and analysis of it, observation of students' interactive behaviour, and consideration and examination of the final negotiated advertisement.

Development and extensions Extension activities may include: a visit to an advertising company, having a visiting speaker from an advertising office, or television or radio station, making an annotated collection of effective advertisements and using the World Wide Web to see how different groups and associations advertise their products.

CONFLICT MANAGEMENT

Tensions inevitably arise when people come together in interactive situations. The way they adjust to conflict will vary but usually a particular person or group has more power over the other and tends to dominate the other. Eventually a consensus may be reached but this may involve a long and, at times, difficult process, particularly for the less powerful person or group. The conflict management may involve resolution, negotiation, compromise, consensus or arbitration. Each of these conflict management processes requires the employment of complex skills and involves students in making value judgements which are then translated into action. Conflict should be viewed as part of a productive process and involvement in conflict management scenarios can be an effective learning experience. Situational conflicts which arise within the school or classroom setting can provide students with powerful possibilities for handling conflicting values and complex emotional reactions with sensitivity. Conflict should be regarded as potentially positive and transformative rather than as negative and as a problem to be solved. Hence, here the term conflict management is deliberately used instead of conflict resolution. The latter implies that conflict can be fixed while the former implies that it can be used positively and is inevitable in social life.

Activity 12 Conflict management in educational settings
Age: 5 to tertiary

Purpose   To allow students to justify publicly their position in relation to violence in schools. To examine their ability and willingness to make public affirmations about positive approaches to conflict management.

Theoretical context   This activity reflects elements of the theories of Aristotle in relation to role-plays of situations with opposing views, Socrates and Raths in relation to values clarification, Nietzsche in relation to power and authority, Ayer and Stevenson in relation to expounding a position or opinion, Kant in relation to human rights issues and Mill in relation to the development of democratic principles.

Resources   Teachers to develop a series of critical incident cards arising out of incidents from their own school and local community. These cards may include pictures or written incidents relating to violence. Incidents may include examples of power used by groups of children to intimidate others so that they are afraid to play in certain areas of the school yard (examples should include both same-sex groups of students in conflict and girls and boys involved in power struggles). An example of a critical incident card might include the following scenario. One student takes another student's calculator without permission and starts using it. A fight ensues with the student who took the calculator being hurt. The teacher punishes both students equally for misbehaving.

Procedure   Students work in pairs or in small groups. Each student takes a card and is allowed three minutes to take up a position about the incident described on the card and to justify their position to their peers. The other student or students are allowed two minutes to question them and ask for clarification of the speaker's position. Issues for further discussion may include peer group pressure, common causes of conflict, violence and bullying.

Conclusion   Teacher initiates group discussion on the issues raised and the processes involved. The group might then discuss how aspects of conflict management are related to what is currently occurring in their school and classroom. Suggestions can be made as to any changes that may be agreed upon to enhance a supportive classroom environment.

Evaluation of learning Systematic observation of students' behaviour in the classroom and in the playground when assessing students in schools and consideration of anecdotal records of conflict management documented in journals.

Extension activities Some extension activities could include: a poem, a story, newspaper report, interview, radio play (recorded on audio tape), or art and drama activities such as charades, related to conflict management. With older students a video could be produced.

Activity 13 Inter-generational communication and conflict management
Age: 5 to tertiary

Purpose To allow students to explore verbal and non-verbal communication and conflict across a range of age groups and power positions.

Theoretical context This activity reflects elements of the theories of Aristotle in relation to role-plays of situations with opposing views, Socrates and Raths in relation to values clarification, Nietzsche in relation to power and authority, Ayer and Stevenson in relation to expounding a position or opinion and L. Kohlberg in relation to moral dilemmas.

Procedure Students work in groups of three to develop and act out a situation of an inter-generational moral dilemma which involves a power conflict. For example, a group may comprise grandparent, parent and child; principal, teacher and student; dean, lecturer and student teacher; head of a corporation, middle manager and employee. Students discuss and write an outline of a problem to be explored and are then given a set amount of time to role-play the scenario. Students to take on at least two out of the three roles within each role-play activity. It is preferable for the students to develop the moral dilemma situations to be used in the role-play, but in the case of younger students the teacher may create scenarios and present them to the students.

Conclusion Small-group post-role-play discussion would focus on how students felt about the roles they played, the different feelings and reactions of the other participants and the reasons for the way in which participants took up the various positions. Negative and positive strategies for managing conflict could be discussed with an emphasis on positive approaches to conflict management with supportive learning environments being encouraged.

189

Evaluation of learning Students' involvement in class discussion, observation of students' active involvement in the role-plays and the nature and quality of the scenarios.

Development and extensions Students may develop and extend key ideas and concepts which have emerged from the activities. Issues and concepts for further development and discussion might include: encouraging students to write their own moral dilemma stories arising from personal experience and share them with others, examination of fables and classical tales to explore moral dilemmas, and interviewing people from other generations about the moral dilemmas that they faced as students and the methods used for their resolution.

VALUES CLARIFICATION

A value judgement is a decision which involves an assessment of value, of worth or choice-worthiness. The range of value judgements reflects the range of human experiences and the choice it demands of us (Garforth, 1985: 57).

Students are involved on a daily basis in situations which involve making decisions, solving problems and taking action, all of which incorporate value judgements about various situations. Students are provided with potentially bewildering and complex choices and therefore need to develop strategies and approaches to assist them in making appropriate choices in each situation. Teachers and students are required to be aware of the distinction between a value judgement and a value commitment. Students may make a value judgement but have no intention of acting on that commitment. For example, a student may make a value judgement about factors which are affecting river pollution in their local community without making any commitment to cleaning up the pollution in the future.

The values clarification approach is systematic and widely applicable and is based on an approach formulated by Raths *et al.* (1966), who built on the work of Dewey (1933). Raths' concern is with the process of valuing the ways in which people come to hold certain values and how they establish certain behaviour patterns. He suggests that the process involved in reflecting on values may be divided into three areas which include seven sub-processes.

Choosing

A value is freely chosen.
A value is chosen from alternatives.
A value is chosen after careful thought of the consequences of each alternative.

Prizing

> A value is cherished. One is happy with the choice.
> A value is prized enough to be publicly affirmed.

Acting

> A value is acted upon, not just talked about.
> A value is acted upon repeatedly. It is a pattern of life.
> (Model developed by Raths, Harmin and Simons, 1966)

An activity which may be used for values clarification is one where students are asked to consider the strength of feeling they have about specific issues and to discuss it under the headings described above.

The values clarification process is not aimed at providing students with a particular set of values but allows students to use the seven processes outlined under the headings Choosing, Prizing and Acting. The processes involve both a reflective and an action component. In making their own choices and considering the consequences students potentially become more critical in their approach to understanding their own values. The need to clarify values can be linked with the search for knowledge. Values clarification may be integrated with the planned curriculum or used separately in response to particular incidents or issues.

Activity 14 What can we do to clean up the environment?
Age: 8 to tertiary

Purpose   To enable students to reflect on their personal values in relation to action that they may take to clean up the environment both locally and globally.

Theoretical context   This activity reflects elements of the theories of Socrates and Raths in relation to values clarification, Kant in relation to environmental and global issues and Mill in relation to the consequences of actions.

Resources   Art materials.

Procedure   Teacher presents students with a statement related to the environment such as:

- all drinks should be sold in returnable containers;
- supermarkets should not provide free non-biodegradable plastic bags to their customers;
- all local communities should provide recycling bins for all household refuse including glass, plastic and paper separately.

Teacher demonstrates on the board a graphic representation of an environmental issue or problem and the short- and long-term consequences of a particular form of action. In the centre the teacher writes the key statement, such as 'Supermarkets should not provide free non-biodegradable plastic bags to their customers.' Teacher and students discuss short- and long-term consequences of a particular issue or action and write consequences around the key statement with short-term consequences closest to the key statement. See example below.

Birds and fish would not be caught up in non-biodegradable plastic bags (long-term consequence).

There would be less plastic bag pollution in the waterways (long-term consequence).

Plastic bags would not be thrown away after use (short-term consequence).

Supermarkets should not provide free non-biodegradable plastic bags to their customers (key statement).

Supermarkets would save money on plastic bags (short-term consequence).

Savings would be passed on to supermarket customers (long-term consequence).

Conclusion Students decide on a particular issue or topic and graphically illustrate short- and long-term consequences on a poster. Students then discuss and justify their position in pairs and display their posters in the classroom.

Evaluation of learning Students' involvement in class discussion and understanding of short- and long-term consequences, observation and examination of students' representation of an environmental issue.

Extension activity Extension activities to further develop values perspectives could include: a class or school survey on a particular environmental issue, or an interview with other members of the community about their environmental concerns or designing a questionnaire relating to environmental concerns. Questionnaires could be administered to a range of active environmental groups so that the students gain some appreciation of the groups which are active in the local area.

Students may compare their ideas with students in other classrooms or schools both locally or globally. If feasible, students communicate their activities with overseas students and environmental activists at the global level using the World Wide Web or other available technology.

Activity 15 World peace
Age: 8 to tertiary

Purpose   To encourage students to reflect on their values and attitudes to world peace. To allow students to devise a concept map of their feelings and potential action that may be taken in relation to an issue.

Theoretical context   This activity reflects elements of the theories of Socrates and Raths in relation to values clarification, Kant in relation to global issues and Mill in relation to the consequences of actions, Durkheim in relation to group processes and Dewey in relation to integrated approaches.

Resources   Teacher provides an example of how a concept map may be developed.

Procedure   Students individually construct a concept map on a sheet of paper under the headings listed below. Students write a statement or draw a picture under each heading. For example: 'I believe that if everyone respected each other we would have world peace.'

I believe	I feel	I want
	world peace	
I hope	I think	I say

(Adapted from Lemin *et al.*, 1994)

Conclusion   Teacher places a large sheet of paper on the classroom wall with the same headings as described above. Student responses to each of the headings are summarized and added to the chart. Whole-class discussion is conducted with an emphasis on local and global perspectives about world peace.

Evaluation of learning   Students' involvement in class discussion, observation of students' individual and group behaviour, and consideration and examination of students' concept maps.

Extension activity   Extension activities include: student discussion about recent media reports on local and international events, interviews with peace activists, and, for older students, viewing films that are both pro- and anti-war. Another activity suitable for students and teacher education students would be to compare their views in relation to world peace with students in classrooms locally and in other national settings through the Internet and through more traditional means such as letter writing.

CONCLUSION

In this chapter an attempt has been made to show the links which exist between the theoretical foundations of values education and the practical implementation of the values dimension of curriculum in schools. The practical activities which are provided here are illustrations of the way educators can devise practical classroom activities which are grounded in legitimate and clearly articulated theoretical or meta-theoretical perspectives regarding values.

It is important, however, that educators devise and create activities which are relevant, appropriate, specific and meaningful in particular contexts. Values education is not susceptible to prescriptions or recipes for activities and it is unwise for educators to transpose uncritically activities which are appropriate in one setting to another setting. The crucial point to be made here is that without a firm understanding of the theoretical underpinnings of values education, and without an appropriate discourse with which to discuss values, educators are handicapped in their efforts to implement consistently and effectively the values education dimension of the curriculum. If practical activities are implemented without a firm and explicit rationale for their inclusion in the curriculum of values education, the resultant programme is likely to be *ad hoc*, eclectic, untheorized and ineffective.

REFERENCES

Baker, P. and Marshall, M. (1986) *Simulation Game 1* (Melbourne, The Joint Board of Christian Education).

Barr, I. and McGhie, M. (1995) 'Values in Education: The Importance of the Preposition', *Curriculum*, 16 (2): 102–8.

De Bono, E. (1992) *Six Thinking Hats for Schools. Resources Books 1–4* (Cheltenham, Hawker Brownlow).

Dewey, J. (1933) *How We Think* (Boston, D.C. Heath & Company).

Dibella, M. and Hamston, J. (1989) *Undercover: Exploring Values Education Using Children's Literature* (Melbourne, Collins Dove).

Garforth, F. W. (1985) *Aims, Values and Education* (North Yorkshire, Christygate Press).

Lemin, M., Potts, H. and Welsford, P. (1994) *Values Strategies for Classroom Teachers* (Hawthorn, Australian Council for Education Research).

Ling, L. (1996) 'I'm from Calathumpia' (unpublished poem).

Raths, L., Harmin, M. and Simons, S.B. (1966) *Values and Teaching: Working with Values in the Classroom* (Columbus, Ohio, Charles E. Merrill).

Thiagarajan, S. (1993) 'Metaphors for Transfer of Values and Attitudes: Six Fast and Powerful Simulation Games', in F. Percival, S. Lodge and D. Saunders (eds) *The Simulation and Gaming Yearbook 1993* (Kogan Page, London).

Values Questionnaire Responses (1994) International Values in Education Research Study.

Part IV

REFLECTIONS

9

VALUES EDUCATION IN THE UNITED STATES OF AMERICA

David Purpel

THE ORGANIZATION OF EDUCATION IN THE USA

The responsibility, direction and oversight of public education in the USA do not constitutionally reside in the federal government but in the individual states. Indeed, the term education does not appear in the US Constitution, and although public education is mandatory in all fifty states, there is no national legal mandate that requires states to provide public education. Each of the states has its own policies and programmes which vary sharply in how much control and budget responsibility is delegated to individual communities within the state.

Despite the local nature of public education, its basic orientation and nature is *de facto* national in character, that is, schools are remarkably much the same from one state to another. This has been caused by a number of factors, such as the effects of school texts developed for a national market; the prevalence of standardized testing; similar admission requirements among colleges and universities; regional accrediting associations concerned with standards for educational institutions; national accrediting associations concerned with standards for various professions; and the absence of a public debate on significant alternatives. Moreover, the federal government does have an important influence on public education through certain legislation that provides funds provided certain standards are maintained (for example, gender equity and appropriate provision for the handicapped). In addition, the US Supreme Court has handed down decisions that have had a very powerful impact on the schools, most notably in the case which declared segregated schools to be unconstitutional.

In addition, we have had on the national level a number of highly publicized and quite sharp criticisms of the schools, in which many social and cultural problems from crime to economic stagnation have been blamed on the inadequacy of the public schools. This has led the two major political parties to add educational policy to their agenda, something which had been missing from past political debate, thus adding to the public visibility of educational issues.

Nowhere has this public and political debate been more heated and pointed than on the topic of the place of values in the schools, a situation which many view with surprise, if not alarm, as if a new and disturbing element were being introduced into the debate on educational policy. However, the early history of education in the United States has been one in which issues of public schools and public morality have always been closely and explicitly linked.

HISTORICAL PERSPECTIVES

Many of the original American colonies were settled by sectarian Christian groups intent on establishing communities deeply grounded in their religious and moral beliefs, perhaps none more enduringly influential than the Puritans. The Puritans mandated schooling early on as an institution designed to extend the role of the family and church in transmitting, nourishing and preserving their theocratic way of life. Although some colonies were not as relentlessly religious as the Puritan enclaves of Massachusetts Bay and there was a diversity of schools in the other colonies, the notion of tax-supported, state-controlled compulsory education directed at preserving the dominant social and cultural institutions became the basis of the movement for public education that was to sweep across the United States in the nineteenth century. The transition from a group of autonomous and competitive, if not hostile, colonies ruled by a distant monarchy to a federated, democratic nation was, of course, enormously difficult and at times disruptive and bloody. The new nation at the beginning of the nineteenth century was faced with very basic problems and questions: would it be possible to bring order, cohesion and unity to this newly united group of separate entities; could and would the people take hold of and adopt the democratic principles enunciated by the Revolution's leaders in the Declaration of Independence and the Constitution? What was to be the shape of a uniquely American culture and how was it to be fashioned? Beyond the extraordinary problems that face those moving from colonization to autonomy, the new nation was confronted with other major phenomena such as a very heavy flow of immigrants with varying languages, religions, cultures and ethnicities; the tremendous westward movement; the rise of industrialism; the growth of cities; the growing power of a slave economy in the South; and the tremendous burst of entrepreneurship and capitalistic ventures.

This era of incredible energy, change and volatility was viewed by many as potentially threatening to social order and to cultural cohesion. For some, public education was seen not only as a powerful mode of warding off these threats but also as a critically important institution for inculcating a new and consensual American consciousness. Indeed, the intense public debate on the desirability and nature of compulsory, tax-supported, state-supervised schooling was a struggle among competing social and cultural groups –

Protestant vs. Catholic; rural vs. urban; and elitist vs. populist. The historian Carl Kaestle has characterized the results of this struggle as a triumph of 'an ideology centred on republicanism, Protestantism, and capitalism' (Kaestle, 1983). According to Kaestle this ideology included concerns for:

> the fragility of the republican polity; the importance of individual character in maintaining social morality; the critical importance of personal industry as determinant of merit; a respected but limited domestic role for women; the critical importance of a strong and appropriate family and social environment (in contrast to those of certain ethnic and racial groups) to character building; the superiority of White American Protestant culture; the grandeur of American destiny; the equality and abundance of economic opportunity; and the necessity of a determined public effort to unify America's polyglot population, chiefly through education.

The similarities between this set of issues and the agenda of the current dialogue on education are as striking as the differences are instructive. We still hear a lot today about the importance of family, personal industry, opportunity, American destiny, and there is considerable debate on multiculturalism and the role of women. Interestingly enough, there is very little rhetoric in our current educational discourse about the necessity of nourishing democracy. Another important difference resides in the recent and rather dramatic increase in the prominence of the concept of character education. Although the public discourse in the nineteenth century on public education was openly and unapologetically moral in character, the more circumspect dominant educational discourse of the twentieth century is one in which moral language is seen as archaic and inappropriate. When every so often (as is the case now) there is a flurry of interest in values education, it is seen as something new and/or controversial, largely because it is seen by many as being rooted in religious sectarianism and hence a threat to freedom and autonomy.

The change from the nineteenth-century discourse is partly a function of the widespread acceptance of principles of legal fairness and impartiality that emerges from the constitutional separation of church and state and a politics of accommodation that reflects the realities of a pluralistic society. Another dimension of the twentieth-century coyness about the moral dimensions of education is intellectual in nature; that is, the dominance of positivism has produced a consciousness of the primacy and necessity of objectivity and neutrality in which moral issues are seen as inevitably and hopelessly 'subjective', and hence irrelevant and disruptive. Another explanation has been offered by Elizabeth Vallance (1973), who argues that the explicitly moral curriculum of the nineteenth century has been so thoroughly assimilated and internalized that it has moved beyond criticism and become absorbed into what we are likely to call the 'hidden curriculum'.

199

This confluence of constitutional limits, political expediency, positivistic epistemology and social amnesia has produced an approach in which education becomes a process of learning information and gaining intellectual insights that are presumed to be independent of moral and political considerations. This has allowed the phenomenon of a 'new' field of moral education to emerge, a field which focused on what was once considered as a central and indispensable aspect of educational dialogue and what had now become a problematic and controversial candidate for being part of the agenda. The question had changed over time from, 'what should the moral grounding of education be?' to 'should education have a moral dimension?' thereby allowing moral education to be seen as a possibility rather than an inevitability.

VALUES EDUCATION TODAY

The situation as far as values education in the USA in the mid-1990s is concerned can be described as swirling and confused. In some ways, paradoxically enough, this would seem to be a time of great energy and creativity in the area even though (with important exceptions) this is also a time when the term moral or values education has less *cachet* than it did just a few years ago. The late 1970s and early 1980s was a time of considerable excitement in the field with the emergence of at least two major moral education orientations, namely Values Clarification and the Kohlberg moral developmental approach. Interest in these programmes has essentially dissipated, leaving behind a legacy of scepticism and disenchantment, if not dismissal not only of these particular orientations but of the broader notion of the concept of values education *per se*. The most important exception to this fall from grace is the Character Education Movement (Lickona, 1991).

I would have to say that this is the only self-consciously systematic values education programme that, at least for the moment, has currency in the USA. This approach, unlike the values education programmes of the 1970s and 1980s, does not try to avoid being programmatic and prescriptive as it affirms a set of presumed universal values and behaviours worthy of inculcation. These values include honesty, civility, hard work, perseverance and respect for authority. The instructional emphasis is less on study and reflection and much more on encouraging students to behave in line with these time-tested virtues. The programme is presented as both innovative and traditional; that is, an urgent call for a return to traditional family values, a call made necessary because of their exclusion from the school curriculum and the deterioration of public morality. This approach, of course, resonates very strongly with the rightward swing of American politics, for what sets off this programme from those of the 1970s and 1980s is that it does not primarily emerge from the profession. Indeed, it has the support of a number of groups (including trade unions, business organizations and non-partisan organizations) and much of its ideology and rhetoric comes from the neo-conservative movement.

Although there is, generally speaking, no place in the traditional formal curriculum for values education and very little support for giving it parity with the usual requirements (English, science, mathematics, history and foreign languages), a number of school systems have mandated some form of 'character education', emphasizing moral instruction and behaviour change, usually on a modest basis (for example, thirty minutes per week) and/or by integrating it into existing courses. However, it seems very unlikely in the foreseeable future that the majority of schools will make such programmes a major or permanent feature of the standard curriculum.

There are other pressures on the schools, however, that complicate the issues and make for caution and indecision by school leaders on how they are to respond to a public concern for values education. There are the conflicts that derive from the increasingly intense pressures from the Religious Right who insist that schools respond to their demands for such matters as school prayer and book censorship, as well as from the counter-pressures of those who demand that schools adhere to a strict policy of church and state separation. In addition, there is the continuing debate on multicultural education and the pressures on the one hand to nourish diversity and difference and the countervailing fears that this exacerbates divisiveness and fosters fractionation. Add to this the extremely volatile and contentious debates on sex education, AIDS prevention, and education on substance abuse, and the school usually finds itself often making bland compromises, side-stepping controversy and ambiguity, or in a state of educational gridlock as school leaders struggle to respond to a number of conflicting constituencies with varying moral outlooks.

However, the picture for values education is a lot brighter in the theoretical world even though, as I have said, there is a significant erosion in the interest in capital V or M Values or Moral Education. For one thing, there is growing sensitivity to moral aspects of education and much less reluctance in the professional literature to address the moral aspects of social and educational policies. For example, those writing in the traditions of critical pedagogy are far more likely to include moral concepts and even to use the term than they were ten or fifteen years ago. What had once been considered by many to be part of the discourse of organized religion or superstition is, at minimum, becoming an important element of educational discourse.

Moreover, there are a number of contemporary writers who are clearly speaking directly to issues implicit in values education even though they do not present themselves explicitly as moral educators. Perhaps the most prominent are two educators who are strongly influenced by feminist thought, Nel Noddings and Jane Roland Martin. Noddings' work focuses on the critical importance of caring, both as a focus of instruction and as informing school climate; that is, she urges teachers to be caring in their relationships with students and to teach children to be caring and compassionate with each other. She has written extensively not only about her theoretical orientation but quite concretely on how such a programme could be integrated into the existing curriculum (Noddings, 1992). Jane Roland Martin also emphasizes the importance of supportive relationships in her thesis that the ideal family life in which nurture, love and connection are central provides us with an appropriate educational model. Martin has also supplemented her theoretical framework with concrete curricular examples on how this might look in actual practice (Martin, 1992).

There are other curriculum projects that have a strong values component as reflected, for example, in the growing interest in what is called service education in which students are given opportunities to be involved in such activities as working in soup kitchens, clinics, tutorials and clean-up projects. Indeed, there are a number of schools which now require such participation for graduation. In addition, there are a number of schools which have introduced into the curriculum programmes in techniques of conflict resolution. In many of these programmes students are trained in mediation techniques and then go on to serve on student panels organized to deal with individual cases of student conflict either with other students or with staff. Another example of values-oriented curriculum is in the area of student governance of which perhaps the most well-developed example is the Democratic Classroom Programme based on the theories of Lawrence Kohlberg and designed by Ralph Mosher and his colleagues in which students actually take (not pretend to take) major responsibilities for school governance.

In addition, there continue to be writers who directly approach moral education from a philosophical perspective, arguing that moral education requires careful analysis and open dialogue grounded in logic and rationality (Heslep, 1995). Perhaps the most intriguing and potentially significant trend is the growing emergence of interest in the relationship between spirituality and education. This is clearly a reflection of the huge growth in public interest in the USA in religious and spiritual matters. Although there has been continuing interest in religiously oriented education among various sectarian groups, it has only been fairly recently that a new literature has begun to appear, one that is clearly not sectarian but that seeks instead to integrate spiritual concerns with education. Some of this takes the form of religion and spirituality as legitimate objects of study but increasingly it deals more with the spirit as a source of insight and of development. James Moffett has proposed that spiritual development become the prime focus of the school curriculum and has suggested specific techniques and programmes which are largely grounded in the spiritual traditions of the East (Moffett, 1994). Other, the more Western-oriented approaches for spiritual education for the schools have come from such writers as Kathleen Kesson (1996), Dwayne Huebner (1996) and Parker Palmer (1983). Such works are not to be confused with religious instruction or with religious studies but represent attempts to provide a holistic perspective to human learning in that they all posit the presence and significance of certain phenomena (the soul, spirit, or inner life, and the transcendent) normally denied and/or ignored by traditional education.

REACTIONS TO THE STUDY

For a variety of reasons, there was no study done in the United States parallel to the ones presented and discussed in this book. In lieu of such a study I have been asked to comment on and react to, from the perspective of an American working in this area, the data, interpretations and ideas that have emerged from the research undertaken by the other authors. My responses, therefore, will necessarily be heavy on the interpretative and personal side as I make no claim that my reactions are any more representative than that of my own experience and perspective.

My own experience and sense is that there is very little if any attempt in the United States to provide systematic training directly concerned with issues of values for either teachers-to-be or experienced teachers. On the other hand there is an increasing sensitivity to the significance of values issues among those involved in the professional preparation of educational practitioners. For example, one of the standards for initial teacher preparation set by the voluntary, private and very powerful national group which accredits teacher education programmes requires that students 'acquire and learn to apply knowledge about [among other things] the social, historical, and philosophical foundations of education, including an understanding of the moral, social, and political dimensions of classrooms, teaching, and schools' as well as 'an understanding of professional ethics'.

Beyond this, my own very strong sense (without any empirical evidence) is that the mainstream of American teachers and prospective teachers would have a great deal in common with the respondents of the research described in this book when it comes to attitudes towards values education. My reading of the research results is that there is a strong intuitive sense among the respondents that values are an inevitable and critical dimension of education but that it is an issue so deeply fraught with cultural conflicts, political dangers and intellectual perplexities that one is extremely reluctant to take hold of this tiger's tail. Moreover, there seems to be a general consensus that a spirit of tolerance, acceptance and pluralism within a context of democracy and goodwill should be the grounding for values education. There also seems to be a high degree of confidence among the respondents and contributors that well-thought-out and appropriately applied programmes of deliberate values education would have a salutary effect on the students and on their society. I would not expect that there would be any significant deviation from these general attitudes among teachers and teacher trainees in the United States.

My guess is that most teachers in America feel (as do the teachers in the other nations described in the book) the pain and frustration that emerge from the dilemma of balancing individual autonomy with preserving certain cultural, particularly moral, traditions, as well as the difficulties of having to respond to the demands of a diverse student body and of conflicting social and political pressures. Our teachers also feel both relatively vulnerable and helpless as they are asked to deal with these incredibly difficult and volatile issues with few, if any, specialized professional resources and little intellectual mastery. I would also note, regretfully, that teachers in the United States are also extremely reluctant to affirm a moral vision beyond that of tolerance and acceptance of all. It is very likely, however, that they, like their colleagues in the studies discussed in this book, yearn to get help in the form of public understanding and solid intellectual discourse, as well as appropriate teaching resources and materials.

These observations are both very broad and highly speculative but I should like to take advantage of this opportunity to supplement them with some of my own views on these matters. For starters, I want to say rather emphatically that some of the important dilemmas implicated in values education are best left in tension and unresolved. The conflict between individual rights and social order, between personal creativity and cultural continuity, and between individual fulfilment and social responsibility are inherent, inevitable and, I dare say, eternal dimensions of human existence. Our constant challenge is to reinterpret the particular configuration of these conflicts in the context of a particular time, place and setting, knowing that circumstances will determine our most thoughtful, albeit temporary, response. The genuine threat to this struggle lies much more in certainty than in uncertainty, for certainty precludes the necessity for reflection, humility and forbearance. As long as the tension remains, we retain the possibility of open and productive dialogue and of responding appropriately as situations change. The major moral dilemmas are easy to describe, impossible to solve; inevitably and persistently present, they represent a permanent agenda in ever-changing forms, requiring that we be flexible in how we act on our enduring but conflicting commitments.

It is possible to be fanciful and to conjure up the possibility that these dilemmas are not inevitable and by some miracle they could be legitimately resolved. Even if one were to entertain such a fantasy, surely that day is far off and hence it is cruel and unfair to expect teachers and students to be able to do what has eluded our greatest thinkers since the beginning of history. An intellectually honest, morally sound and politically sensible beginning point for any values education programme, therefore, is one of humility in which we accept as a given that moral issues reflect inherent and inevitable conflicts, ambiguities and uncertainties. Such uncertainties and ambiguities can surely be frustrating but they can also be liberating to the extent that they absolve us from the absurd demand that we can resolve them either by being godlike or by being all things to all people.

Having said that, let me quickly say that I am not at all advocating anything like equivocation and neutrality for I believe very strongly that educators have a responsibility to affirm strongly the social and moral vision that grounds their educational outlook. Not only is it intellectually impossible to be ultimately objective and neutral on moral and political issues, it is morally irresponsible either to attempt to be non-committal or to avoid confronting the issue of affirmation. Moral issues not only are matters to be studied (they are surely that) but are the very basis of who we are and what we do. Paradoxically enough, to be non-committal is a political and moral act and its consequences are equivalent to acting on strong commitments. One of the tasks of values educators is to address the importance and problematics of moral commitment and they need to model how thoughtful people respond to rather than run away from this opportunity and responsibility.

This is not at all to gainsay the difficulty of making commitments in the face of the ambiguities and complexities noted above as well as the incipient dangers of dogmatism and authoritarianism in making affirmations. Such dangers are very real and we must always be on guard that our commitments are tempered by humility and regard for the dignity and autonomy of others. However, there are parallel dangers to being non-committal, namely paralysis, wishy-washiness, inaction, and the preservation of the status quo. We must be willing to risk the dangers of being affirmative because it allows us the opportunity to ground our work in meaning rather than in expediency, and to teach students to struggle for the good rather than cope with the bad. At the same time, we must also be mindful of the terrible things that have been done in the name of righteousness and perhaps be guided by Sharon Welch's admonition that we act with 'absolute commitment and infinite suspicion'.

I want also to point out that I am not at all limiting myself to 'educational commitments'; that is, I reject the tendency of many educators to focus in on the schoolhouse to the exclusion of the social and political context. There is a curious anomaly that I find among American educators that seems to be mirrored in the attitudes reported in the research studies of this book having to do with the relationship between the moral condition of the society and the responsibilities of the schools for values education. On the one hand, many educators are very aware of the inevitability and pervasiveness of values not only in schools but in the larger community. On the other hand, many of these same educators speak to the necessity and desirability of schools providing programmes of systematic values education, thus belying the claim of inevitability and pervasiveness of values education. There is in this anomaly a suggestion that schools would likely be more systematic and coherent in their efforts if that task were clearly assigned to them. Moreover, it would seem to reflect a naive and unrealistic confidence and reliance in the power of educational methodology. This suggests an outlook that claims that if we only had the right curriculum and the proper pedagogy we could provide meaningful values education and have a powerful and positive impact on the larger society. The difficulty I have with this optimism is its blindness to the overwhelming influence of the other dominant social, economic, political and cultural institutions which control not only the schools but the shape of the entire society.

My response to this anomaly is to urge educators to give up on reifying education as if it were some autonomous entity poised to reform the outside world. Instead of identifying ourselves as educators we ought to consider ourselves to be social, cultural and moral leaders who happen to work in the realm of educational institutions. We need to develop a discourse in which there are no educational problems *per se*, but instead only moral, political, social, cultural problems that get expressed in educational forms. In this way we recognize the relationship between and the integration of educational matters with larger political, moral and economic ones. This also would serve to be a check on the naiveté and romanticism of educators that is, at least in part, a function of their isolation and alienation from the broader social and political contexts. To argue that the moral climate in the society can be changed by values education in the schools is a poignant denial of the immense power of the dominant culture and its relentless determination to preserve its position.

PERSPECTIVES ON VALUES EDUCATION

My view is that those of us interested in moral issues would be better served if we gave up the discourse of 'values education'. This concept is seriously problematic partly because it deflects us from the deeper moral issues that are rooted in the society and partly because it makes an insupportable distinction between values education and education. This has allowed those on the right to adopt a discourse of 'we must return values to the schools' as if values are elements to be added or withheld like ingredients in a recipe. Of course, in reality this discourse is a code for a *particular* values orientation (one that celebrates hard work, respect for authority, obedience, etc.), leaving those opposed to this particular value code seemingly to favour a valueless education. This is not only a disingenuous discourse but a distracting one, for it displaces the possibility of a critically important public dialogue on what moral vision(s) should guide our society and moves it to the relatively narrow and technical professional and essentially meaningless argument about whether or not there should be values education in the schools. One of the contradictions of the current Character Education Movement in the United States lies between its discourse of diagnosis, which is broadly social and cultural in character ('there is lawlessness, incivility, lasciviousness and indolence in the land'), and its discourse of remediation, which is narrowly educational in character ('we must restore values to the schools'). The implication here is that moral transformation will come when the schools change but all other social, political, cultural and economic institutions remain the same. The discourse of school-based values is a language of stasis, for such programmes will inevitably become, at best, peripheral and at worst co-opted.

However, this is certainly not to say that educators should abandon their concerns for the moral for, indeed, we must greatly intensify our efforts and speak with the urgency and passion that the times demand.

I can summarize my own views on what might constitute a more prod-uctive endeavour than designing values education programmes with a quota-tion from a prior publication:

> Perhaps it is time to put an end to efforts at explicit moral education programmes. They have not only failed in their own goal of being integrated into the schools; they have also had the deleterious effect of reification and reductionism. What we need instead of moral educa-tion is much more moral discourse and analysis, but not just on the specific ethical implications of living in schools as in what happens when students cheat or steal. We also need to ground our educational policies and practices in a larger moral analysis of our culture and society. We need to confront the intersection of moral beliefs and educational policies and practices in such questions as the balance between individual autonomy and social responsibility; between the values of competition and co-operation; we need to confront the moral problematics of testing, excellence, grading, tracking, and hier-archy. We *don't* need more moral education programmes; we *do* need a moral mode of analysis for education, one that helps us to understand our moral needs and aids us in responding as educators to them. Yet, this is still not enough. We also need to ground that language in a moral vision, a far more demanding, more problematic, and more vital requirement than analysis. Moral education without affirmations is a contradiction in terms, an evasion, and an act of irresponsibility. Edu-cators have a marvellous opportunity to participate in the most important cultural project of our time – the creation of a renewed common vision. Elements of such a vision are available from our traditions of fundamental commitments to love, human dignity, and social justice grounded in a quest for a life of meaning. An education that is fully dedicated to this quest is what will make it moral. Nothing else will do.

(Purpel, 1991)

207

REFERENCES

Heslep, Robert (1995) *Moral Education for America* (Westport, Praeger Press).

Huebner, Dwayne (1996) 'Education and Spirituality', *Journal of Curriculum Theorizing*, 11 (2): 13–33.

Kaestle, Carl (1983) *Pillars of the Republic* (New York, Hill & Wang).

Kesson, Kathleen (1996) 'The Foundations of Holism', *Holistic Education Review*, Summer: 14–24.

Lickona, Thomas (1991) *Educating for Character: How Our Schools Can Teach for Character* (New York, Bantam).

Martin, Jane Roland (1992) *The Schoolhome* (Cambridge, Mass., Harvard University Press).

Moffett, James (1994) *The Universal Schoolhouse* (San Francisco, Jossey-Bass).

Mosher, Ralph and Kenny, Robert (1994) *Preparing for Citizenship* (Westport, Praeger Press).

Noddings, Nel (1992) *The Challenge to Care in Schools: An Alternative Approach to Education* (New York, Teachers' College Press).

Palmer, Parker (1983) *To Know as We Are Known: A Spirituality of Education* (San Francisco, Harper & Row).

Purpel, David (1991) 'Moral Education: An Idea Whose Time Has Gone', *Clearing-House*, 64, May: 305–12.

Vallance, Elizabeth (1973) 'Hiding the Hidden Curriculum: An Interpretation of the Language of Justification', in *Curriculum Theory Network* 4 (1): 61–78.

10

CONCLUSION

Lorraine Ling

In comparing the findings from the various socio-cultural contexts in which the studies reported here have been undertaken, some common findings emerge. One of the most compelling reasons for the commonality of findings across different social, economic and political contexts may be that the current era of globalization breaks and blurs traditional boundaries between cultures, time, space, ideologies and nations. The last decade of the twentieth century is marked by a break with tradition and the failure of grand narratives upon which nations were hitherto founded. This transformation period may variously be described as a divide, an interregnum and a transition. It is an era where traditional social processes are called into question and thus we could be seen to have entered a post-traditional era. In discussing this concept, Giddens (1994: 104) states:

> Tradition is effectively a way of settling clashes between different values and ways of life. . . . Tradition incorporates power relations and tends to naturalize them. The world of 'traditional society' is one of traditional societies, in which cultural pluralism takes the form of an extraordinary diversity of mores and customs – each of which, however, exists in privileged space.

The current era marks a shift or transition from such traditional societies to a period which exhibits features which are unlike those of previous eras. The rise of technology and communication, and the impact which this has upon globalization and the reducing of time and space, may be perceived to be the dominant reason for social, political and economic globalization. It follows, then, that in a post-traditional era such as is currently occurring across the world, previous traditional values will be challenged, questioned and may be found to be anachronistic, inappropriate and irrelevant. It may not be surprising, given this explanation, that in many of the countries involved in this study of values education, a trend towards a moral vacuum model was discerned. Giddens (1994: 104–5) states:

The post-traditional society is quite different. It is inherently globaliz-
ing, but also reflects the intensification of globalization. In the post-
traditional order cultural pluralism, whether this involves persisting or
created traditions, can no longer take the form of separated centres of
embedded power.

Within a post-traditional era it is inevitable that clashes of values will
occur and that there will be a confusion and a multiplicity of discourses
about values at the social, political and economic levels. Educators are
thus faced with a complex challenge regarding the teaching of values in
educational institutions.

Four typologies were employed as an interpretative framework for the
findings in the final phase of the study into values in education. Three of
these typologies are based upon Hill (1991). These are: religious monopolism, moral universalism and consensus pluralism. A fourth typology was
added during the study to describe an emerging trend whereby in the Australian context the moral vacuum model appeared to be gaining momentum.
While each of these categories was seen to exist in each of the contexts
within which this study was implemented, there was, in most cases, a pre-
dominance of one category over another. What appears clear from the findings of each country is that there were elements of all categories present
concurrently.

It has been stated in the findings which have emerged from this study
that it appears that educators lack a discourse to express their ideas about
values and to conceptualize the area of values in education. This stems,
largely, from the lack of theoretical knowledge and experience educators
possess in this area. While there is much in the literature of education
especially in the area of philosophy and moral education, it is not an
integral and explicit part of the training which most teachers undergo. In
many instances, the area of values and moral education is seen to be so
embedded in all of the curriculum areas that it is not necessary to address it
as a discrete subject which is explicitly part of the curriculum programme. It
is likely that the lack of discourse and the tentativeness which characterize
values education in the curriculum of schools and teacher education
courses may be attributable in part to the inadequate theoretical knowledge
of those who plan and implement the curriculum in this area. Overarching
this theoretical deficit is the more pervasive and radical concept of post-
traditional society. Educators, in reflecting the broader social context in
which they function, experience the same clashes of values, the same
uncertainties and confusions about social and moral values, as do all other
sectors of society. Thus, the notion of a trend towards the moral vacuum,
where there is a multiplicity of diverse values, eclecticism in the way the
systems of values which prevail are constructed and a hesitancy to commit
to a particular values stance, may be viewed as a global trend. It is not

peculiar to educators or indeed to any other section of the population, nor is it a local or a national phenomenon. The moral vacuum model transcends boundaries and transcends ideologies.

> What applies in the area of personal relations and everyday life applies also to the global order and all levels between. The post-traditional era is an ending; but it is also a beginning, a genuinely new social universe of action and experience. Social bonds have effectively to be made rather than inherited from the past – on the personal and more collective levels this is a fraught and difficult exercise, but one that also holds out the promise of great rewards.
>
> (Giddens, 1994: 107)

It is clear, then, that old approaches to values education will not do in the current era and into the next century. A discourse for educators to address the area of values in education is urgently required if the existing confusions, inconsistencies and inadequacies are to be replaced with clear philosophies, rational approaches and time- and space-appropriate approaches for the new era.

One of the effects of globalization is the diminution of the effect of local contexts and their cultures so that a global culture is created. The rise of abstract systems where the face-to-face contact between people is severely reduced is one of the features of globalization and the post-traditional society. In faceless encounters which involve human beings interacting with machines and technology rather than with each other, values underpinning relationships in society are transformed. Relationships of time and space are recast and the notion of 'action at a distance [where] absence predominates over presence' (Giddens, 1994: 96) is central. It is not only inevitable but essential, given the features of the new era, that a new system of values emerges.

While it is vital that the local contexts remain strong and are sustained it is also equally vital that, concurrent with this, the global context is continuously constructed and reconstructed. Thus at the same time as we engage in reconstruction and transformation of local cultural values, we are impelled to construct and reconstruct global values. The dialectical relationship between the local and the global values, then, forms the framework for the area of values education. It is necessary for educators to reflect critically upon the era in which they and the learners are to function and thus to formulate a structured, coherent, era-appropriate curriculum for values education. This curriculum will need to address the local and the global values and stress the dialectical relationships between them. It will need to be transformative, radical, empowering, reconstructive. New relationships and bonds and thus new value systems are required. We as educators cannot rely upon past approaches, nor can we bury our heads in the sand and pretend that the new era is not upon us. Radical action is essential.

REFERENCES

Giddens, A. (1994) 'Living in a Post-Traditional Society', in V. Beck, A. Giddens and S. Lash (eds) *Reflexive Modernization – Politics, Tradition and Aesthetics in the Modern Social Order* (Cambridge, Polity Press).

Hill, B.V. (1991) *Values Education in Australian Schools* (Melbourne, ACER).

Appendix I

VALUES EDUCATION DURING THE TRAINING OF ASPIRING TEACHERS FOR THE SECONDARY GRADE I AT THE UNIVERSITY OF BERNE

Hans Ulrich Grunder

A survey was also attempted in Switzerland at the University of Berne, where the initial questionnaire was given to graduates; that is, former students of the training institution for secondary school teachers. In 1995 the final questionnaire was sent to students on the secondary training course at the University of Berne as well as to graduates from the same institution. Unfortunately, in both cases, too few completed questionnaires were returned to undertake a full study for this book. However, what responses there were indicate that there were similarities of opinion and practice with those expressed by students and teachers in other countries.

From the first project the function of the teacher as a model was repeatedly emphasized: 'One's own attitude should serve as a good example to the students (and not just talk about moral attitudes).' 'The teacher makes it possible for adolescents to see how to react in certain situations. Especially with regard to tolerance towards those with different views, the teacher can set an example.' 'The more consistently the teacher realizes his or her own ideals, the more the pupils will think these ideals worth imitation.' 'What is the use of a well-intentioned discussion about ecology or even of a fantastic action poster about the same topic if the teacher involved drives home in a (prestige) car shortly afterwards? All the commitment is as good as useless. As the teacher determines the class atmosphere, she/he has to stand up for the observation of his/her own values in action.' One of the respondents went into details: As a teacher, she notices not only the decay of values, the observation of values, the building up of values but also the shifting of values. The atmosphere of a class is to be judged on that scale. An ethos is created even if the teacher is not conscious of the problem. Issues regarding discipline, learning and working attitudes, morals and ethics as well as religion were thought to be dependent on the class and the teacher as well as on the location of the school and the teaching staff.

The respondents, however, regretted the declining relevance of the teacher with regard to values education. The system of subject teachers allows for too little influence although every teacher could consciously encourage values during his or her own (few) lessons. One of the answers stated that values education does not take place in the classroom only. In addition, respondents mentioned that those moral attitudes which have been neglected under the parental roof have to be transmitted to the children in the form of re-education. These include such issues as, for example: 'protection of the environment, garbage disposal, social relations with teachers and fellow-pupils, language, consumer behaviour, considerate handling of materials'. Besides the parents, the teacher plays the role of a very important reference person for adolescents, especially for the children of the lower and intermediate grades.

The following defining factors for the teacher with respect to values education were mentioned: the teacher's personality, character and charisma, the selection and rating of topics within individual subjects, the explicit and personal expression of the teacher's opinion, the teacher's ways of working and ability to lead discussions, as well as the teacher's reaction to opinions expressed by the pupils and by third persons. In this context, one of the answers claimed that the teacher has to reveal his or her implicit or explicit moral attitudes as openly as possible. Teachers not only have to allow discussions about moral attitudes but even have to initiate and to encourage them. There was one reference to the multicultural aspect of schools. Whenever there is a class with children of different cultural backgrounds, the teacher takes on a particular co-ordination function.

When asked about the problems they expected with regard to the transmission of moral attitudes in classrooms, the teachers suspected that the pupils (in this regard, the parents are also mentioned once) would either be indifferent to this or not accept it. They also questioned the degree of co-operation between the teaching staff, parents and the authorities when it comes to acting in a value-educational way at school. With regard to the teacher, they said clearly: 'In the field of values education, the teacher could act as a landmark, provided he or she has found a pattern of values for which he or she can stand up.' But on the other hand teachers are neutral. However, on the side of the children and adolescents there will be a tendency towards the decay of values in the classroom because of the teacher's lack of a unifying pattern of values. Another one cautioned against an 'active transmission of values' as 'this could be delicate and dangerous'. However, if a pluralistic point of view with regard to values is accepted, 'moral attitudes will have to be respected'.

With regard to didactics, the teacher should transmit values rather by 'presenting and explaining' than by 'imposing and manipulating'. There is no magic formula. 'Values education should not aim at forcing an opinion or a value upon the pupils.' Thus a know-all manner as well as any politicizing are excluded, as the delicate brinkmanship of values education requires the teacher's sympathetic understanding as well as a 'central inner concern'. 'The transmission should not appear artificial' as it would then equal a dull passing on of pseudo-values. It was furthermore claimed that the most efficient transmission of values is done by daily setting an example, but values are less clearly exemplified in classroom situations. It finally depends on the spirit of the school whether a unified canon of values can be transmitted in a plausible way. Despite all the well-meant attempts to vary teaching methods and include a range of material, the different familial, national and ethnic backgrounds of the children of today's multicultural school stand in the way of the value-educational activities of the teacher. If there is no longer any common denominator, the teacher's task becomes even more difficult.

The statements in the questionnaires returned in the results of this first survey were not unanimous. Even though all the teachers were convinced that values education is indispensable in class, they shied from transmitting values categorically. In this connection, they referred to the adolescents' growing maturity regarding their own concepts of values as well as to the role of the teacher as a model for moral attitudes.

For the final stage of the joint project the survey was carried out in two phases, but supplementary telephone interviews were not carried out because of lack of time. Results, however, suggested that the teachers who did respond understood their function as a model for the adolescents. With the exception of a few respondents, the students wanted to commit themselves to the development of values and moral attitudes of their students at their future places of employment. On the other hand, the students already doubted their ability to have an effective role in this respect. Considering the rapid change of values, several of them even spoke of a decay of values. They did not see themselves in a position to transmit consistent moral attitudes (or, presumably, to set an example). They had difficulty in dealing with competing value systems and the transmission of these to the generation growing up.

The future teachers asked themselves how they should explain to children that rigid value conceptions very rarely lead to solutions on which an all-encompassing point of view could be based. But, on the other hand, how could this understanding of the existence of competing value systems and the practicability of a life under such circumstances be taught within a school and teaching context?

The students seemed to be insecure with regard to their competence in the transmission of such facts. They clearly recognized the dilemma of being caught between the necessity of building up one's own moral attitudes and having the necessary flexibility in dealing with them within the teaching context. In addition, they accepted the child as an individual whose own immediate values and norms are first to be respected and not necessarily to be changed immediately.

As future teachers, the students appeared to manoeuvre between personal orientations, didactic needs and respect for the child's psyche. The students saw this not only in respect to values education. Their training seems to have sharpened their view of the complexity of the problem without having given them the tools needed to tackle the decisive questions relating to values together with the pupils. The students all agreed that their studies were largely inadequate to further the development of personal values. At best, there were, in their opinion, few of their university courses that prepared them for their function as mediators of values. In order to improve this situation, they suggested more alternatives in their studies as well as more interdisciplinary courses. They did recognize, however, the central goals in the Bernese school curriculum in relation to values education as being those principles which were to be respected. These include the development of self-competence, social competence and expertise. They considered a range of working and teaching modes as being suitable for the building up of moral attitudes. They considered 'missionary teacher' behaviour as counter-productive. They would prefer to lead the children in the discussion of questions regarding value-educational questions through their own joy of life and that of the children. They felt that this should generally happen within human science and arts subjects. They would like to encourage the children to build up moral attitudes on the basis of their own experiences. The students suggested that their academic studies should deal with more human subject matters, such as choices, grief, temptation, ethical dilemmas. They also claimed that the curricula were too charged and yet lacked explicit value-educational contents and that the lecturers acted as doubtful models as they themselves shied away from taking a stand. If they were to act in a value-educational way, ecological, ethnological, religious, peace-educational, media studies and family educational subject matters should be integrated into the training of future teachers. This is already the case in the introduction to media studies. In this context, some students proceeded on the assumption that a compensatory values education programme should be followed with those children whose moral education had been neglected at home. Others underlined the multicultural field within which the school as an institution is acting nowadays. They stressed a new task for teachers which has so far been given little attention within the debate about values education at school. Teachers, considering the genesis of moral attitudes at school to be essential, should see themselves not so much as transmitters of definite positions but rather as having a co-ordinating function towards children coming from very different cultural backgrounds. Here, however, we are faced with another problem. Students wondered how to decide which values of a society are to be encouraged, which are worth preserving or which are in need of being altered. The students consulted thought that an eventual refusal by the pupils of the value-educational efforts of the teacher was the main problem of all teaching aimed at the genesis of moral attitudes.

Those respondents already working as teachers were less uncertain about the issues mentioned and less sceptical of an instruction aimed at value-educational goals. Like the students, they referred to the generation of self-competence as well as social competence and expertise which should further the building up of a critical and constructive moral attitude in adults. Like only a few students, one teacher mentioned the instruction of the Western Christian tradition as a value-educational basis. The teachers participating in the study wanted to encourage adolescents to examine critically their own moral attitudes, to discuss them, to tolerate other moral attitudes and to have experience of being faced with moral dilemmas, as a means of generating their own moral attitudes. As far as the strategies aimed at these goals are concerned, those respondents who were already teachers referred to numerous methodologies. Besides a wide range of working and teaching techniques, they mentioned contracts with the students, class hierarchy and delegating responsibility to the pupils.

It appears that the more practical experience the teachers had, the more freely they dealt with values education. They had, in any case, more didactic strategies at their disposal than teachers who had had only very little school experience or than students. All those who answered the questionnaire were basically prepared to work in a value-educational way. Notwithstanding their doubts as to the validity of the necessary knowledge as well as their scepticism about their effectiveness as a model for the pupils, the respondents were ready to discuss with the children the difficulties a relativist position could cause. The manner in which questions of moral attitudes are eventually tackled in class should be revealed by a survey which does not concentrate on a questionnaire but on class observation and analysis.

ACKNOWLEDGEMENT

This text presents a version, with additional data, of the paper given at the conference of Association for Teacher Education in Europe, Prague, 1994. The present paper has been prepared with the assistance of Karma Lobsang, Research Department for School Pedagogics and Subject Didactics at the University of Berne.

Appendix II

THE QUESTIONNAIRE

Question 1 Briefly state three essential principles upon which you make decisions with regard to the teaching and development of values in the curriculum programme.

Question 2 Outline four specific classroom strategies (two informal and two formal) which you employ in the area of values development and teaching within your classroom context.

Question 3 List five of the predominant cultural issues which you perceive exert major influence upon the values dimension of curriculum in your context.

Question 4 Write one brief comment on these four questions as they relate to values development and teaching in your context.

a) whose knowledge forms the basis of the course?
b) how is the knowledge organized for the learners?
c) how is the knowledge imparted to the learners?
d) to which individuals or groups of learners is the knowledge pertaining to the values dimension of the curriculum available?

Question 5 What are five of the most important elements which a) values teaching in schools, and b) values education components of teacher education courses, should address?

INDEX

219